Corliss K. Slack
August 2005

THE HISTORY OF AL-ṬABARĪ

AN ANNOTATED TRANSLATION

VOLUME X

The Conquest of Arabia

THE RIDDAH WARS

A.D. 632–633/A.H. 11

The History of al-Ṭabarī

Editorial Board

Ihsan Abbas, University of Jordan, Amman

C. E. Bosworth, The University of Manchester

Franz Rosenthal, Yale University

Everett K. Rowson, The University of Pennsylvania

Ehsan Yar-Shater, Columbia University (*General Editor*)

Estelle Whelan, *Editorial Coordinator*

Center for Iranian Studies

Columbia University

SUNY

SERIES IN NEAR EASTERN STUDIES

Said Amir Arjomand, Editor

The preparation of this volume was made possible in part by a grant from the National Endowment for the Humanities, an independent federal agency.

Bibliotheca Persica
Edited by Ehsan Yar-Shater

The History of al-Ṭabarī

(Ta'rīkh al-rusul wa'l mulūk)

VOLUME X

The Conquest of Arabia

translated and annotated
by

Fred M. Donner

The University of Chicago

State University of New York Press

Published by
State University of New York Press, Albany

Printed in the United States of America

For information, address the State University of New York Press,
90 State Street, Suite 700, Albany, NY 12207
Library of Congress Cataloging-in-Publication Data
Ṭabarī, 838?–923.
[Ta'rīkh al-rusul wa-al-mulūk. English. Selections]
The Conquest of Arabia / translated and annotated by
Fred M. Donner.
p. cm.—(The History of al-Ṭabarī = Ta'rīkh a-rusul wa'l
mulūk; v. 10) (Bibliotheca Persica) (SUNY series in Near Eastern studies)
Translation of extracts from: Ta'rīkh al-rusul wa-al-mulūk.
Includes bibliographical references and index.
ISBN 0–7914–1071–4.—ISBN 0–7914–1072–2 (pbk.)
1. Riddah Wars. 2. Islam—History. 3. Arabian Peninsula—
History. I. Donner, Fred McGraw, 1945– . II. Title.
III. Series. IV. Series: Ṭabarī, 838?–923. Ta'rīkh al-rusul
wa-al-mulūk. English; v. 10. V. Series: Bibliotheca Persica
(Albany, N. Y.)
DS38.2. T313 1985 vol. 10
[DS38.1]
909'. 1 s—dc20 91–35989
[953'. 02] CIP
10 9 8 7 6 5 4 3 2 1

Preface

THE HISTORY OF PROPHETS AND KINGS (*Ta'rīkh al-rusul wa'l-mulūk*) by Abū Ja'far Muḥammad b. Jarīr al-Ṭabarī (839–923), here rendered as the *History of al-Ṭabarī*, is by common consent the most important universal history produced in the world of Islam. It has been translated here in its entirety for the first time for the benefit of non-Arabists, with historical and philological notes for those interested in the particulars of the text.

Al-Ṭabarī's monumental work explores the history of the ancient nations, with special emphasis on biblical peoples and prophets, the legendary and factual history of ancient Iran, and, in great detail, the rise of Islam, the life of the Prophet Muḥammad, and the history of the Islamic world down to the year 915. The first volume of this translation contains a biography of al-Ṭabarī and a discussion of the method, scope, and value of his work. It also provides information on some of the technical considerations that have guided the work of the translators.

The *History* has been divided here into thirty-eight volumes, each of which covers about two hundred pages of the original Arabic text in the Leiden edition. An attempt has been made to draw the dividing lines between the individual volumes in such a way that each is to some degree independent and can be read as such. The page numbers of the Leiden edition appear on the margins of the translated volumes.

Al-Ṭabarī very often quotes his sources verbatim and traces the chain of transmission (*isnād*) to an original source. The chains of transmitters are, for the sake of brevity, rendered by only a dash (—) between the individual links in the chain. Thus, "According to Ibn Ḥumayd—Salamah—Ibn Isḥāq" means that al-Ṭabarī received the report from Ibn Ḥumayd, who said that he was told by Salamah, who said that he was told by Ibn Isḥāq, and so on. The numerous subtle and important differences in the original Arabic wording have been disregarded.

The table of contents at the beginning of each volume gives a brief survey of the topics dealt with in that particular volume. It also includes the headings and subheadings as they appear in al-Ṭabarī's text, as well as those occasionally introduced by the translator.

Well-known place names, such as, for instance, Mecca, Baghdad, Jerusalem, Damascus, and the Yemen, are given in their English spellings. Less common place names, which are the vast majority, are transliterated. Biblical figures appear in the accepted English spelling. Iranian names are usually transcribed according to their Arabic forms, and the presumed Iranian forms are often discussed in the footnotes.

Technical terms have been translated wherever possible, but some, such as dirham and imām, have been retained in Arabic forms. Others that cannot be translated with sufficient precision have been retained and italicized, as well as footnoted.

The annotation aims chiefly at clarifying difficult passages, identifying individuals and place names, and discussing textual difficulties. Much leeway has been left to the translators to include in the footnotes whatever they consider necessary and helpful.

The bibliographies list all the sources mentioned in the annotation.

The index in each volume contains all the names of persons and places referred to in the text, as well as those mentioned in the notes as far as they refer to the medieval period. It does not include the names of modern scholars. A general index, it is hoped, will appear after all the volumes have been published.

For further details concerning the series and acknowledgments, see Preface to Volume I.

Ehsan Yar-Shater

Contents

Abbreviations

Aghānī: al-Iṣfahānī, ʿAlī b. al-Ḥusayn, *Kitāb al-aghānī*

B: Berlin Mss. of al-Ṭabarī (nos. 9414–22), used by editors of Leiden edition; Ms. 9416 covers the *riddah*

BGA: *Bibliotheca Geographorum Arabicorum*

C: Istanbul ("Constantinople") Ms. Köprülü 1040 of al-Ṭabarī, used by editors of Leiden edition

Cairo: al-Ṭabarī, *Taʾrīkh*, Cairo edition

EI²: *Encyclopaedia of Islam*, 2nd edition. Leiden: E. J. Brill, 1960–

Emendanda: M. J. De Goeje, *Annales quod scripsit Abu Djafar Mohammed ibn Djarir al-Ṭabarī: Introduction, Glossarium, Addenda et Emendanda*. Leiden: E. J. Brill, 1901, p. DLXXIII–DCCCIII

Glossary: M. J. De Goeje, *Annales quod scripsit Abu Djafar Mohammed ibn Djarir al-Ṭabarī: Introduction, Glossarium, Addenda et Emendanda*. Leiden: E. J. Brill, 1901, p. CI–DLXXII

IK: Possibly a reference to passages in Ibn Khallikān's *Wafāyāt al-aʿyān* cited by P. De Jong, editor of this section of text in the Leiden edition. In the introduction to the Leiden edition (see *Glossary*, p. LXIII) Ibn Khallikān is mentioned in the *stemma* of manuscripts, but no mention of Ibn Khallikān or any other source to which the siglum IK might refer is included in discussion of the manuscripts and sources used by De Jong (pp. LII–LIII).

Kos: J. K. L. Kosegarten, ed., Greifswald partial edition of al-Ṭabarī, cited in notes to Leiden edition

TAVO: *Tübinger Atlas des vorderen Orients*, Wiesbaden: Dr. Ludwig Reichert Verlag, 1977–

Text: al-Ṭabarī, *Ṭaʾrīkh*, Leiden edition

Translator's Foreword

This volume of al-Ṭabarī's *History*, corresponding to pages 1837–2016 in the prima series of the Leiden edition, covers only part of the year A.H. 11/A.D. 632–33. It is devoted to two main themes: the *saqīfah* incident, during which the young Muslim community selected a leader following the death of Muḥammad, and the wars of the *riddah* or apostasy, during which the first caliph, Abū Bakr, led the government in Medina as it subjected all of Arabia. Some accounts of the *saqīfah* incident are also found at the end of volume IX of the translation (pp. 1820ff. of the text); on the other hand, all al-Ṭabarī's material on the *riddah* wars is included in volume X, constituting the overwhelming bulk of it.

Both the *saqīfah* incident and the *riddah* were crucial events in the development of the early Islamic state. Immediately after the death of the Prophet Muḥammad, the community of Muslims in Medina was in danger of falling apart. Old tribal tensions and rivalries among the Prophet's closest supporters, which the Prophet himself had been able to keep under control by the force of his personality and the authority of his message, threatened to break once again into the open. The Medinan *Anṣār*, or "Helpers" of the Prophet, and the *Muhājirūn*, or "Emigrants" who had come with the Prophet from Mecca, had sometimes felt keen rivalry toward one another. Early converts to Islam and old supporters of the Prophet—both *Muhājirūn* and *Anṣār*—resented some of the late converts from Mecca, who had been shown great favor by the Prophet in his last years, despite their long and bitter opposition to him and his message. Upon the Prophet's death, some of the leading clans of the Medinan *Anṣār* gathered to plan for their future and were on the verge of selecting one of their number to be leader of the Medinan Muslims, assuming that the Meccan Muslims would choose another chief for themselves. The gathering—which took place on a portico (*saqīfah*) of one of the Medinan clans, hence the name of the incident—was visited by a few of Muḥammad's earliest Meccan followers, who pleaded successfully for a unified leadership. The result was the acclamation of Abū Bakr, an early Meccan convert and close confidant of the Prophet, to be the first caliph (*khalīfah* "successor," sometimes "vicegerent").

In agreeing to recognize Abū Bakr as their leader following the Prophet's death, the Muslims also decided that they were to continue not only as a religious community but also as a unified polity. This decision was of the utmost importance. Had they decided otherwise, it is fair to assume that Islam would never have spread as it did, for the initial Islamic conquest movement was not primarily the expansion of a new faith, but rather the expansion of a new state—albeit a state whose coalescence was intimately linked with the new faith, which would come to be called Islam. It was under the shelter of this state ruled by Muslims that Islam first struck deep roots outside Arabian soil; without this shelter, Islam might well have remained a purely local Arabian cult, very different from what it eventually became as a result of its later evolution in the highly cultured regions of Mesopotamia, Syria, Egypt, and Iran.

If the *saqīfah* incident can be taken as the moment when Muslims committed themselves to being a unified political community, the *riddah* wars can be seen as the first test of that commitment. Even as the core of the Muslim community—the Prophet's Meccan and Medinan followers—was deciding to remain under united leadership, many other groups whom the Prophet had brought into his community in various parts of Arabia were deciding to end their submission to Medina. Some tribes claimed that they wished to remain Muslims in the religious sense—by performing prayer, for example—but would not send to Abū Bakr the tax payments that Muḥammad had requested of them in his last years. Others repudiated both the political and the religious leadership of Medina; they wished simply to go their own way, now that the Prophet was dead, in some cases choosing to follow other figures who claimed, like Muḥammad, to be prophets (and whom the Muslim tradition, naturally, condemns as "false prophets"). Still others, it seems, hoped simply to take advantage of the turmoil in Medina to raid the town, enriching themselves with plunder and ending what they perhaps felt to be vexatious demands for tribute. All of these movements are termed *riddah* "apostasy" by the Muslim sources, even in cases where the opponents of Medina showed no desire to repudiate the religious aspects of the faith. Abū Bakr vowed to fight them all until they were subdued and dispatched several armies to deal with the main rebellions. Indeed, the campaigns did not limit themselves to the reconquest of Arabian tribes that had previously had some contact with Muḥammad; they spilled over the whole of Arabia, and many tribes and groups that had had no contact with the Prophet at all, and who certainly had not been allied to or subjected by him, were conquered for the first time. The Arabic sources classify these wars, too, as wars against the *riddah*, even though they involved neither apostasy nor rebellion—only resistance to expansion of the new islamic state based in Medina.[1] The *riddah* wars constitute, in effect, the first chapter in the early Islamic conquest movement that led to the establishment throughout the Near East of a new imperial state ruled by Arabian Muslims.

The large amount of space that al-Ṭabarī dedicated to the *riddah* wars reflects the importance accorded the *riddah* theme in early Islamic historiography. It was a theme closely related to the theme of *futūḥ* (conquest by the Islamic state), which dominates the next several volumes in this translation of al-Ṭabarī. Both the *riddah* and the *futūḥ* were seen retrospectively by Muslims as signs of God's favor for the new Islamic faith, which is why they became such central themes in early Islamic historiography. But, unlike the *futūḥ* theme, the secondary

1. There are occasional passages where this classification is not enforced, however; e.g., I, 1961 top (from Sayf), which carefully distinguishes "apostates" from "non-apostates who were still unbelievers."

purpose of which was to explain and justify the Muslims' sovereignty over their non-Muslim subjects, the *riddah* theme was intended to affirm the superiority of the companions of the Prophet (*ṣaḥābah*) and of certain tribes and lineages over others.

In relating the stories of the *saqīfah* and the *riddah*, al-Ṭabarī relied on existing narratives conveyed to him by his predecessors in the historiographical enterprise—above all on the Kūfan compiler Sayf b. ʿUmar, whose accounts make up about 90 percent of this volume. As in other parts of al-Ṭabarī's history, then, very little in this volume represents original material written by al-Ṭabarī himself. This approach is hardly surprising, for al-Ṭabarī was first and foremost a traditionist and subscribed to the principle that true knowledge was what had been received via sound transmission from reliable earlier authorities, who had been closer to the events described. In the face of such transmitted evidence, al-Ṭabarī would have argued, what could later ideas made without support of sound transmission be but rank speculation? This does not mean, however, that al-Ṭabarī simply repeats everything he receives from his predecessors or that he had no point of view of his own. On the contrary, it seems clear that al-Ṭabarī screened his accounts carefully and so projected his particular interpretation of events by editorial manipulation, arrangement, and omission.[2]

Because of this method, al-Ṭabarī's point of view often becomes clear only when his treatment of a particular episode is compared with that of other compilers. For example, in relating the episode of Mālik b. Nuwayrah and the tribe of Tamīm, al-Ṭabarī tells us relatively little about how Mālik, who had been appointed tax agent over the Banū Ḥanẓalah by the Prophet, came to be considered a quasi-apostate and how he earned his nickname "al-Jafūl." These things are related much more fully by other compilers, like al-Diyārbakrī and al-Balansī. On the other hand, al-Ṭabarī dwells at length on Mālik's eventual death while captive in the hands of the troops of Khālid b. al-Walīd. He also focuses on Khālid's hasty marriage with Mālik's widow, on

---

2. On this aspect of al-Ṭabarī's editorial work, see the pioneering study by M. G. S. Hodgson, "Two Pre-Modern Muslim Historians."

the angry reaction of 'Umar b. al-Khaṭṭāb to this act, and on Abū Bakr's handling of the case. The latter issues are legal and political ones but, above all, questions of personal morality and its relation to political authority, which often seems to be what interested al-Ṭabarī most. When compared with the accounts in al-Balansī (pp. 50ff.), for example, al-Ṭabarī's narratives, derived from Sayf b. 'Umar, read like an effort to divert the reader's attention from the questionable behavior of Mālik b. Nuwayrah that led to his captivity in the first place. This might be considered simply another example of Sayf's desire to exculpate his tribe, Tamīm, for responsibility for the *riddah*, as noted long ago by Wellhausen.[3] On the other hand, Sayf's account—unlike that in al-Balansī—also exonerates Khālid b. al-Walīd from direct personal responsibility for killing Mālik. The point here is not to show that one or another of these alternative points of view is better but simply to demonstrate how al-Ṭabarī and other authors were able to guide their readers' attention to the issues—and perhaps, to the conclusions—that they wished by means of editorial manipulation and selection.

Al-Ṭabarī uses the "cut and paste" method of *khabar* history,[4] in which discrete accounts (*akhbār*, sing. *khabar*) on specific events are arranged one after another to provide fuller treatment of events. Because synthetic reformulation of material from various sources is eschewed, the compilation often suffers from poor coordination of the narrative and contains little, if any, analysis at all. For example, al-Ṭabarī likes to begin his examination of the *riddah* of a particular tribe (person, group) by relating what contacts, if any, that tribe had had with the Prophet Muḥammad and Islam before the Prophet's death. This material is presumably included to establish for certain that the tribesmen were, in fact, apostates who had given up the true faith after having acknowledged it. However, it is often not clearly set off from accounts of the *riddah* proper, so that it may be confusing to the reader, who encounters information about the events of the *riddah* in the year 11 and about events in

---

3. Wellhausen, *Skizzen*, VI, 1–7.
4. The term is that of F. Rosenthal, *A History of Muslim Historiography* (2nd ed. Leiden: 1968), pp. 66ff.

earlier years jumbled together in successive *akhbār*.[5] In other instances, the straitjacket of *khabar* history sometimes leads al-Ṭabarī to mention in an incidental way characters who only later receive a proper introduction into the narrative. For example, in relating Ṭulayḥah's rebellion, ʿUyaynah b. al-Ḥiṣn is mentioned along with Ṭulayḥah (p. 62, below), without any clarification of who ʿUyaynah was and what role he played in the *riddah*; this comes only later (p. 68, below). As a given body of material may be covered in several different *akhbār*, moreover, overlaps, repetitions, verbatim repeats, and the like are common, even in different accounts by one and the same transmitter.[6] Of course, between accounts related on the authority of different transmitters, overlaps are often multiple and extensive.

The disjointed nature of al-Ṭabarī's presentation becomes especially clear when we compare his text with others in search of parallels. Frequently, al-Ṭabarī's accounts do not provide a very complete or balanced overview of a particular event from the narrative point of view. His accounts of the battles at Buzākhah, Buṭāḥ, and even al-Yamāmah, though including much, also leave out much, knowledge of which is nonetheless implied or assumed in the accounts he does include. This means that accounts in other sources often provide the key to understanding the meaning of obscure or elliptical references in al-Ṭabarī's narratives.

On the other hand, al-Ṭabarī also sometimes includes material not found elsewhere; for example, his several accounts comparing miracles performed by the Prophet with failed efforts by Musaylimah to duplicate them (p. 110, below, from Sayf) do not occur in the other sources I have consulted.

Al-Ṭabarī's heavy reliance on the narratives of Sayf b. ʿUmar in recounting the events of this volume warrants some comment here. Sayf has been severely criticized by Wellhausen and other scholars for the apparent tribal chauvinism and chronological absurdity of his accounts, which these scholars

---

5. See, for example, I, 1892–93 on Ṭulayḥah's rebellion and its background.
6. An example is the phrase *bi'sa ʿawadtum anfusakum*, introduced in two accounts of Ibn Isḥāq, at pp. 118 and 122, below.

have dismissed as "historical novels" of little value to the modern historian.[7] Recently, a number of scholars have softened this criticism considerably, arguing that some of Sayf's presumed shortcomings are merely reflections of the kind of popular narrative he collected, that the chronology of other authors has little more claim to veracity than that of Sayf, and that his narratives do not so much contradict accounts by other transmitters, as they complement them by viewing events from a completely different vantage point.[8]

Sayf's narratives on the *riddah* (and on the conquests to follow) were evidently the fullest available to al-Ṭabarī. Other transmitters, like Ibn Isḥāq and Abū Mikhnaf, also provided al-Ṭabarī with some material, but its bulk is dwarfed by that coming via Sayf. It may be that al-Ṭabarī preferred Sayf's material because it conformed to the political and theological perspective that he himself wished to convey.[9] On the other hand, we must recall that al-Ṭabarī, as a traditionist, would have insisted that his sources meet the strict standards imposed by traditionists in evaluating transmitted material; one of his main purposes in writing his history seems to have been to establish the writing of history on the same systematic basis found in the study of *ḥadīth*, where the study of transmitted accounts had first been scientifically pursued. Al-Ṭabarī's heavy reliance on Sayf's material, then, can in some measure be taken as an affirmation of its perceived reliability in the eyes of one of the leading intellectual figures of the day.

Al-Ṭabarī's fondness for Sayf poses a definite handicap for the translator, however, because Sayf's narratives are frequently much more difficult to understand—and hence to translate—than those of other transmitters. The accounts of Ibn Isḥāq or of

---

7. E.g., Wellhausen, *Skizzen*, VI, pp. 1–7; M. J. De Goeje, *Mémoire sur la conquête de la Syrie*; Murtaḍā al-ʿAskarī, *Khamsūn wa miʾah ṣāḥābī mukhtalaq*.

8. On chronology, see Donner, *Conquests*, pp. 142ff. Landau-Tasseron, "Sayf b. ʿUmar in Medieval and Modern Scholarship," surveys the literature on Sayf and offers several cogent reasons why his compilations deserve serious consideration as sources.

9. On this aspect of al-Ṭabarī's selection of material, see Donner, "The Problem of Early Arabic Historiography in Syria," esp. pp. 21ff.

Ibn al-Kalbī (from Abū Mikhnaf), for example, often come as welcome interludes of lucidity amid long stretches of Sayf's vexing prose. Without going into great detail, we can note five specific features of Sayf's prose style that make it especially difficult.[10] First, Sayf's narratives often include elliptical phrases that can be virtually opaque unless the fuller context to which the phrase refers is known from another account. Related to this is his penchant for using numerous pronouns in long passages, leaving it unclear at times who or what the antecedent of the various pronouns may be. Second, Sayf sometimes uses a verb in one form to signify an action usually referred to by a verb of another form, for example *wāʿada bi-* (III) for "to threaten" instead of the usual *awʿada bi-* (IV).[11] Third, he sometimes employs known words with unknown meanings or with prepositions not associated with them in the dictionaries.[12] Fourth, verb and subject sometimes seem not in grammatical agreement, or verbs have no apparent subject. Fifth, Sayf sometimes seems to use certain particles, like *ḥattā, thumma*, etc., with unorthodox meanings.[13]

These and other anomalies of Sayf's narrative style may be more than just a headache for the translator, however; they may also be clues to the origins of his material. For they suggest that Sayf was not engaged mainly in polishing his narratives into an acceptable literary style but was, rather, intent on relating a variety of stories he had collected from informants hailing from diverse tribes—tribes whose differing dialects may be responsible for the grammatical and stylistic anomalies of Sayf's accounts. We have seen that Sayf was criticized harshly by Wellhausen for presenting a picture of events that favored his own tribe of Tamīm, but the chains of informants Sayf prefaces

10. The following observations are impressionistic and not meant to be either conclusive or exhaustive.

11. This occurs at p. 72. Cf. *ijtāza ʿalā* (p. 92), meaning "to commit aggression against," instead of the usual *jāwaza ʿalā*; *kharraṭa ʿalā* (p. 125), cf. dictionaries' *ikhtaraṭa* "to draw [the sword]"; *aqāma li* (p. 146) "to resist (?)."

12. E.g., *istabraʾa* (p. 105) "to mop up" in military context (?); *ramā bi-* (p. 92) "to shoot" [someone]; *intalaqa bi-* (p. 110) "to take [something] away"; *ikhtalafa bayna* (p. 97) "to serve as intermediary between."

13. E.g., pp. 110, 57 bottom, *thumma* as "so, so that."

to his accounts reveal that his informants came from many tribes in addition to Tamīm, and it seems likely that Sayf (or some of his immediate informants) made a concerted effort to collect tribal oral traditions that had never been written down. Other clues, too, point to possible oral origins of much of Sayf's narrated material—not only the generally rough and disjointed nature of the overall compilation but also such details as occasional lapses into the "narrative present" in tales otherwise couched in the past.[14]

Sayf's rendition of the *riddah* in the Yemen offers an interesting case in point. In general, the section is very confusing, as the material on al-Aswad's rebellion is related in tandem with material on the Prophet's appointment of tax agents and his death in a way that makes the chronological relationship of the different events quite unclear. In fact, al-Ṭabarī includes not one but two quite lengthy narrations of the beginnings of the *riddah* in the Yemen on Sayf's authority (pp. 18–34, 34–38), and, though these two versions of Sayf's have many common features (enough to make each of some help in decoding the other), they also display considerable divergence in detail.[15] Both are cast in an unusually problematic Arabic, and it seems likely that we are faced here with two oral variants of a common tribal tradition about the killing of al-Aswad.

Given the frequent difficulties of Sayf's Arabic, the search for close parallels to his accounts in texts other than al-Ṭabarī offers the hope of finding clearer wordings for awkward phrases. What is most interesting, however, is that the search for parallels reveals that Sayf's Arabic was almost as problematic to medieval

---

14. E.g., p. 179, where Sayf has the imperfect, *lā tuḥdithu . . . , lā tajidu. . . .* It is worth noting that Ibn al-Athīr's almost verbatim quote from this passage (*Kāmil*, II, 380) changes the verbs from the imperfect (denoting incomplete action) to the jussive (denoting completed action): *lam yuḥdith . . . lam yajid. . . .*

15. There is actually a third summary of events on Sayf's authority at pp. 158–61, but it is very different from the two noted above.

16. Cf. Balādhurī, *Futūḥ*, pp. 94ff., on the apostasy of *al-ʿarab*, referring to the largely nomadic groups of Sulaym, ʿĀmir b. Ṣaʿṣaʿah, Asad, Fazārah, Tamīm, etc., but with separate sections on the apostasy of Kindah and al-Aswad al-ʿAnsī and his followers, both groups of sedentary people. Cf. also Balansī, 5, where the *muhājirūn* say to Abū Bakr, when Usāmah is away, "We don't have the power to fight the Arabs," referring to the nomads of Fazārah.

Arab historians as it is to us. This offers us only the cold comfort of knowing that our problem in deciphering a given passage lies more with the text than it does with our knowledge of classical Arabic; for the parallels often do not assist us at all in our goal of achieving a satisfactory translation of al-Ṭabarī's text.

Passages in most authors who deal with the *riddah* were only occasionally useful in clarifying the precise wording of a passage but were frequently helpful in clarifying the general context of events. Most useful in this respect were al-Balansī, al-Diyārbakrī, and al-Balādhurī's *Futūḥ al-buldān*. The longest sustained parallel to al-Ṭabarī's text on the *riddah* is provided by Ibn al-Athīr in his *al-Kāmil fī al-ta'rīkh*, for he relied heavily (indeed, almost exclusively) on al-Ṭabarī for his account. According to De Goeje's *stemma* of the manuscripts of al-Ṭabarī, Ibn al-Athīr relied on an earlier manuscript, now lost, that was also the source for the Berlin, Oxford, and one of the Istanbul manuscripts on which the Leiden edition of the text was partially based. Ibn al-Athīr is thus occasionally helpful but more frequently frustrating; though long, straightforward passages from al-Ṭabarī are quoted by him verbatim, problematic passages are often simply dropped altogether, and the remnants harmonized into a plausible narrative or condensed in summaries that, though clear in meaning, really represent merely Ibn al-Athīr's commentary on what al-Ṭabarī's text might have meant. Moreover, we do not always agree with Ibn al-Athīr's judgment; at p. 107, for example, Ibn al-Athīr fills in the subject of the phrase *wa kāna yantahī ilā amri-hi* as Musaylima, but it seems to me more likely to refer to Nahār "al-Rajjāl."

Of course, Ibn al-Athīr's evasion of many textual difficulties means that the manuscript he used already contained many of the same problems we face. This may, of course, simply be the result of corruptions creeping into the text in the manner normal in a manuscript tradition, but I think that it is really further evidence that the texts on the *riddah*, particularly those related from Sayf, are in fact archaic—in both origin and language—and hence not well understood already in al-Ṭabarī's day, much less in Ibn al-Athīr's. The fact that virtually all the really problematic spots occur in Sayf's narratives, rather than in those related by other informants, argues against the random hand of manuscript corruption as the source of most difficulties.

Volume 19 of the Cairo (1975) edition of al-Nuwayrī's *Nihāyat al-arab fī funūn al-adab* also has a long section on the *riddah* that is derived, primarily, from al-Ṭabarī. Although a few of al-Nuwayrī's circumlocutions are helpful in establishing the sense of al-Ṭabarī's text, he seems even more determined than Ibn al-Athīr to evade opaque passages.

The problematic nature of many passages in the text has had several practical implications. First and foremost, of course, it means that the translation offered here can be considered only a provisional one. We can hope that someday, when scholars have undertaken a much more thorough examination of the text on the basis of all available manuscripts (and perhaps even on the basis of new manuscripts yet to be discovered), a much surer edition of the text can be prepared, on the basis of which a definitive translation can be prepared. In the meantime, readers must be warned that, despite my efforts and those of several very learned Arabists who kindly agreed to consider rough passages with me, there remains considerable scope for distortion or outright error in this translation.

A second practical implication of the text's complexity is that instead of noting all the many manuscript variants noted by the Leiden edition, I have chosen only a few that seemed to me significant in clarifying the meaning of the passage or in suggesting a plausible different meaning. The reason for this is simply the sheer number of manuscript variants—sometimes exceeding twenty per page. To have included all of them would have added at least two thousand additional notes to the volume, most of little consequence for the translation. The Arabist who uses the translation, however, and who is interested in a particular passage of text must still refer back to the Arabic text itself to see whether or not some variant that I have not noted may bear important implications for his or her work.

I have been most fortunate to have had the kind assistance of several very learned colleagues, who reviewed my translation of problematic passages and suggested a large number of changes. First and foremost I wish to thank Dr. Ella Landau-Tasseron of the Hebrew University, a fine Arabist and without doubt the leading specialist on the history of the *riddah* in our generation of scholars. With the careful attention she displays in all her work, she reconsidered many thorny passages and offered extensive and meticulously detailed corrections and improvements, both linguistic and historical. My colleagues at Chicago, Dr. Farouk Mustafa and Dr. Wadad al-Qadi, sat with me for many hours and helped me to gain a better understanding of many passages (particularly of poetry) the import of which, or some important nuance of which, had escaped me in part or completely. To all of them I offer my heartfelt thanks for having so generously shared their time (so limited) and knowledge (so extensive) in a way that has immeasurably improved the reliability and accuracy of the translation presented here. As none of these colleagues reviewed the entire text of the translation, however, the errors and oversights that doubtless remain in it must redden my ears alone. I also wish to thank my editor, Dr. Estelle Whelan, who saw this volume through the press.

In closing, I list a few relatively common words, the translation of which from classical Arabic is often problematic, with my explanation of the way I have translated them (or, in some cases, refused to do so). I hope this may help Arabists and general readers alike to get a better sense of some passages where these words are used.

> *al-ʿarab*. I have generally rendered this simply as "Arabs," but the word does not, of course, have the modern nationalist meaning, which has been known only since the nineteenth century. Rather, it means either "nomads," that is, nonsedentary pastoral people,[16] or "speakers of Arabic"; not infrequently, the text is ambiguous as to which meaning is intended, for which reason it seemed advisable to leave the term untranslated.
>
> *amr*. The basic meaning is either "affair, matter" or "order, command," but it is used in a wide variety of contexts and so requires very flexible rendering. It is variously translated "situation," "cause," "purpose," "something," "leadership", or "authority."
>
> *al-nās*. Basically "people" (according to *Glossary*, actually "chiefs, noblemen" or "horsemen"), in many cases it is

best translated "the army," always referring to one's own side.

al-qawm. Basically "group, tribe, people," it often means "the enemy," that is, the other side.

dīn. Sometimes rendered "religion," e.g. *dīn Allāh*, p. 56, but sometimes, especially in political contexts, best rendered "obedience." At times *dīn Allāh* seems to mean "obedience to God," especially when *dīn* is juxtaposed with *islām* "submission," as on p. 57.

Fred M. Donner

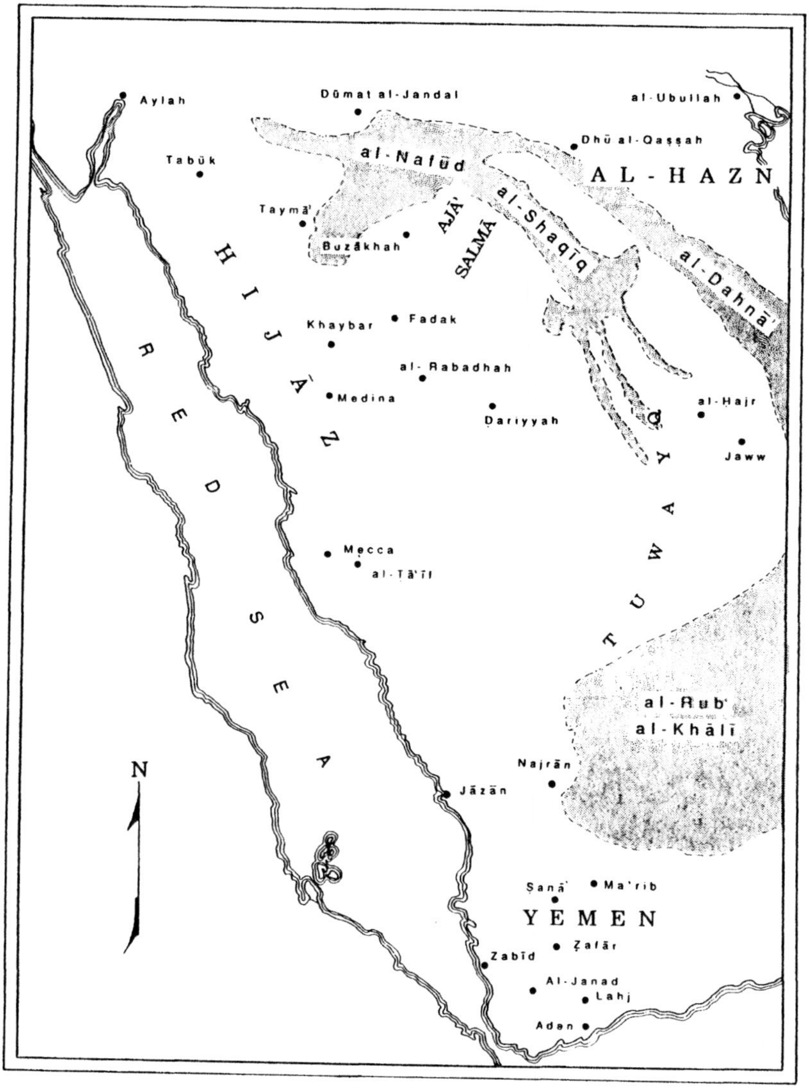

Map 1. Western Arabia at the Time of the Riddah

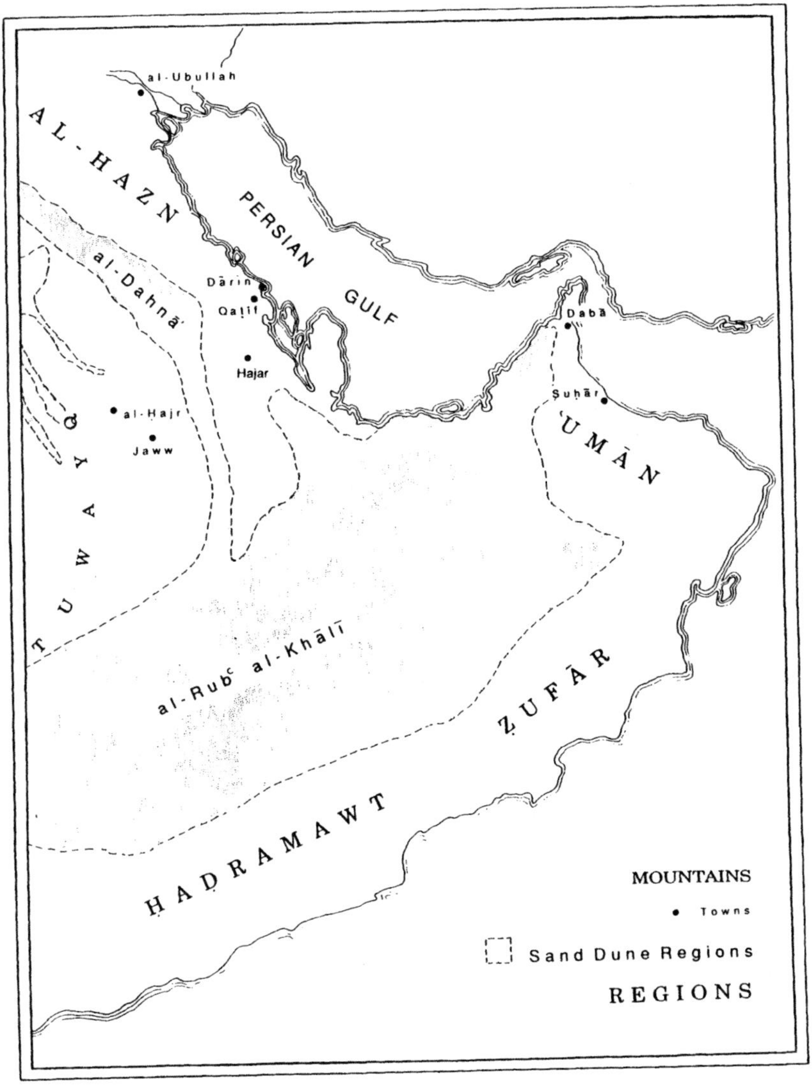

Map 2. Eastern Arabia at the Time of the Riddah

The Events of the Year

11 (cont'd) [1837]

(March 29, 632–March 17, 633)

What Took Place between the Muhājirūn and the Anṣār over the Matter of Leadership at the Portico of the Banū Sā'idah[1]

According to Hishām b. Muḥammad—Abū Mikhnaf—'Abdallāh b. 'Abd al-Raḥmān b. Abī 'Amrah al-Anṣārī:[2] When the Prophet passed away, the Anṣār gathered on the portico of the Banū Sā'idah said, "Let us appoint Sa'd b. 'Ubādah[3] to be in charge of

1. The Muhājirūn (often translated as "Emigrants," but see note 81, below, on *hijrah*) were mainly those people of the Meccan tribe of Quraysh—the Prophet's tribe—who emigrated to Medina to join the Prophet's community there, but they included some people of other groups who embraced Islam and settled in Medina; the Anṣār ("Helpers") were the Medinan converts to Islam, comprising mainly the rival Medinan tribes of Aws and Khazraj; the Banū Sā'idah b. Ka'b were a clan of he Khazraj. For an analysis of the traditions on Abū Bakr's election, see Caetani, 521–33.

2. Ibn Abī al-Ḥadīd, *Sharh nahj al-balāghah*, I, 302–3, summarizes pp. 1–10; cf. Nuwayrī, 29–31 (as far as p. 15). Cf. Caetani, 514–15.

3. A chief of the Khazraj tribe of Medina and one of the twelve *naqībs*, or guarantors, of the Medinan Anṣār chosen by the Prophet during the meeting at al-'Aqabah, before the *hijrah*; cf. Ibn Sa'd, III/2, 134–35, 142–45.

our affairs after Muḥammad." They made Saʿd come out to them; but he was sick, and after they had gathered he said to his son or to one of his cousins, "Because of my illness I cannot make my words heard by all the people. Take my speech from me and make them hear it." So he spoke, and the man memorized what he said and said [it] in a loud voice so that his [1838] companions would hear it. After praising and extolling God, he said:

> Company of the Anṣār! You have precedence in religion and merit in Islam that no [other] tribe of the Arabs can claim. Muḥammad remained ten-odd years in his tribe, calling them to worship the Merciful and to cast off idols and graven images, but only a few men of his tribe believed in Him, and they were able neither to protect the Apostle of God, nor to render His religion strong, nor to divert from themselves the oppression that befell them all; until, when He intended excellence for you, He sent nobility to you and distinguished you with grace. Thus God bestowed upon you faith in Him and in His Apostle, and protection for him and his companions, and strength for him and his faith, and battle (jihād) for his enemies. You were the most severe people against his enemies who were among you, and the most troublesome to his enemies who were not from among you, so that the Arabs became upright in God's cause, willingly or unwillingly, and the distant one submitted in abject humiliation, until through you God made great slaughter in the earth[4] for His Apostle, and by your swords the Arabs were abased for him.[5] When God took (the Prophet) to Himself,[6] he was pleased with you and consoled by you. [So] keep [control of] this matter to yourselves, to the exclusion of others, for it is yours and yours alone.

---

4. Reading ʾathkhana . . . fī al-ardı, ınstead of the text's and Nuwayrī's (p. 30) athkhana . . . al-arda. Cf. Qurʾān 8:67.
5. Translatıng the verb dānat as transıtıve, rather than ıntransıtıve.
6. I.e., at the time of the Prophet's death.

They answered him all together, "Your opinion is right, and you have spoken correctly. We will not diverge from your opinion, and we shall put you in charge of this business. For indeed, you are sufficient for us and satisfactory to whoever is righteous among the believers." But then they began to debate among themselves, and [some] said, "What if the Muhājirūn of Quraysh refuse, saying, 'We are the Muhājirūn and the first companions of the Apostle of God; we are his kinsmen and his friends.[7] So why do you dispute this matter with us after him?'" [Another] group of (the Anṣār) said, "Then we should say, 'let us have a leader from among ourselves, and you a leader from among yourselves,' for we should never be satisfied with less [1839]
than this leadership." When Sa'd b. 'Ubādah heard this, he said, "This is the beginning of weakness."

'Umar learned of this and went to the Prophet's house and sent to Abū Bakr, who was in the building.[8] Now 'Alī b. Abī Ṭālib[9] was working busily preparing the Apostle [for burial], so ['Umar] sent a message to Abū Bakr to come out to him. Abū Bakr sent back that he was occupied, but ['Umar] sent him another message, saying, "Something has happened that you must attend to in person." So he came out to him, and ['Umar] said to him, "Didn't you know that the Anṣār have gathered at the portico of the Banū Sā'idah intending to put Sa'd b. 'Ubādah in charge of this affair? [Even] the best of them is saying, 'A leader for us and a leader for Quraysh.'" So the two of them hurried toward them; they met Abū 'Ubaydah b. al-Jarrāḥ,[10] and the three of them marched toward them. [On

---

7. *'Ashīratuhu wa awliyatuhu*. Ibn Abī al-Ḥadīd, I, 302, has *awliyā'uhu wa 'itratuhu*; Nuwayrī, 30, has *'ashīratuhu wa awliyā'uhu*.

8. Cf. Ibn Hishām, 1013 (from Ibn Isḥāq), 1015–16; Diyārbakrī, II, 168 (from Ibn Isḥāq); and Ṣan'ānī, V, 442 (al-Zuhrī—'Ubaydallāh b. 'Abdallāh b. 'Utbah—Ibn 'Abbās). Ibn Hishām, 1015–16, seems to be a condensed version of pp. 3–8.

9. 'Alī b. Abī Ṭālib was the Prophet's cousin and the husband of the Prophet's daughter Fāṭima; he would later be the fourth caliph or successor to the Prophet as head of the Muslim community. 'Umar ibn al-Khaṭṭāb and Abū Bakr, in the preceding sentence, were early converts and close associates of the Prophet and would later serve as the second and first successors of the Prophet, respectively.

10. An early convert to Islam from Quraysh, who played a major role in the Islamic conquest of Syria after the Prophet's death; cf. *EI*[2], s.v. "Abū 'Ubayda b. al-Djarrāḥ" (H. A. R. Gibb). Diyarbakrī, II, 167–68 (from Ibn Isḥāq) makes no

their way] they were met by ʿĀṣim b. ʿAdī and ʿUwaym b. Sāʿidah,[11] who said, "Go back, for it will not be as you wish." But they refused [to turn back] and arrived while [the Anṣār] were gathered.

According to ʿUmar b. al-Khaṭṭāb: We came to them, and I had pieced together[12] a speech that I wanted to deliver to them; but, when I had pushed in among them and was about to begin my address, Abū Bakr said to me, "Easy does it, ʿUmar, until I have spoken; then afterward say whatever you wish." So he spoke [first], and there was nothing that I had wanted to say that he did not come to, or amplify it.

According to ʿAbdallāh b. ʿAbd al-Raḥmān:[13] Abū Bakr began by praising and extolling God. Then he said, "Verily God sent Muḥammad as an Apostle to His creatures and as a witness to his community, that they should worship God and affirm His
[1840] oneness. For they had worshiped various deities other than Him, alleging that [those deities] were intercessors before Him on their behalf and were beneficial for them. [Those gods] were of carved stone and hewn wood." Then he recited, "And they serve beside God that which can neither harm nor help them, saying: 'These are our intercessors before God.'"[14] And they said, "We worship them only that they may make us nearer to God."[15] [Abū Bakr continued,] "Now the Arabs found it most distressing that they should leave the religion of their forefathers; so from among his tribe God singled out the first Muhājirūn, by having

---

mention of him and has only Abū Bakr and ʿUmar proceeding to the Anṣār, but later in the account he mentions the raising of the hands of ʿUmar and Abū ʿUbaydah to swear allegiance to Abū Bakr.

11. The names vary in different accounts. Ibn Hishām, 1016 (Ibn Isḥāq—al-Zuhrī—ʿUrwah b. al-Zubayr); Ibn Abī al-Ḥadīd, I, 293; Ṣanʿānī, V, 445 (al-Zuhrī—ʿUrwah); and Diyārbakrī, II, 167, give the first name as Maʿn b. ʿAdī; the last gives the second name as ʿUwaymir b. Sāʿidah. Ṣanʿānī, V, 442, gives simply "two righteous men of the Anṣār" and has them saying "Go and settle your affairs among yourselves."

12. Reading *zawwartu* (instead of *zawwaytu* ["I cast off?"] or *rawītu* ["I related"] of the manuscripts), as suggested by De Goeje in *Emendanda*, Ibn al-Athīr *Kāmil*, II, 327; Ibn Abī al-Ḥadīd, I, 293; Ibn Hishām, 1015–16; and Nuwayrī, 32. Ṣanʿānī, V, 443, has *rawwaytu* "I asked [s.o.] to recite"(?).

13. Cf. Nuwayrī, 33–36, as far as p. 8.

14. Qur'ān 10:18.

15. Qur'ān 39:3.

them affirm that he spoke the truth and by their belief in him, and consoling him and enduring patiently with him the harsh insults their tribe [directed] against them and (their tribe), calling them liars. All the people were opposed to (the Muhājirūn) and rebuked them; but they were not distressed by their small numbers or by the hatred of the people for them or by (the people's) single-minded opposition to them, for they were the first who worshiped God on the earth and who believed in God and the Apostle. They are his friends and kinsmen[16] and the most deserving people in this matter after him; only a wrongdoer would dispute that. Oh company of the Anṣār, your superiority in religion and great precedence in Islām are undeniable. May God be satisfied with you as helpers (*anṣār*) for His religion and His Apostle. He made his *hijrah* to you, and the majority of his wives and his companions are among you; so—after the first Muhājirūn—there is no one among us who is in your station. We are the leaders, and you the helpers;[17] matters shall not be settled without consultation, nor shall we decide on them without you."[18]

Then al-Ḥubāb b. al-Mundhir b. al-Jamūḥ[19] stood up and said, "Oh company of the Anṣār, take command of yourselves, for you overshadow [other] people.[20] No one will dare oppose you [1841]
[if you do], nor will the people[21] proceed, except in accordance with your opinion. You are the people of power and wealth, numerous and strong in resistance and experienced, having boldness and courage. The people look only to what you do; so do not differ among yourselves, lest your judgment (*ra'y*) be spoiled and your cause (*amr*) collapse.[22] This one [i.e., Abū Bakr]

---

16. *'Ashīratuhu*. Ibn Abī al-Ḥadīd, I, 302: *'itratuhu* "his family."

17. *Wuzarā'*, here using *wazīr* in the Qur'ānic sense of "helper, assistant"; cf. Qur'ān 20:29, 25:35.

18. A loose parallel in Ibn Sa'd, III/1, 129, ll. 4ff., makes clear the idea of shared power.

19. A leader of Khazraj, prominent at Badr and other battles of the Prophet. Cf. Ibn Sa'd, III/2, 109–10.

20. Lit., "the people are in your shade and shadow."

21. Ibn Abī al-Ḥadīd, I, 302: "anyone."

22. Ibn Abī al-Ḥadīd, I, 302, has "lest you spoil your affairs (*umūr*) for yourselves."

insisted on what you have heard.[23] So [let us have] a leader from among us, and [they] a leader from among them." At this ʿUmar said, "Absolutely not; two cannot come to agreement in a joining.[24] By God, the Arabs will not be content to give you the leadership when their Prophet was not one of you; but they would not prevent their affairs from being led by one of those among whom prophethood [had appeared] and from whom the guardian of their affairs [was chosen]. In that [fact] is manifest argument and clear proof[25] for us against those Arabs who deny [it]. Who would attempt to wrest from us the sovereignty (*sulṭān*) of Muḥammad and his authority (*imārah*), seeing that we are his friends and his kinsmen, except someone advancing falsehood, inclining to sin, or hurtling into destruction?" [But] al-Ḥubāb b. al-Mundhir stood up [again] and said, "Oh company of the Anṣār, take charge of your own affairs[26] and do not listen to what this one and his companions say, for they would do away with your share in this matter. If they refuse to give you what you ask for, then drive them out of this country, and seize control of these matters despite them. For you are more deserving of this authority[27] than they are, as it was by your swords that those who were not yet converted came to obey this religion.[28] I am their much-rubbed little rubbing post, and their propped little palm tree loaded with fruit.[29] By God, if you wish to return it as a stump [then do so!]" ʿUmar said, "Then may God kill you!" and (al-Ḥubāb) replied, "Rather may He kill

23. Lit., "denied everything except what you heard." Ibn Abī al-Ḥadīd, I, 302, has "If this one has insisted . . . , then let us have. . . ." Cf. Diyārbakrī, II, 169 top.

24. This phrase is, at best, laconic. Ibn Abī al-Ḥadīd, I, 302, has "two swords cannot be joined in one scabbard"; Al-Ṣanʿānī, V, 444, has "two swords are not suitable in one scabbard." The idea, in any case, is that one community cannot be led by two people.

25. *Al-sulṭān al-mubīn.*

26. Lit., "grasp upon your hands."

27. *Imārah*; but cf. Nuwayrī, 35 top: *amr* "affair."

28. *Dāna li-hādhā al-dīn man dāna mimman lam yakun yadīnu*, lit., "those who came to obey of those who had not [yet] obeyed came to obey this religion."

29. I.e., "I am sought out by those needing advice as camels with mange seek the scratching post, and I have a numerous family to defend me" (Lane, *Arabic-English Lexicon*, s.v. "*jidhl*"). Cf. Ibn Hishām, 1016; Diyārbakrī, II, 168, 169; Nuwayrī, 32 bottom, 35 top.

you!" At this Abū 'Ubaydah said, "Oh company of the Anṣār, you were the first who helped and strengthened, so do not be the [1842] first to substitute and change for the worse."[30]

Then Bashīr b. Sa'd,[31] father of al-Nu'mān b. Bashīr, stood up and said, "Oh company of the Anṣār, if indeed by God we were the first in merit in battling the polytheists and in precedence in this religion, we would want by (these deeds) only [to gain] our Lord's pleasure, and obedience to our Prophet, and sustenance for ourselves; it is not appropriate for us to exalt ourselves over [other] people. Let us not seek by it some transitory thing of the world, for indeed God is the One Who provides (such things) for us out of His grace.[32] In truth Muḥammad was from Quraysh, and his people are more entitled to [hold] (authority) and more suitable. I swear by God that He shall never see me contesting this matter (*amr*) with them. So fear God and do not oppose them or dispute with them."

At this Abū Bakr said,[33] "This is 'Umar, and this is Abū 'Ubaydah; render the oath of allegiance to whichever of them you wish." But they both said, "No, by God, we shall not undertake [to hold] this authority over you, for you are the best of the Muhājirūn, the "second of two when they were in the cave,"[34] and the Apostle of God's deputy (*khalīfah*) over the prayer; and prayer is the most meritorious obedience (*dīn*) of the Muslims. So who should precede you or undertake this authority over you? Extend your hand so we may render the oath of allegiance to you!"

When[35] the two of them went forth to render the oath of allegiance to him, Bashīr b. Sa'd went to him ahead of them and swore allegiance to him [first]. At this al-Ḥubāb b. al-Mundhir shouted to him, "Oh Bashīr b. Sa'd, you are in op-

---

30. I.e., as the Muslim community was united and strong before, a change to disunity will be a setback.

31. An early follower of Muḥammad from Medina. Cf. Ibn Sa'd, III/2, 83–84.

32. Lit., "God is the benefactor of grace upon us by that."

33. Cf. Al-Diyārbakrī, II, 168, 169.

34. A quotation from Qur'ān 9:40, considered by Muslim exegetes to refer to an episode when Abū Bakr made the *hijrah* with the Prophet.

35. Cf. Diyārbakrī, II, 169.

position [to your kinsmen];[36] what drove you to [do] what you have done?[37] Did you envy your cousin[38] the sovereignty?" He replied, "By God, no! But I abhorred contending with a group for a right that God had given them." Now when the Aws saw what Bashīr b. Saʿd had done and what Quraysh had called for and what the Khazraj were demanding by way of giving sovereignty
[1843] to Saʿd b. ʿUbādah, they said to one another (and among them was Usayd b. Ḥuḍayr, one of the *naqībs*):[39] "By God, if once you appoint the Khazraj over you, they will always have the advantage over you on that account, and will never give you any share in it with them. So stand up and render the oath of allegiance to Abū Bakr." So they came forth to him and rendered the oath of allegiance to him. Thus that which Saʿd b. ʿUbādah and the Khazraj had agreed to do was defeated.

Hishām—Abū Mikhnaf—Abū Bakr b. Muḥammad al-Khuzāʿī:[40] Aslam[41] approached *en masse* until the streets were packed with them, and they rendered the oath of allegiance to Abū Bakr. ʿUmar used to say, "It was not until I saw Aslam that I was certain we had won the day."[42]

Hishām—Abū Mikhnaf—ʿAbdallāh b. ʿAbd al-Raḥmān.[43] People approached from all sides swearing allegiance to Abū Bakr, and they almost stepped on Saʿd b. ʿUbādah. Some of Saʿd's associates said, "Be careful not to step on Saʿd!" At this ʿUmar said, "Kill him; may God slay him!" Then he stepped on his head, saying, "I intend to tread upon you until your arm is

36. Reading, with Cairo, *ʿaqqatka ʿaqāqī*, for *ʿaqaqta ʿaqāqī* in the text. Cf. Ibn Manẓūr, X, 257, for the idiom.

37. Reading *mā akhrajaka* for *mā aḥwajaka*, as suggested by P. De Jong in notes to text. However, Nuwayrī, 36, has the same reading as the text.

38. I.e., his fellow tribesman of Khazraj, Saʿd b. ʿUbādah.

39. On the *naqībs* see note 2, above. On Usayd, a chief of the Aws tribe who had led them in battle against the Khazraj at the battle of Buʿāth before Islam, see Ibn Saʿd, III/2, 135–37.

40. Cf. Nuwayrī, 36–38, as far as p. 10.

41. A tribe associated with Khuzāʿah, living west and southwest of Medina and among Muḥammad's earliest backers after his arrival in Medina. Cf. Watt, *Muhammad at Medina*, 82ff.

42. Lit., "that I was certain of victory."

43. Cf. Diyārbakrī, II, 169; Nuwayrī, 36–37.

dislocated."[44] At this Saʿd took hold of ʿUmar's beard and said, "By God, if you remove a single hair from it you'll return with no front teeth in your mouth." Then Abū Bakr said, "Take it easy, ʿUmar; compassion[45] would be more effective at this point." So ʿUmar turned away from him. Saʿd said, "By God, if I had the strength to get up, you would have heard from me in the regions and streets [of Medina], roaring in a way that would make you and your companions take cover; by God, I shall join to you a group among whom you[46] would be a follower, not a leader. [Now] carry me from this place." So they carried him and took him into his house. He was left for several days; then[47] [1844]
he was sent to [and told] that he should come to render the oath of allegiance, for the people [generally] had done so and his tribe as well. But he said, "By God, I shall not do it, before I have shot at you with whatever arrows are in my quiver, and have reddened the head of my spear, and struck you with my sword, as long as my hand controls it. I will fight you with my family and those who obey me of my tribe. I swear by God, [even] if the jinn gathered to you with the people,[48] I would not render the oath of allegiance to you, until I am brought forth[49] before my God and know what my reckoning is."

When Abū Bakr was informed of this, ʿUmar said to him, "Pester him until he renders the oath of allegiance." But Bashīr b. Saʿd said, "He has refused; he has made up his mind, and wouldn't render the oath of allegiance to you even if he were

---

44. Reading *ʿaḍudaka* with Cairo edition and *Emendanda*, instead of the text's *ʿiḍwaka* "your limb." The emendation does not solve all the problems in the text, however, as the context immediately before and after the word refers to Saʿd's head (e.g., "if you remove a single hair from it"), not his arms. In view of this, one might expect here that ʿUmar may have threatened to break Saʿd's neck (i.e., dislocate his head?).

45. Or, perhaps, "gentleness" or "tact": *rifq*.

46. Reading with *Emendanda*, instead of "among whom I was a follower" in the text.

47. Ibn Saʿd, III/2, 144, ll. 24ff., provides a close parallel to the remainder of this paragraph and the following one.

48. An echo of the Qurʾānic "men and jinn," meaning all creatures (e.g., Qurʾān 17:88); a loose English rendering might be something like "even if man and beast joined in supporting you."

49. Reading *uʿraḍu* with Ibn Abī al-Ḥadīd, I, 303; Nuwayrī, 37; and Cairo ed.

killed; and he would not be killed without his children and family and a party of his kinsmen being killed with him. So leave him alone; leaving him won't harm you, he is only one man,"[50] So they left him alone. They came to accept the advice of Bashīr b. Saʿd, consulting him whenever it seemed right to them to do so.

Saʿd[51] [b. ʿUbādah] used not to pray in their [daily] prayer or congregate with them [for Friday prayer]; he performed the pilgrimage [to Mecca] but did not press on with them in the multitudes.[52] He continued thus until Abū Bakr died.

According to ʿUbaydallāh b. Saʿd[53]—his uncle—Sayf b. ʿUmar—Sahl and Abū ʿUthmān—al-Ḍaḥḥāk b. Khalīfah: When al-Ḥubāb b. al-Mundhir stood up, he drew his sword and said, "I am their much-rubbed little rubbing post and their propped little palm tree loaded with fruit.[54] I am [like] the father of a cub in the lion's den, related to the lion [as son to father]." Then ʿUmar attacked him, striking his hand so that the sword dropped out,
[1845] and picked it up. Then he pounced upon Saʿd [b. ʿUbādah]; and they all fell upon him. The people rendered the oath of allegiance successively [to Abū Bakr]; and Saʿd rendered the oath of allegiance. It was an action taken without consideration, like those of the *jāhiliyyah*.[55] Abū Bakr stood up before them. Someone said, when Saʿd was being trampled, "You have killed Saʿd," to which ʿUmar replied, "God killed him, for he is a hypocrite"; and ʿUmar struck the sword on a stone, breaking it.[56]

---

50. Ibn Abī al-Ḥadīd, I, 292, has a similar phrase, but applied to ʿAlī b. Abī Ṭālib as the one holding out against Abū Bakr.

51. Cf. Diyārbakrī, II, 169.

52. Referring to the multitudes surging to and from ʿArafah during the culmination of the pilgrimage rituals on the eighth-tenth days of the month of Dhū al-Ḥijjah.

53. Text has Saʿīd; cf. *Emendanda*, Cairo edition, manuscript C of Leiden edition.

54. Cf. p. 6, above.

55. The pejorative term for the pre-Islamic age in Islamic historiography; roughly "age of barbarism," i.e., before the enlightenment of Islam had arrived.

56. The text is difficult, but similar passages help clarify the meaning. In Ibn Abī al-Ḥadīd, I, 315, ʿUmar seizes the sword of al-Zubayr b. al-ʿAwwām as he is about to recognize ʿAlī b. Abī Ṭālib and breaks it on a stone; in Ibn Abī al-Ḥadīd, I, 291, and Nuwayrī, 39, al-Zubayr's sword is taken away and broken on a rock at

According to ʿUbaydallāh b. Saʿd[57]—his uncle Yaʿqūb—Sayf—Mubashshir—Jābir:[58] Saʿd b. ʿUbādah said to Abū Bakr on that day, "Oh company of Muhājirūn, you begrudge me sovereignty (*al-imārah*), and you and my tribe have compelled me to render the oath of allegiance." At this they replied, "If we had compelled you to division and then you had come to unity (*jamāʿah*) [of your own accord] you would be in a comfortable position; but we forced [you] to unity, so there is no going back on it.[59] If you withdraw a hand from obedience, or divide the union, we will strike off your head."[60]

According to ʿUbaydallāh b. Saʿd[61]—his uncle—Sayf; and according to al-Sarī b. Yaḥyā—Shuʿayb b. Ibrāhīm—Sayf b. ʿUmar—Ibn Ḍamrah—his father—ʿĀṣim b. ʿAdī: Two days after the Apostle of God's death, Abū Bakr's public crier called out so that the mission (*baʿth*) of Usāmah[62] could be completed: "Up now! No one from Usāmah's army should remain in Medina, but should go out to his camp at al-Jurf."[63] And [Abū Bakr] stood up among the people, praised and extolled God, and said,[64] "Oh people, I am like you. I do not know, perhaps you will impose on me that which the Apostle of God was able to do. God chose Muḥammad above [all] the worlds and protected him from evils; but I am only a follower, not an innovator (*mubtadiʿ*). If I am [1846]
upright, then follow me; but, if I deviate, straighten me out.[65] The Apostle of God died with no one of this community having

---

ʿUmar's request when al-Zubayr wants to recognize ʿAlī; in Diyārbakrī, II, 169 (from Mūsā b. ʿUqbah), ʿUmar breaks al-Zubayr's sword when he refuses to recognize Abū Bakr. Cf. Caetani, 515–16.

57. See note 53, above.

58. Cf. Nuwayrī, 38.

59. Lit., "there is no cancellation in it." The concept of *jamāʿah*, or political unity of the Muslim community, was from the start an important one in Islamic political discourse.

60. Lit., "we will strike off that in which are your eyes"; cf. Lane, V, 2215.

61. See note 53, above.

62. Usāmah b. Zayd, the Prophet's freedman, was sent by him to raid the Balqāʾ region of southern Syria just before the Prophet's final illness overtook him; cf. Ibn Hishām, 970, 999; Wāqidī, *Maghāzī*, 1117ff.

63. A place three miles from Medina in the direction of Syria (Yāqūt, s.v.).

64. For widely divergent "accession speeches" of Abū Bakr, see Ibn Hishām, 1017; Ibn Abī al-Ḥadīd, I, 314; Ibn Saʿd, III/1, 129.

65. Cf. Ibn Abī al-Ḥadīd, I, 314.

a claim against him concerning anything wrongfully taken [for which the punishment would be] one lash of the whip or [even] less. I have a Satan who takes possession of me; so when he comes to me, avoid me so that I may have no [evil] effect [even] on your hair and your skins.[66] You come and go [in this life] at an appointed time, knowledge of which is hidden from you; so if you are able [to ensure] that this appointed time elapses only while you are engaged in good works, do so. But you will only be able to do that through God; so compete in putting off your appointed times, before your appointed times surrender you to the interruption of [your] works. Verily, a tribe that forgets their appointed times, and lets others do the [good] deeds—beware being like them. Haste! Hurry! Salvation! For behind you is one who searches swiftly, an appointed time whose passage is rapid. Beware of death; be forewarned by [your deceased] fathers and sons and brothers, and do not envy the living except on account of that for which you envy the dead."

He also stood up and said, after praising and extolling God: "God only accepts those works through which His countenance was desired; so strive for God in your works. Know that whatever you sincerely direct to God is among your [good] works: obedience you have rendered, or a sin you have overcome, or taxes you have paid,[67] or a good work you have sent forward from ephemeral days to others that endure, to the time of your poverty and need.[68] Servants of God, be forewarned by whoever
[1847] among you has died, and think on those who were before you. Where were they yesterday, and where are they today?[69] Where are the tyrants, and where are those who were renowned for fighting and victory on the fields of war? Time has abased them, and they have become decayed bones upon whom have been perpetuated gossip—"loathsome women for the loathsome men, and loathsome men for the loathsome women."[70] Where are the kings who tilled the earth and cultivated it? They have perished, and mention of them is forgotten, and they have become as

66. I.e., so that I may not harm you in any way.
67. *Ḍarā'ib ataytamūhā.*
68. I.e., to the Day of Judgment.
69. On this theme see C. H. Becker, "Ubi sunt, qui ante nos in mundo fuere."
70. Qur'ān 24:26.

nothing; but God has preserved the consequences [of their evil deeds] against them and cut them off from the desires [of this world], and they have passed away. The deeds [they did] are [still reckoned] their works, but the world is the world of others. We remained after them; and, if we take warning from them, we will be saved, but, if we are deceived by them, we will be like them. Where are the pure ones with beautiful faces, captivating in their youthfulness? They have become dust, and what they neglected to do before has become a source of grief for them. Where are those who built cities and fortified them with walls and made in them wondrous things? They have left them to those who follow after them; those are their residences, empty,[71] while they [themselves] are in the darkness of the grave. "Do you perceive any one of them, or hear a sound from them?"[72] Where are those sons and brethren of yours whom you know, whose appointed times have elapsed? They have arrived according to what they had sent forward, alighting upon it and abiding for misery or happiness after death. Between God, Who has no associate, and between [any] one of His creatures there is no means of access by which He may grant him grace or divert evil from him—unless it be through obedience to Him and following His command. Know that you are requited servants[73] and that what is with Him is only attained through obedience to Him. What seems good is not good if its consequence is [hell]fire, and what seems evil is not evil if its consequence is paradise."[74]

ʿUbaydallāh b. Saʿd[75]—his uncle—Sayf; al-Sarī—Shuʿayb— [1848]
Sayf—Hishām b. ʿUrwah—his father:[76] After the oath of allegiance had been rendered to Abū Bakr and the Anṣār had come together on the matter over which they had differed, he said that Usāma's mission should be completed. Now the Arabs[77] had

71. A paraphrase of Qur'ān 27:52.
72. Qur'ān 19:98.
73. Cf. Qur'ān 37:53.
74. Lit., "There is no good in a good thing that is followed by [hell]fire," etc.
75. See note 53, above.
76. Cf. Caetani, 588–89. Close parallels to the following section (through p. 17) are found in Ibn al-Athīr, *Kāmil*, II, 334–36; and Nuwayrī, 46–47.
77. Here and a few lines farther on, the word *al-ʿarab* seems to have the sense

apostasized, either generally or as particular individuals in every tribe. Hypocrisy appeared, and the Jews and Christians began to exalt themselves, and the Muslims were like sheep on a cold and rainy night because of the loss of their Prophet and because of their fewness and the multitude of their enemy.[78] So the people said to (Abū Bakr), "These[79] are the majority of the Muslims. The Arabs, as you see, have mutinied against you, so you should not separate the troop of Muslims from yourself." At this Abū Bakr replied, "By Him in Whose hands is Abū Bakr's soul, even if I thought that beasts of prey would snatch me away, I would carry out the sending of Usāma just as the Apostle of God ordered. Even if there remained in the villages no one but myself, I would carry it out."

ʿUbaydallāh—his uncle—Sayf; and al-Sarī—Shuʿayb—Sayf—ʿAṭiyyah—Abū Ayyūb—ʿAlī; and al-Ḍaḥḥāk—Ibn ʿAbbās: Then some of the tribes who had been absent in the year of [the truce of] al-Ḥudaybiyah gathered about Medina and rose in rebellion. The people of Medina had gone out in the army of Usāma; so Abū Bakr detained[80] whoever remained of those tribes that had made *hijrah* within their territories,[81] so that they became armed outposts (*masāliḥ*) around their tribes, but they were few.

[1849] ʿUbaydallāh—his uncle—Sayf; and al-Sarī—Shuʿayb—Sayf—Abū Ḍamrah, Abū ʿAmr, and others—al-Ḥasan b. Abū al-Ḥasan al-Baṣrī:[82] Before his death, the Apostle of God had imposed a campaign on the people of Medina and those in their vicinity, among them ʿUmar b. al-Khaṭṭāb. He had put Usāmah b. Zayd in charge of them, but the last of them had not yet crossed the

---

78. Cf. Balansī, 1, where this phrase is related on the authority of Ibn Isḥāq—ʿĀ'ishah; cf. also Ibn al-Athīr, *Kāmil*, II, 334; Balādhurī, *Futūḥ*, 95; Diyārbakrī, II, 201.

79. I.e., those assigned to the army of Usāmah b. Zayd.

80. Ibn al-Athīr, *Kāmil*, II, 334, following Mss. C and B of Ṭabarī, has "formed [them] into an army."

81. The text refers to the act of joining the Muslim community, which in the early days was done by emigrating to and settling in Medina. This procedure was called *hijrah*. At some point, the Prophet seems to have allowed certain tribes to become recognized members of the community without making *hijrah* in Medina. On *hijrah* as emigration to a place or to a powerful group in order to secure its protection, see Robert Bertram Serjeant and Ronald Lewcock, *Sanʿāʾ*, ch. 5. "Ṣanʿāʾ the 'Protected,' *Hijrah*," pp. 39–43.

82. Cf. Nuwayrī, 47–48; Caetani, 589–91.

ditch[83] when the Apostle of God passed away. So Usāmah stopped with the army[84] and said to ʿUmar, "Return to the caliph of the Apostle of God and ask his permission for me to return with the army; for the chiefs of the army are with me along with their forces,[85] and I am uneasy lest the polytheists snatch away the caliph and the Apostle of God's household and the households of the Muslims." The Anṣār added, "And if he insists that we proceed, convey to him our request that he appoint in command of us a man older than Usāmah." So ʿUmar went out on Usāmah's order and came to Abū Bakr and informed him of what Usāmah had said. Abū Bakr replied, "Even if the dogs and wolves were to snatch me off, I would not reverse a decision the Apostle of God had made." Then ʿUmar said, "The Anṣār ordered me to inform you that they would like to request that you put in charge of them a man older than Usāmah." At this Abū Bakr sprang up—he had been seated—and seized ʿUmar's beard, saying, "May your mother be bereft of you and destitute of you, Ibn al-Khaṭṭāb! The Apostle of God appointed him, and you order me to dismiss him?" So ʿUmar returned to the army. They said to him, "What did you do?" And he replied, "Proceed, may your mothers be bereft of you! I didn't receive [anything] for your cause from the caliph."

Then[86] Abū Bakr went out until he reached them; he made [1850]
them go forth, and he followed after them on foot while Usāmah was riding and ʿAbd al-Raḥmān b. ʿAwf[87] led Abū Bakr's mount. Usāmah said to him, "By God, oh caliph of the Apostle of God, either you ride or I shall dismount." But Abū Bakr said, "By God, don't dismount; nor, by God, will I ride. It will not hurt me to get my two feet dusty for an hour in God's way; but, for each

---

83. The ditch on the edge of Medina, dug during the siege by Quraysh in A.H 7. Cf. Watt, *Muhammad at Medina*, 35ff.

84. Or perhaps "the people" (*al-nās*), here and later in the paragraph. Diyārbakrī, II, 114, states that all the notables (*wujūh*) of the Muhājirūn and Anṣār went on the raid.

85. The editor of text suggests *aw julluhum* "or most of them" for *wa ḥadduhum*; Nuwayrī has *waḥdahum* "by themselves."

86. Cf. Ṣanʿānī, V, 199–200 (no. 9375).

87. An early convert from Banū Zuhra of Quraysh. Cf. *EI*², s.v. "ʿAbd al-Raḥmān b. ʿAwf" (M. Th. Houtsma—W. M. Watt).

step the warrior takes, seven hundred beauties are destined for him, and seven hundred steps[88] are made visible to him, and seven hundred sins are lifted from him." Until, when he was done, (Abū Bakr) said to (Usāmah): "If you think you might help me out [by lending me the services of] 'Umar, then do so." So Usāmah gave him permission to do that.[89] Then (Abū Bakr) said, "Oh army, stop and I will order you [to do] ten [things]; learn them from me by heart. You shall not engage in treachery; you shall not act unfaithfully; you shall not engage in deception; you shall not indulge in mutilation; you shall kill neither a young child nor an old man nor a woman; you shall not fell palm trees or burn them; you shall not cut down [any] fruit-bearing tree; you shall not slaughter a sheep or a cow or a camel except for food. You will pass people who occupy themselves in monks' cells;[90] leave them alone, and leave alone what they busy themselves with. You will come to a people who will bring you vessels in which are varieties of food; if you eat anything[91] from [those dishes], mention the name of God over them. You will meet a people who have shaven the middle of their head and have left around it [a ring of hair] like turbans;[92] tap them lightly with the sword. Go ahead, in God's name; may God make you perish through wounds and plague!"[93]

---

88. Reference to the steps or stages to, and the beautiful companions in, paradise.

89. That is, Usāmah allowed 'Umar to remain behind with Abū Bakr in Medina, rather than marching on the campaign.

90. Al-Ṣan'ānī, V, 199–200 (no. 9375), has "people who allege that they imprison themselves" (i.e., as monks, for God).

91. The text reads *shay'an ba'da shay'in* "something after something," but this may be a conflation of two separate variant readings: *shay'an* "a thing" and *ba'ḍa shay'in* "some thing."

92. Reference to a monk's tonsure.

93. The text is difficult; Ibn al-Athīr's version, *Kāmil*, II, 336, is identical, and both are closely paralleled by Ṣan'ānī, V, 199–200 (no. 9375). Although these passages are in substantial agreement that Muslims should smite shaven-headed monks with the sword, they do not fit the larger context of the accounts in which they occur, in which Abū Bakr warns the Muslim warriors *not* to abuse certain categories of people, including monks in their cells, thus directly contradicting the passage in question. Ṣan'ānī, V, 200 (no. 9377:—Ma'mar—al-Zuhrī), may preserve a more accurate version: "You will find people who have shaved their heads with the sword, and those who lock themselves up in cells: leave them alone in their sins." The sentence about wounds and plague, missing

According to al-Sarī—Shuʿayb—Sayf; and according to ʿUbaydallāh—his uncle—Sayf—Hishām b. ʿUrwah—his father:[94] Abū Bakr went out to al-Jurf and followed Usāmah and sent him off. He asked Usāmah for ʿUmar [b. al-Khaṭṭāb], which he agreed to. He told Usāmah, "Do what the Prophet of God ordered you to do: Begin with the Quḍāʿah[95] country, then go to Ābil.[96] Do not fall short in anything that the Apostle of God commanded, but do not hurry because of what you have not [yet] attained of his injunction." So Usāmah advanced quickly to Dhū al-Marwah[97] and the valley[98] and ended up doing what the Prophet had ordered him to do by way of dispersing horsemen among the Quḍāʿah tribes and raiding Ābil. He took captives and booty, and his completion [of the mission] was within forty days, excepting [the time of] his encampment and his return.[99] [1851]

According to al-Sarī b. Yaḥyā—Shuʿayb—Sayf; and according to ʿUbaydallāh—his uncle—Sayf—Mūsā b. ʿUqbah—al-Mughī-

---

in Nuwayrī's account, is Abū Bakr's backhanded way of wishing that all the warriors might attain paradise, as according to Islamic law those who die fighting the infidel and those who die from plague are deemed martyrs whose place in paradise is assured. E. Landau-Tasseron observes that this "blessing" is a reference to the prophetic *ḥadīth*, "My community will vanish through wounds and plague" (personal communication). Caetani, 590–91, observes that variants of this speech appear in *topos*-like fashion in several other contexts and ascribed to different speakers.

94. Cf. Diyārbakrī, II, 154–55; Nuwayrī, 49; Caetani, 591.

95. A group of tribes living north of Medina as far as Syria, including Juhayna, ʿUdhrah, Balī, Bahrāʾ, Kalb, al-Qayn (Bal-Qayn), Tanūkh, Salīḥ, and Saʿd Hudhaym, as well as Nahd and Jarm in South Arabia and ʿUmān. See *EI*², s.v. "Ḳudāʿa" (M. J. Kister); Caskel, II, 470.

96. Diyārbakrī, II, 154; Wāqidī, *Maghāzī*, 1117ff.; and Yāqūt, s.v. "Ubnā" call this place Ubnā. De Goeje argued that the name Ubnā was a corruption of Ābil, referring to the ancient town of Abıla in Gaulanitis: Ibn Rusṭah (*BGA*, VII), 329 note c. Robert Schick, *The Fate of the Christians of Palestine*, s.v. "Ābil," cites Ṭabarī, I, 2081, which places Ābil in association with Zīzāʾ and Qasṭal during the conquest of the Balqāʾ region of Syria; on this basis he argues that Ābil in these accounts of the conquest is not Abila at all but a corruption of Arabic Ubnā, which he therefore localizes near the other two places, just south of modern ʿAmmān. Yāqūt places Ubnā in the Balqāʾ, near Muʾtah.

97. A village in Wādī al-Qurā "the valley of villages," north of Medina (Yāqūt, s.v. "al-Marwah").

98. Presumably Wādī al-Qurā.

99. Diyārbakrī, II, 155: Usāmah raids Quḍāʿah as far as Muʾtah, then raids people of Ubnā; takes booty and captives; kills the killer of his father, Zayd; and returns within forty days.

rah b. al-Akhnas; and according to the two of them—Sayf—'Amr b. Qays—'Aṭā' al-Khurasānī: a similar account.

Remainder of the Account Regarding al-'Ansī the Liar[100]

According to what we have learned, when Bādhām[101] and the Yemen embraced Islam, the Apostle of God placed in Bādhām's hands the governorship of all the Yemen, putting him in charge of all its districts; and he continued to be the Apostle's governor all the days of his life. The Apostle did not dismiss him from it or from any part of it, nor did he place in it any associate with him, until Bādhām died. After he died, the Apostle divided governorship of the Yemen among a group of his companions.

According to 'Ubaydallāh b. Sa'īd[102] al-Zuhrī—his uncle—
[1852] Sayf; and according to al-Sarī b. Yaḥyā—Shu'ayb b. Ibrāhīm—Sayf—Sahl b. Yūsuf—his father—'Ubayd b. Ṣakhr b. Lawdhān al-Anṣārī al-Salmī (who was one of those whom the Prophet sent with the governors of Yemen):[103] in the year 10, after he had performed the "completion pilgrimage"[104] [and after] Bādhām had died, the Prophet accordingly divided up his governorship among the following: Shahr b. Bādhām, 'Āmir b. Shahr al-Ham-

---

100. For the beginning of this account, see Ṭabarī, I, 1795ff.; tr. I. K. Poonawala, *The History of al-Ṭabarī*, IX, 164ff. A parallel version of this segment as far as p. 34, is found in Ibn al-Athīr, *Kāmil*, II, 336–41; another as far as p. 20, is in Nuwayrī, 50–51. Ṭabarī returns to the *riddah* in Yemen, p. 158, below. The rebel's cognomen was "al-Aswad" ("the black one"); his tribe, 'Ans b. Mālik, was a settled tribe of Madhḥij living mainly in the northern highlands of Yemen and in part near Najrān; cf. Caskel, II, 190. On his proper name, see note 172, below.

101. One of the Abnā' ("sons"), descendants of Persians sent to Yemen around A.D 570 by the Sasanian king Khusraw Anūshirwān. Balansī, *infra*; Ibn al-Athīr, *Kāmil*; and Ibn al-Athīr, *Usd*, I, 163, give his name as Bādhān; Balādhurī, *Futūḥ*, 105ff., has Bādhām. On the name (properly Bādhān) see Justi, 56.

102. See note 53, above.

103. Cf. Diyārbakrī, II, 153.

104. *Hijjat al-tamām*, presumably another term for the Prophet's last pilgrimage of the year A H 10, more usually called the "farewell pilgrimage" (*hijjat al-wadā'*), during which he is reported to have said, "Today I have completed for you your faith." It is apparently also called "pilgrimage of Islam" (*hijjat al-islām*). I thank E. Landau-Tasseron for clarifying the relationship of these terms (personal communication).

dānī,[105] 'Abdallāh b. Qays Abū Mūsā al-Ash'arī,[106] Khālid b. Sa'īd b. al-'Āṣ,[107] al-Ṭāhir b. Abī Hālah,[108] Ya'lā b. Umayyah,[109] and 'Amr b. Ḥazm;[110] and over the Ḥaḍramawt country Ziyād b. Labīd al-Bayāḍī;[111] and 'Ukkāshah b. Thawr b. Aṣghar al-Ghawthī[112] over the Sakāsik, Sakūn, and Mu'āwiyah b. Kindah.[113] And he sent Mu'ādh b. Jabal[114] as teacher to the people of the countries of Yemen and Ḥaḍramawt.

According to 'Ubaydallāh—his uncle—Sayf b. 'Umar—Abū 'Amr, *mawlā* of Ibrāhīm b. Ṭalḥah—'Ubādah b. Qurṣ b. 'Ubādah b.[115] Qurṣ al-Laythī: The Prophet returned to Medina after completing the pilgrimage of Islam,[116] having arranged the government of the Yemen. He divided it among [a number of] men, making each man unchallenged in his territory. He arranged [also] the command of Ḥaḍramawt, dividing it among

---

105. Ibn al-Athīr, *Usd*, III, 83, says merely that he was a Yemeni tribesman, one of the Prophet's governors of Yemen, who later settled in al-Kūfah.

106. Yemeni tribesman who came to the Prophet in 7/628; he later had an important military and political career. See EI^2, s.v. "Al-Ash'arī, Abū Mūsā" (L. Veccia Vaglieri).

107. An Umayyad of Quraysh, one of the earliest Muslims; the Prophet sent him to Yemen as a collector of taxes with the Yemeni convert Farwah b. Musayk. He later had a controversial military and political career. See EI^2, s.v. "Khālid b. Sa'īd" (H. Loucel).

108. Son of the Prophet's first wife, Khadījah, considered a member of the tribe of Tamīm, which was allied with the 'Abd al-Dār clan of Quraysh; Ibn al-Athīr, *Usd*, III, 50. Diyārbakrī, II, 153, omits his name from the list.

109. A Tamīmī, ally of the Banū Nawfal of Quraysh, who embraced Islam at the conquest of Mecca. This passage and another from Sayf (p. 158, below) suggest that he was sent to Yemen by the Prophet, but Ibn al-Athīr, *Usd*, V, 128–29; Ibn Ḥajar, *Iṣābah*, s.v.; and even another account by Sayf (Ṭabarī, I, 2162) suggest that he may not have gone to Yemen until the time of Abū Bakr or 'Umar.

110. He seems to have been a Khazrajī of Banū al-Najjār from Medina; cf. Caskel, I, Table 186, II, 176. However, Ibn al-Athīr, *Usd*, IV, 98–99, provides several alternative genealogies for him.

111. A Khazrajī from Medina, he emigrated to Mecca and embraced Islam before the Prophet's *hijrah* to Medina; Ibn al-Athīr, *Usd*, II, 217; Ibn Sa'd, III/2, 131.

112. Other sources add nothing to what is given here by Sayf.

113. Three tribes of Ḥaḍramawt, genealogically subdivisions of Kindah but at this time politically independent; cf. Caskel, I, Table 233, II, 413, 503.

114. An early Medinan convert to Islam renowned for his religious knowledge; Ibn Sa'd, III/2, 120–26.

115. Reading *ibn* for *'an*, following *Emendanda*.

116. *Hijjat al-islām*; cf. note 104, above.

three [persons], each one of whom he made unchallenged in his territory. Over Najrān[117] he appointed ʿAmr b. Ḥazm; Khālid b. Saʿīd b. al-ʿĀṣ he appointed over what was between Najrān and Rimaʿ and Zabīd;[118] ʿĀmir b. Shahr he appointed over Hamdān;[119] over Ṣanʿāʾ, [he placed] Ibn Bādhām; over ʿAkk and the Ashʿarīs,[120] [he placed] al-Ṭāhir b. Abī Hālah; over Maʾrib,[121] [he placed] Abū Mūsā al-Ashʿarī; and over al-Janad,[122] [he placed] Yaʿlā b. Umayyah. Muʿādh [b. Jabal] was the teacher,
[1853] who used to make the rounds in the district of each governor of the Yemen and Ḥaḍramawt.[123] And [the Prophet] appointed to the governorships of Ḥaḍramawt: ʿUkkāshah b. Thawr over the Sakāsik and Sakūn; over Muʿāwiyah b. Kindah, ʿAbdallāh[124] or al-Muhājir,[125] who then fell ill and did not go until Abū Bakr sent him;[126] and over Ḥaḍramawt[127] [he appointed] Ziyād b.

---

117. An important town on the northern edge of the Yemen, renowned for its Christian population on the eve of Islam; cf. Yāqūt, s.v.

118. Zabīd was the main town of the Yemeni Tihāmah or coastal plain, situated about 100 km north of the Bāb al-Mandab. According to Balādhurī, *Futūḥ*, 105, Khālid (or al-Muhājir b. Abī Umayyah?) governed Ṣanʿāʾ. Ibn al-Athīr, *Kāmil*, II, 336, does not mention Rimaʿ, a valley leading down to the Red Sea coast about 20 km north of the city of Zabīd and its valley (cf. Yāqūt, s.v. "Zabīd"; Hamdānī, 71; *TAVO* B VII 1; Wilson, 31).

119. Large tribe and territory north of Ṣanʿāʾ: *EI*², s.v. "Hamdān" (J. Schleifer—W. M. Watt); *TAVO* B VII 1.

120. Ashʿar was a tribe of the Tihāmah coastal plain located between Mukhah (Mocha) and Zabīd; ʿAkk lived in the Tihāmah north of Ashʿar. Cf. Caskel, II, 150, 200; *EI*², s.v. "ʿAkk" (W. Caskel).

121. Important town on the eastern desert edge of the Yemeni highlands, ca. 140 km due east of Ṣanʿāʾ (*TAVO* B VII 1); in antiquity the capital of the kingdom of Sabaʾ (Sheba).

122. Large town in Yemen about 200 km due south of Ṣanʿāʾ and, with Ṣanʿāʾ and Ḥaḍramawt, normally one of the three administrative seats of southwestern Arabia (Yāqūt, s.v.).

123. I.e., to teach Qurʾān and prayer?

124. Wellhausen, *Skizzen*, VI, 146, proposed that this was Abū Mūsā al-Ashʿarī; note, however, that Abū Mūsā figures as governor of Maʾrib in the immediately preceding list.

125. Balādhurī, *Futūḥ*, 105, identifies this as al-Muhājir b. Abī Umayyah; he was of the Makhzūm clan of Quraysh and full brother of the Prophet's wife Umm Salamah (Ibn al-Athīr, *Usd*, IV, 322–23).

126. Ibn al-Athīr, *Kāmil*, II, 336–37, suggests that this refers to the Prophet's illness, having delayed the dispatch of the governor.

127. I.e., over the valley of Ḥaḍramawt proper, as opposed to the whole province of the same name?

Labīd al-Bayāḍī, who assumed [also] the governorate of al-Muhājir. So, when the Apostle of God died, these were his governors over the Yemen and Ḥaḍramawt, excepting those who had been killed in fighting al-Aswad or had [otherwise] died—those being Bādhām, who died and because of [whose death] the Prophet divided up his governorate, and his son Shahr b. Bādhām, against whom al-Aswad marched to fight him, killing him. This account was [also] related to me according to al-Sarī—Shuʿayb b. Ibrāhīm—Sayf—Abū ʿAmr, *mawlā* of Ibrāhīm b. Ṭalḥah; then the rest of the account was according to his *isnād* like the account of Ibn Saʿd[128] al-Zuhrī.

According to al-Sarı—Shuʿayb b. Ibrāhīm—Sayf—Ṭalḥah b. al-Aʿlam—ʿIkrimah—Ibn ʿAbbās: The first ones who resisted al-ʿAnsī and tried to match his numbers[129] were ʿĀmir b. Shahr al-Hamdānī,[130] in his district, and Fayrūz and Dādhawayh[131] in their districts. Then there followed those who had been assigned commands.

According to ʿUbaydallāh b. Saʿd[132]—his uncle—Sayf; and according to al-Sarī—Shuʿayb—Sayf—Sahl b. Yūsuf—his father—ʿUbayd b. Ṣakhr:[133] While we were in al-Janad,[134] having [1854]
laid out for them what [conditions] were necessary and having drawn up agreements between us, a letter arrived from al-Aswad. [It said:] "Oh you who are marching against us: Grasp firmly against us that which you have taken of our land, and hold back that which you have gathered, for we are more entitled to it, as long as you are [in the situation] you are." So we asked the messenger from where he had come. He replied:

---

128. Reading with Cairo edition and *Emendanda*; text has Saʿīd.

129. Text: *kātharahu*; Ibn al-Athīr, *Usd*, III, 83, has *kābarahu* "strove to overcome him," which makes more sense. Cf. Caetani, 678.

130. Ibn al-Athīr, *Kāmil*, II, 337, says it was Shahr, not ʿĀmir b. Shahr.

131. Both were of the Abnāʾ and embraced Islam under the Prophet; cf. Ibn Saʿd, V, 389–90. The names are of Middle Persian origin, cf. F. Justi, *Iranisches Namenbuch*, 100, 247 (s.v. Pērōz) and 75–76 (s.v. Dādhōē).

132. See note 53, above.

133. Cf. Nuwayrī, 51–53 (to p. 25); al-Masʿūdī, 276–77; Caetani, 678–80.

134. Reading with Cairo ed. and Wellhausen, *Skizzen*, VI, 146, for "with the army" given in the text.

"From the cave of Khubbān."[135] Then he directed himself toward Najrān until he took it ten [days] after coming out [in rebellion], and the bulk of Madhḥij submitted to him.[136] So, while we were taking care of our business and gathering our force, someone came to us and said, "This al-Aswad is in Shaʿūb."[137] Shahr b. Bādhām had gone out against him twenty days after the beginning [of his revolt], and while we were awaiting the news of who would be defeated, we learned that (al-Aswad) had killed Shahr and routed the Abnāʾ[138] and taken possession of Ṣanʿāʾ, twenty-five days from his uprising. Muʿādh [b. Jabal] fled until he passed by Abū Mūsā while he was in Maʾrib, and the two then rushed to Ḥaḍramawt.[139] Muʿādh settled among the Sakūn, and Abū Mūsā among the Sakāsik that are adjacent to al-Mufawwur,[140] with the desert between them and Maʾrib. The other commanders withdrew to al-Ṭāhir [b. Abī Hālah], except for ʿAmr and Khālid,[141] who returned to Medina. Al-Ṭāhir at that time was in the midst of the ʿAkk country, facing Ṣanʿāʾ.[142] Al-Aswad subdued [the territory] between Ṣayhad—the desert of Ḥaḍramawt[143]—to

---

135. Yāqūt, s.v. "Khubbān," evidently on the basis of this report or one like it, describes it as a village in a valley of the same name near Najrān. Cf. Al-Hamdānī, 101, on *wādī* Khubbān.

136. Or "aided him": *ṭābaqahu*; but the verb often has a sexual connotation; cf. Ibn Manẓūr, X, 211. Ibn al-Athīr, *Kāmil*, II, 337, has "followed him." Cf. Diyārbakrī, II, 155, bottom; Balansī, 151ff. Madhḥij was a large tribe or tribal confederation of the Yemen, which later played an important role in the Islamic conquests in Egypt and Syria. Cf. *EI*², s.v. "Madhḥidj" (C. E. Bosworth—G. R. Smith).

137. Yāqūt, s.v.: a high fortress near Ṣanʿāʾ.

138. Cf. note 101, above; Balādhurī, *Futūḥ*, 105.

139. Diyārbakri, II, 156, ll. 9–10.

140. The editor notes that the reading is uncertain. Kosegarten offered "Aẓfūr." Neither al-Mufawwar nor Aẓfūr was known to Hamdānī or Yāqūt. Nuwayrī omitted the phrase.

141. I.e., ʿAmr b. Ḥazm and Khālid b. Saʿīd. Diyārbakrī, II, 156 l. 10, has "ʿAmr b. Khālid."

142. Ibn al-Athīr, *Kāmil*, II, 337, has "in the mountains of Ṣanʿāʾ." Neither reading is entirely satisfactory from the point of view of content, as the ʿAkk lived not near Ṣanʿāʾ but in the Tihāmah coastal region; cf. two sentences farther on in text and note 120, above.

143. Text, Nuwayrī, 52, and all manuscripts read *ṣ.h.y.d*, and Cairo ed. has Ṣahīd, but this must refer to the well-known desert district. Cf. p. 182, below,

the province of al-Ṭā'if [to the north], to al-Baḥrayn in the direction of Aden.[144] The Yemen submitted to him, while the [1855] ʿAkk in the Tihāmah were resisting him, and [his movement] began to advance like wildfire. The day he met Shahr [in battle] he had with him seven hundred horsemen, in addition to the camel riders; his commanders were Qays b. ʿAbd Yaghūth al-Murādī,[145] Muʿāwiyah b. Qays al-Janbī,[146] Yazīd b. M.h.r.m., Yazīd b. Ḥuṣayn al-Ḥārithī, and Yazīd b. al-Afkal al-Azdī.[147] His rule became stable; his order was considered harsh. Some of the coastal districts submitted to him—Jāzān [and] ʿAthr and al-Sharjah and al-Ḥirdah and Ghalāfiqah and Aden;[148] and al-Janad

---

where Sayf describes "*ṣ.h.y.d*" as "the desert between Ma'rib and Ḥaḍramawt"—i.e., Ṣayhad. Cf. Hamdānī, index; and Ibn Manẓūr, III, 260.

144. Wellhausen, *Skizzen*, VI, 146, notes that no place named al-Baḥrayn is known in the region of Aden. There seems to be some problem with the text here. Perhaps it read "to al-Baḥrayn *and* in the direction of Aden," so that al-Baḥrayn could be taken to refer to the well-known district of that name in eastern Arabia, for the sentence seems at this point to be enumerating regions beyond the Yemen highlands that were following al-Aswad. Cf. Nuwayrī, 50, who states that al-Aswad overcame the area from Ṣanʿā' to ʿUmān to al-Ṭā'if—i.e., the whole southern half of the Arabian peninsula. Cf. also note 148, below. Although in Islamic times the term "al-Baḥrayn" came to be used for the whole east Arabian littoral from the head of the Persian Gulf to ʿUmān, in earlier usage it referred to the largest oasis cluster of northeastern Arabia, ca. 60 km inland from the coast near the modern country called al-Baḥrayn. Its main center was the oasis of Hajar. Cf. Thilo, s.v. "Baḥrayn"; Wüstenfeld, "Bahrein und Jemâma," 175–76.

145. Originally of the tribe of Bajīlah, but an ally of the Murād clan of Madhḥij, for whom he became an important warrior. There is confusion about his name, which sometimes appears as Qays b. Hubayra "al-Makshūḥ," Qays b. ʿAbd Yaghūth b. Makshūḥ, or more commonly, simply Qays b. al-Makshūḥ: cf. Balādhurī, *Futūḥ*, 105–6; Ibn al-Athīr, *Kāmil*, II, 337; Ibn al-Athīr, *Usd*, IV, 222, 227–28; p. 165, below; and *Emendanda*, where Qays b. Makshūḥ b. ʿAbd Yaghūth is proposed.

146. Caskel, II, 257, lists Janb as a group of Madhḥij living near modern Khamīs Mushayṭ.

147. I have found no other references to any of these three Yazīds.

148. Text has "Ḥāz ʿAthr." These places were along the Red Sea coast north of Aden, as mentioned in Hamdānī, 52, ll. 9–15, which even offers them in the same sequence (in reverse) and clarifies that "Ḥāz" and ʿAthr (also ʿAththar; cf. Hamdānī, 54 l. 11 and index) are two places. There were several places named Ḥāz, Ḥāzzah, etc., in Yemen; they seem to have been situated in the mountains, not along the coast, but their names may have caused a copyist to corrupt the name Jāzān to "Ḥāz." Cf. Hamdānī, index, s.v. "Ḥāz" (there misprinted as "Jāz"!); Wilson, 125–26. On Jāzān (modern Jīzān or Jayzān, in southern Saudi Arabia) see *EI*², s.v. "Djayzān" (G. Rentz).

and then Ṣanʿāʾ to the province of al-Ṭāʾif [and] to al-Aḥsiyah[149] and ʿUlayb.[150] The Muslims dealt with him out of fear;[151] the apostates dealt with him out of disbelief and turning back from Islam. His lieutenant among Madhḥij was ʿAmr b. Maʿdīkarib.[152] He based his command on a group of warriors; as for the command of his army, it was in the hands of Qays b. ʿAbd Yaghūth, and he put command of the Abnāʾ in charge of Fayrūz and Dādhawayh. Then, after he had made much slaughter in the land, he made light of Qays and Fayrūz and Dādhawayh and married the wife of Shahr,[153] who was Fayrūz's niece. [In Ḥaḍramawt][154] we were on the verge of Muʿādh's marriage into the Banū Bakr, a clan of Sakūn, to a woman named Ramlah, whose maternal uncles were the Banū Zankīl,[155] so
[1856] that they had become fond of us because of his kinship [with them]. Muʿādh admired her greatly; indeed he used to say when he prayed to God, "Oh God, raise me up on Judgment Day with the Sakūn," and sometimes, "Oh God, be forgiving to

149. This toponym was unknown to Hamdānī; Yāqūt knew of it directly from accounts of the *riddah* and related that, when al-Aswad expelled the Prophet's governors in Yemen, Farwah b. Musayk, who had been the Prophet's governor over the Murād clan, set up camp in al-Aḥsiyah. This part of the text, however, is suspiciously similar to a passage several lines earlier that also begins with the phrase "to the province of al-Ṭāʾif" (cf. note 144, above); one wonders whether the otherwise unknown "al-Aḥsiyah" is not actually a copyist's error for al-Aḥsāʾ, the oasis district in the region of al-Baḥrayn, and whether ʿUlayb—the localization of which was evidently a problem for the geographers (see note 150, below)—is not an erroneous reading of ʿAdan/Aden. Or should we, following the principle of *lectio difficilior*, propose that the errors proceeded the other way around, so that al-Aḥsiyah and ʿUlayb came to be misread as al-Aḥsāʾ (then revised to al-Baḥrayn) and Aden? In any case, the possibility that one of these phrases represents a dittography should be noted.

150. Apparently a place in the Tihāmah (Yāqūt, s.v.) or in the Sarāt mountains north of Yemen (Hamdānī, 181 ll. 12ff.), perhaps as far north as Mecca or Medina. Nuwayrī, 52, has "and elsewhere" (*wa-ghayrihā*).

151. Reading *taqiyya*, with *Emendanda*, for *baqiyya* in the text and Nuwayrī.

152. Leading chief, warrior, and poet of the Zubayd clan of Madhḥij, said to have embraced Islam in Medina shortly before the Prophet's death; cf. *EI*[2] s.v. "ʿAmr b. Maʿdīkarib" (C. Pellat); Caskel, II, 178.

153. Cf. Diyārbakrī, II, 156 ll. 11–12; Balansi, 151: al-Aswad marries the wife of Shahr's father, Bādhān.

154. At this point an enormous sentence has been broken into several parts in the translation and the clauses rearranged.

155. Thus the text, but probably Zankabīl; cf. Caskel, II, 605.

Sakūn." While we were in this state in Ḥaḍramawt and not free from fear that al-Aswad might march against us or send an army against us, or that some rebel might arise in Ḥaḍramawt demanding what al-Aswad demanded, lo and behold, letters reached us from the Prophet. In them he commanded us to send men to seek out (al-Aswad) by deceit, or to assault him [openly], and to tell about that, on the Prophet's behalf, everyone who desired anything from him. Muʿādh accordingly undertook what he was ordered to do, so that we grew powerful and became confident of victory.

According to al-Sarī—Shuʿayb—Sayf; and according to ʿUbaydallāh—his uncle—Sayf—al-Mustanīr b. Yazīd—ʿUrwah b. Ghaziyyah al-Dathīnī—al-Ḍaḥḥāk b. Fayrūz; and according to al-Sarī—Jushaysh[156] b. al-Daylamī; and according to ʿUbaydallāh b. Jushaysh b. al-Daylamī:[157] Wabr b. Yuḥannis[158] came to us with the Prophet's letter, in which he ordered us to stand firm in our religion[159] and to rise up in war and to take action against al-Aswad either by stealth or by brute force.[160] [And he ordered] that we inform on his behalf anyone whom we thought to be of help and obedient; so we did accordingly, and we saw that the matter was difficult. And we saw that (al-Aswad) was resentful toward Qays b. ʿAbd Yaghūth, who was in command of his army. So we said [to ourselves] that (Qays) would be in fear for his life, so he would be ready to be invited[161] [to join our cause], so we invited him, telling him of the matter and informing him on the Prophet's behalf. It was as if we had descended upon him from heaven while he was in perplexity and sadness over his situation, so he responded [affirmatively] to what we wished in [1857]

156. Ibn al-Athīr, *Kāmil*, II, 338, and Kosegarten have "Jishnas"; but cf. Ibn al-Athīr, *Usd*, I, 283, s.v. "Jushaysh al-Daylamī." Wellhausen, *Skizzen*, VI, 146, proposed Jushnas (< Middle Persian "Gushnasp"). Cf. Dhahabī, *Mushtabih*, 186.

157. Cf. Diyārbakrī, II, 156–57, and Nuwayrī, 53–58, for loose paraphrases of this account as far as p. 33, below. Cf. also Caetani, 680–85.

158. One of the Abnāʾ who embraced Islam; cf. Ibn Saʿd, V, 388–89, Ibn al-Athīr, *Usd*, V, 83; Balansī, 152; Ibn Ḥajar, *Iṣābah*, s.v. His name (Wabr or Wabar or Wabrah?) and exact identity are somewhat confused.

159. Or, possibly, "in our obedience": *dīn*.

160. Lit., "by clashing."

161. *Fa-huwa la-awwalu daʿwatan.*

that. Wabr b. Yuḥannis came to us, and we wrote to the people calling them [to Islam].

Satan told (al-Aswad) something [about this], so he sent to Qays and said, "Oh Qays, [do you know] what this one [i.e., Satan] is saying?" (Qays) said, "[No,] what is he saying?" (Al-Aswad) replied, "He is saying [to me], 'You relied on Qays and honored him, to the point that he had your complete trust[162] and had become like you in power. Then he inclined toward your enemy and schemed after your kingship and because of treachery determined that he would say, "Oh Aswad, oh Aswad, shame, shame!"[163] Pluck the top of him and take from Qays his highest part; if not he will dispossess you or pluck the top of you.' "[164] At this Qays, swearing a [false] oath, said—"Oh Dhū al-Khimār,[165] you are too important to me and too illustrious that I should be envious of you." Whereupon (al-Aswad) said, "How crude of you! Do you [dare] call the angel[166] a liar? The angel spoke the truth; now I know that you have repented because of what (Satan) made known about you."

Then (Qays) went out and, coming to us, said, "Oh Jushaysh and Fayrūz and Dādhawayh, there were words between us; what is [your] opinion?" So we said, "We should be wary." We were in that [state] when (al-Aswad) sent to us, saying, "Did I not honor you above [others in] your tribes? Did (Satan) not keep me informed about you?" To this we said, "Forgive us this time." Whereupon he replied, "Don't let me hear [anything] about you or I shall kill you."[167] So we got away, barely, while he was

162. Lit., "entered every entering from you." This whole passage, with its quotation within a quotation, is awkward to render.

163. Or perhaps "you prick, you prick"; *yā saw'ah yā saw'ah*.

164. I.e., Satan tells al-Aswad to behead Qays before Qays beheads him. Cf. note 174, below.

165. The text has "By Dhū al-Khimār," but Dhū al-Khimār, "the one with the veil," was the nickname of al-Aswad himself (see Balādhurī, *Futūḥ*, 105), and it seems unlikely that Qays would have sworn an oath on his name. However, making this emendation removes from the sentence the formal oath, which the context requires. Perhaps the original was "By God, Oh Dhū al-Khimār."

166. Al-Aswad here refers to Satan as his "angel." One wonders if the text might originally have had *malik*, "king", instead of *mal'ak* or *malak* ("angel").

167. Reading with Cairo ed., following Kosegarten, for "dismiss you" (*uqīlaka*) in the Leiden text. Ibn al-Athīr, *Kāmil*, II, 338, avoided the difficulties

in doubt over our situation and that of Qays, and we were in doubt and great danger. Then [news] reached us of the opposition against him on the part of ʿĀmir b. Shahr and Dhū Zūd and Dhū Murrān and Dhū al-Kalāʿ and Dhū Ẓulaym;[168] they wrote to us and offered us help, and we wrote back to them and instructed them not to put anything in motion until we should [1858] arrange the matter thoroughly. They only became agitated over that when the letter of the Prophet arrived. The Prophet wrote to the people of Najrān, to their Arabs and to the non-Arab inhabitants of the country, so they stood firm and regrouped[169] and gathered in a single place. Learning of that, (al-Aswad) sensed disaster. We hatched a plan, and accordingly I went to visit Āzād, (al-Aswad's) wife,[170] saying to her, "Oh my cousin, you know the misfortune this man represents for your people; he has killed your husband, made excessive slaughter among your people, humiliated those who remained of them, and disgraced the women. So might you have some conspiracy against him?" At this she replied, "To what end?" I said, "To expel him." She added, "Or to kill him?" I replied, "Or to kill him." She said, "Yes, by God. God has created no one more hateful to me than he is. He does not attend to what is right [even] for the sake of God, nor does he refrain from what is forbidden[171] for His sake. So when you have resolved [what to do], let me know so that I may inform you of how this may be

---

(as usual) and gave the following gist of this passage: "He sent to us, threatening us, so we made excuses to him and barely saved ourselves from him, he being in doubt about us and we being wary of him."

168. Cf. p. 165, below. These are all epithets used as names, evidently referring to South Arabian chiefs. ʿUmayr "Dhū Murrān" was a chief of Hamdān who had had written contact with the Prophet (Hamdānī, 99 ll. 4–5; cf. Harding, 542, on the name D̲MRN in Minaean inscriptions); Dhū al-Kalāʿ was the most powerful tribe of South Arabia on the eve of Islam, probably represented here by its chief, Samayfaʿ b. Nākūr "Dhū al-Kalāʿ al-Aṣghar" (Caskel, II, 236, 510); Dhū Ẓulaym was a clan of the Alḥān b. Mālik tribe that lived southwest of Ṣanʿāʾ, probably represented here by its chief Ḥawshab b. Yazīd (Caskel, II, 152, 322). I could find nothing on Dhū Zūd besides the reference on p. 165, below.

169. Lit., "turned aside."

170. Azād or Azādh had been the wife of Shahr b. Bādhām and was the cousin of Fayrūz; Ibn al-Athīr, *Usd*, III, 6, s.v. "Shahr b. Bādhām." Her name is Iranian (< Azāta "free, noble"); cf. Justi, 54.

171. Or, perhaps, "from womenfolk." Cf. Ibn al-Athīr, *Kāmil*, II, 338.

accomplished." And so I was going out, [when] all of a sudden there were Fayrūz and Dādhawayh waiting for me. Qays came, and we wanted to rise against (al-Aswad), but then a man [arrived and] said to (Qays), before he could sit with us, "The king summons you." Accordingly (Qays) entered with ten [men] of Madhḥij and Hamdān, so that (al-Aswad) was unable to kill him.

According to al-Sarī in his account: Then ʿAyhalah b. Kaʿb b. Ghawth[172] said, (or, according to ʿUbaydallāh in his account, "ʿAbhalah b. Kaʿb b. Ghawth said")[173] "Do you fortify yourself against me with men? [i.e., "How dare you fortify yourself against me with men?] Did I not tell you the truth, whereas you lie to me? (Satan) says, 'Shame! shame! If you do not cut the hand from Qays he will cut the heights from your head.' "[174] [He
[1859] went on like this], until (Qays) thought that (al-Aswad) would kill him. Whereupon (Qays) said, "Indeed, it was not right for me to kill you, as you are an apostle of God, so do with me what you will. As for fear and terror, I am in both of them [anyway], in dread [that you will kill me].[175] Kill me, for one death is easier for me than deaths I die every day (or, according to al-Zuhrī: and as for your killing me, one death is easier)." At this, (al-Aswad) took pity on (Qays) and sent him out. So (Qays) came out to us and told us [what had happened] and stayed with us and said, "Do your deed."

(Al-Aswad)[176] came out against us with a group, so we stood at attention for him. [Now] at the gate were one hundred cows and camels, so he stood up and drew a line so that they were

---

172. I.e., al-Aswad. Ibn al-Athīr, *Kāmil*, II, 336; and Al-Balādhurī, *Futūḥ*, 105, state that his proper name was ʿAyhalah, but he was called by his nickname "al-Aswad," "the black," because of his color. Diyārbakrī, II, 155; and Nuwayrī, 49, 55 (as well as Tabarī, I, 1795) also have the form ʿAbhalah.

173. Text has "Oh ʿAyhalah," so that the subject of "he said" must be someone other than al-Aswad. I have followed the suggestion of Wellhausen, *Skizzen*, VI, 147, who proposed that the vocative particle "oh" should be dropped, as the context makes it clear that the words spoken immediately after must have been uttered by al-Aswad, not to him.

174. Text has *yaqṭaʿu qunnataka al-ʿulyā* "he will cut off your highest part," i.e., "your head;" Ibn al-Athīr, *Kāmil*, II, 339, suggests *raqabataka* "your neck." Cf. note 164, above.

175. This emendation is introduced in the Cairo ed. from Nuwayrī.

176. This seems to be the beginning of another version of the narrative, not very neatly integrated into the story told so far.

situated behind it and he stood before it. Then he cut their throats, [they being] neither corralled nor bound, [but] none of them plunged across the line. Then he let them go, so that they roamed around until they passed away. I have never seen a more repulsive scene than that or a more brutal day. Then he said, "Is what I have learned about you true, Fayrūz?" and he pointed the lance at him. "I had intended to cut your throat, making you follow this beast." At this (Fayrūz) said, "You chose us to be your in-laws and gave us precedence over the [rest of the] Abnā'. [Even] if you had not been a prophet we would not have sold our share with you for anything; so how [could we reject you], after the promise[177] of [both] an afterlife and a present life[178] has been gathered to us by you? You should not believe what you have heard about us, for indeed we are where you wish."[179] At this (al-Aswad) said, "Divide this, as you are most knowledgeable of whoever is hereabouts." Then the people of Ṣanʿā' began to gather to me, so I began to order that the slaughtered camels be given to the clan, the cows to the family, [1860] and the equipment to the needy,[180] until the people of each district[181] had taken their share. Then, before he reached his house—while he was watching me[182]—a man overtook him who denounced Fayrūz to him. (Al-Aswad) was listening closely to him, and Fayruz overheard him while he was saying, "I will kill him tomorrow with his companions, so come to me early in the morning." Then (al-Aswad) turned and, lo and behold, there was (Fayrūz). So he said [to the man], "Shhh!"[183] Then [Fayrūz] informed him of what he had done [by way of distributing the meat], at which (al-Aswad) said, "Excellent work." Then (al-Aswad) struck his riding animal and went in. (Fayrūz) returned

177. Lit., "matter" (*amr*).
178. Nuwayrī, 55, has "a faith" (*dīnan*).
179. I.e., our loyalties are with you.
180. The three terms are *rahṭ* (clan), *ahl al-bayt* (family), and *ahl al-khallah* (needy), respectively. Nuwayrī, 56, and Cairo edition, following Kosegarten, read "people of the settlements" (*ahl al-ḥillah*).
181. *Nāhiyah*.
182. Or "standing over me" (*wa-huwa wāqifun ʿalayya*).
183. Or "hold it!" (*mah!*). Alternatively, we might construe this as "So he said [to Fayrūz], "Yes?" as seems to be suggested by Wellhausen, *Skizzen*, VI, 147.

to us and told us the news. At this we sent to Qays, [telling him] that he should come to us. Together they agreed[184] that I should return to the woman to inform her of our decision, so she might tell us what she would order [us to do]. So I went to the woman and said, "What do you think?" She replied, "He is cautious and [closely] guarded. Every part of the palace is surrounded by the guard, except this room; the rear of it is at such-and-such a place on the street, so, when evening has come, break into it; you will then be inside the guard, and nothing will stand in the way of killing him." Then she said, "In [the room] you will find a lamp and weapons." Then I went out; but, when al-Aswad met me coming out of one of his residences, he said to me, "What are you doing here?"[185] and slapped my head so [hard] that I fell down, for he was powerfully built. The woman screamed so that he was startled away from me; but for that he would have killed me. She said, "My cousin came to visit me, but you have treated me meanly!" At this he said, "Shut up, you nobody![186] I hereby give him to you." So she spared me.[187] So I came to my companions, saying, "Help! Get away!" and I told them the news. We were in this state, confused, when all of a sudden [the woman's] messenger came to me, [saying], "Don't give up what
[1861] you were going to do when I left you, for I will continue to be with him until he goes to sleep." So[188] we said to Fayrūz, "Go to her and make sure of her. As for me, there is no way for me to enter after being thrown out [by al-Aswad]."[189] He did so; he was more clever than I. So after she had informed him [of the

---

184. Lit., "their council agreed."

185. Lit., "What brought you to visit me?"

186. Or, "You bastard!" lit., "May you have no father!"

187. *Fa-tazāyalat ʿannī*. Wellhausen, *Skizzen*, VI, 147, proposed that the text should read *fa-tazāyala*, with al-Aswad as the subject; De Goeje, *Glossary*, wished to leave the text unchanged and proposed that it meant "she hid herself from me." The act of handing a captive over to a petitioner who had requested him was a common gesture of magnanimity among chiefs of pre-Islamic and early Islamic Arabia. The idea was that the petitioner could decide the captive's fate—either to free him, as in this instance, or to inflict a more hideous punishment on him than the king might have, in the case of a captive who was a personal enemy of the petitioner.

188. The following eight sentences are omitted from Nuwayrī, 56.

189. Lit., "there is no way for me to enter after the prohibition (*al-nahy*)."

plan], he said,[190] "And how may we break into lined rooms?"[191] [She replied,[192]] "We must remove the lining of the room." So the two of them entered and removed the lining, whereupon they locked it and he sat with her as if he were a visitor. Then (al-Aswad) came to visit her and became consumed with jealousy, but she explained to him (Fayrūz's) kinship and foster-relationship with her [and that] he was within the forbidden degrees of consanguinity.[193] At this, (al-Aswad) screamed at him and threw him out, and he brought us the news. When it was evening we put our plan into effect, our partisans having agreed with us [beforehand]. We went ahead before making contact with the Hamdānīs and Ḥimyarīs[194] and broke into the room from the outside. Then we entered and in it was a lamp under a large bowl. We protected ourselves [by letting] Fayrūz, who was the bravest and strongest of us, [go first][195] and said: "Look [and see] what you can see." So he went out, while we were between (al-Aswad) and the guards that were with him in the compound. When (Fayrūz) got near the door of the room, he heard a loud snoring, and, lo, there was the woman, sitting up. Then, when (Fayrūz) stood by the door, Satan made (al-Aswad) sit up and address him with his tongue. He was snoring as he sat and also saying, "I have nothing to do with you, oh Fayrūz!" At this (Fayrūz) feared that if he went back he and the woman would be

---

190. Cairo ed. has "she said"; this change would eliminate the need for the emendation introduced later in the sentence (see Note 192, below).

191. *Buyūt mubaṭṭanah*, i.e., rooms having a *biṭānah*, or "lining"; cf. next two sentences. The meaning is obscure. E. Landau-Tasseron suggests that this reference may be to a tent, in which case *biṭānah* means an inner divider or wall hanging, but the general sense of the paragraph is that the house was one with solid walls. Perhaps it is simply a way of saying the "inner sanctum" or personal chambers of the ruler in a palace complex; cf. *The Assyrian Dictionary*, II, s.v. "*biṭānu*." The root b–ṭ–n does not seem to be attested in the Sabaic or Sabaean dialect of Old South Arabic.

192. This addition was suggested by Wellhausen, *Skizzen*, VI, 147. Cf. note 190, above.

193. I.e., closely enough related to her so that they could not marry, meaning that he was formally a part of her family and could visit her without arousing suspicion or causing disgrace.

194. Ḥimyar b. ʿĀmir was a large South Arabian nation or tribe that had provided the last Yemeni dynasty of rulers. Cf. Caskel, II, 324.

195. *Ittaqaynā bi-Fayrūz*; translation following Wellhausen, *Skizzen*, VI, 147.

killed. So he acted first and came on him [from behind as if to mount him] like a camel.[196] He took his head and killed him by breaking his neck and placing his knee on his back and breaking it. Then he got up to go out. At this the woman, thinking that he had not killed him, took hold of his robe saying, "Why[197] are you leaving me?" (Fayrūz) replied, "To inform my companions of his death." Then (Fayrūz) came to us, and we went off with
[1862] him wishing to cut off (al-Aswad's) head; but Satan made him move, tossing about so that (Fayrūz) could not restrain him. Whereupon I said, "[All of you] sit on his chest." So two [of us] sat on his chest, and the woman took hold of his hair. We heard a muttering noise, so I bridled him[198] with a rag, and (Fayrūz) passed the knife over his gullet. At this he bellowed, like the loudest bellowing of a bull that I have ever heard, so that the guards hurried to the door—they were around the compound—and said, "What's this? What's this?" Whereupon the woman replied, "It is [only] the prophet, receiving revelations." Then he passed away.[199]

We stayed up all night discussing among ourselves how to notify our supporters, there being none other [present] than the three of us—Fayrūz, Dādhawayh, and Qays.[200] Consequently we agreed to give our war cry that we had with our supporters, and then to make the call to prayer. When the dawn appeared, therefore, Dādhawayh called out the war cry, terrifying [both] the Muslims and the unbelievers. The guards [of al-Aswad] gathered, surrounding us; then I gave the call to prayer. Their horsemen gathered to the guards, so I called out, "I bear witness that Muhammad is the Apostle of God and that ʿAbhalah[201] is a

196. The verb *khālaṭa* here means "to approach from the rear," as animals do when copulating. The text reads, literally, "he approached him, while he was like the camel."

197. Lit., "where."

198. I.e., held him by his head.

199. Or perhaps "Then he calmed down," i.e., ceased bellowing, but the context makes it clear that he died at this time. Ibn al-Athīr, *Kāmil*, II, 340, has "they [i.e., the guards] settled down."

200. Wellhausen, *Skizzen*, VI, 147, remarked that this passage makes clear that the original version of the story was not narrated by Jushaysh (cf. p. 25, above).

201. I.e., al-Aswad. Ibn al-Athīr, *Kāmil*, II, 340; Kosegarten; and Manuscript C: ʿAyhalah.

liar," and we threw his head to them. Then Wabr performed the ritual prayer. The men [of al-Aswad] launched an attack, so we called out, "Oh people of Ṣanʿāʾ, whoever has [one of al-Aswad's men] as a visitor, take hold of him, and whoever [of you] has one of them with him, take hold of him." And I called out to whoever was in the street, "Seize whomever you can." [But] then (al-Aswad's men also) snatched up many boys and seized [things]. Then they departed, going out [of the city]; but, when they emerged, seventy of their horsemen and [camel] riders were missing, and lo! the townspeople[202] had brought them to us. [For our part,] we were missing seven hundred household members. Then we wrote to each other, [agreeing] that they should leave for us what they held and that we should leave for them what we held. So they did this, leaving [Ṣanʿāʾ] without winning anything from us. Then they returned to [the [1863]
region] between Ṣanʿāʾ and Najrān. Ṣanʿāʾ and al-Janad became clear [of them], and God made Islam and its people strong.

We contended among ourselves over [who should] command. The companions of the Prophet returned one by one to their governorates, whereupon we agreed that Muʿādh b. Jabal [should hold authority];[203] he had used to lead us in prayer. We wrote to the Apostle of God with the news—that was during the lifetime of the Prophet. The news reached him the same day;[204] [subsequently] our messengers arrived, but the Prophet had died the morning of that day, so Abū Bakr replied to us.

According to ʿUbaydallāh—his uncle—Sayf; and according to al-Sarī—Shuʿayb—Sayf—Abū al-Qāsim al-Shanawī—al-ʿAlāʾ b. Ziyād—Ibn ʿUmar:[205] The news reached the Prophet from heaven on the night in which [al-Aswad] al-ʿAnsī was killed, that he might bring us the good tidings, so he said, "Al-ʿAnsī was killed

---

202. Lit., "people of the houses and streets."

203. Ibn al-Athīr, *Kāmil*, II, 340–41; Kosegarten; and Manuscript C add "*bi-al-khabar*" or "*bi-khabarihi*," suggesting that the agreement was to let Muʿādh carry the news of the death of al-Aswad to the Prophet. However, two accounts later Muʿādh is clearly still in Ṣanʿāʾ, not a messenger.

204. I.e., the news reached the Prophet miraculously on the same day as al-Aswad's death; see next account. In this passage *laylah* "night" has been translated as "day" because the traditional unit of a day in Arabia began with sundown and was called "a night."

205. Cf. Nuwayrī, 59.

last night; a blessed man of a blessed family killed him." He was asked, "And who [is this]?" He replied, "Fayrūz gained the victory, Fayrūz."

According to ʿUbaydallāh—his uncle—Sayf; and according to al-Sarī — Shuʿayb — Sayf — al-Mustanīr — ʿUrwah — al-Ḍaḥḥāk —Fayrūz:[206] We killed al-Aswad, and our affairs returned to what they had been, except that we sent to Muʿādh [b. Jabal], coming to mutual agreement upon him [as commander]. So he used to lead us in prayer in Ṣanʿāʾ. We had [high] hopes and expectations, as there remained nothing that displeased us except the matter of those horsemen who were going back and forth between us and Najrān; but by God (Muʿādh) only led us in prayer three times, when the news reached us of the Apostle of God's death; whereupon matters became unsettled and we came to disavow many things we used to acknowledge, and the land became disturbed.

[1864] According to al-Sarī—Shuʿayb—Sayf—Abū al-Qāsim and Abū Muḥammad—Abū Zurʿah Yaḥyā b. Abī ʿAmr al-Shaybānī from the province [*jund*] of Palestine—ʿAbdallāh b. Fayrūz al-Daylamī —his father: The Prophet sent them an envoy named Wabr b. Yuḥannis al-Azdī, who resided with Dādhawayh al-Fārisī. Now al-Aswad was a soothsayer who had Satan with him and followed him; so he rebelled and fell upon the king of Yemen, killing its king and marrying his wife. He ruled the Yemen. Bādhām had died before that, leaving his son in charge of his affairs; so (al-Aswad) killed him and married [his wife].[207] At this, Dādhawayh and Qays b. Makshūḥ al-Murādī and I met with Wabr b. Yuḥannis, the envoy of the Prophet of God, plotting to kill al-Aswad. Subsequently al-Aswad ordered the people to gather in an open area of Ṣanʿāʾ; then he came out so that he stood in their midst, [carrying] with him the javelin of the king. Then he called for the king's horse; and he speared it in the mouth with the javelin and then let it go, so that [the horse] began to run loose in the city as it bled, until it died. [Then] he stood up in the midst of the open area and called for sacrificial

206. Cf. Nuwayrī, 59.

207. The confused syntax and evident repetitions suggest that two or more separate accounts have been combined here. Cf. Caetani, 680–85.

camels from behind the line;[208] whereupon he made them stand with their necks and heads behind the line but not crossing it. Then he met them with his javelin, slitting their throats so that they scattered from him until he was done with them.[209] Then he seized his javelin in his hand, then fell upon the earth in a fit and, raising his head, said that he (that is, his Satan, who was with him) [had told him], "Ibn Makshūḥ is one of the oppressors, oh Aswad; cut off his head."[210] Then he cast his head [down] again to contemplate [and] then raised his head and said that [his Satan] had said, "Ibn al-Daylamī is one of the oppressors, oh Aswad; cut off his right hand and his right leg." Now, when I heard him say that, I said [to myself], "By God, I have no surety but that he might call for me so he could slaughter me with his javelin just as he slaughtered these sacrificial camels." So I [1865]
began to hide myself among the people lest he see me, until I went out not knowing in my alarm how I should set out. Then, when I approached my house, one of his people met me and struck me on the neck, saying. "The king summons you, and you sneak off! Go back!" and made me return. When I saw that, I was afraid that he would kill me.

Now hardly ever was any man of us without his dagger, so I slipped my hand in my boot to take hold of my dagger. Then I approached (al-Aswad), wishing to attack him by stabbing him with it until I killed him, and then to kill those with him. But when I drew near him, he saw evil in my face and said, "Stay where you are!" so I stopped. Then he said, "You are the most important of those in this place and the most knowledgeable about the notables of its people, so divide these sacrificial camels among them." [Then] he mounted and left, so I commenced dividing the meat among the people of Ṣanʿāʾ. Whereupon the one who had struck me on the neck came and said, "Give me some of it." But I said, "No, by God, not one bit. Aren't you the one who struck me on the neck?" At this he

---

208. Cf. the account on p. 29, above.

209. I.e., presumably those whose throats had been slit ran away from him one by one. Wellhausen, *Skizzen*, VI, 147 proposed "They fell away on both sides of the line until he was done with them."

210. Lit., "cut the top of his head."

went away angry, so that he came to al-Aswad and informed him of [the treatment] he endured from me and what I had said to him. So, when I had finished, I came to al-Aswad; walking toward him, I overheard the man complaining to him about me, whereupon al-Aswad said to him, "Verily by God I shall slaughter him." Then I said to him, "I have finished what you ordered me to do and have distributed [the meat] among the people." He said, "You have done well" and withdrew; so I left. Then we sent to the king's wife, [saying], "We wish to kill al-Aswad; how [would it be possible] for us [to do so]?" So she sent to me, [saying], "Come on." So I went to her, and she put the servant girl at the door to let us know if (al-Aswad) was coming; and the two of us entered the other house and then dug until we had penetrated [the wall]. Then we came out into the house, letting the curtain drop down; so I said, "Indeed, we shall kill him this very night." Then (the servant girl) said, "Come on!" Then, before I realized it, there was al-Aswad; he had entered
[1866] the house, and there he was with us; whereupon violent jealousy took hold of him, so that he began to strike my neck. I kept him away from me and went out to bring my companions [news] of what I had done. I was sure that our scheme against him was undone; [but] then the messenger of the woman came to us [with her message]: "(Al-Aswad) has not disrupted your plot at all, as long as you are [still] considering [it]. For, after you went out, I said to him, 'Don't you people allege that you are generous and possessors of noble deeds?' He said, 'Of course.' So I said, 'My brother came to greet me and to honor me, and then you fell upon him, striking his neck until you expelled him. So that was your generosity toward him?' And I kept heaping blame on him until he came to blame himself and said, 'He is your brother?' So I told him, 'Yes.' At this he said, 'I didn't realize [that].' So come tonight when you wish."

According to al-Daylamī: So we were reassured. We agreed to come by night, Dādhawayh and Qays and I, in order to enter the farthest house by the breach that we had made. Whereupon I said, "Oh Qays, you are the hero (*fāris*) of the Arabs; enter and kill the man." [But] he replied, "Indeed, powerful trembling overcomes me in the face of harm, so that I fear that I might strike him a blow that would avail nothing. But [rather] you enter, oh Fayrūz, for you are the youngest and strongest of us." So I laid down my sword with the group and entered to see where the man's head was. There was the lamp shining, and there he was asleep on some bedspreads. He was hidden in them, and I didn't know his head from his feet. [But] there was the woman seated with him; she had been feeding him pomegranate until he fell asleep. So I beckoned to her [to tell me] where his head was, whereupon she pointed to it. Then I began to walk until I stood by his head to see. I don't know whether I had [yet] looked at his face or not when all of a sudden he had opened his eyes and looked at me. At this I said [to myself], "If I go back [1867] [to get] my sword, I fear that he will escape me and get a weapon to ward me off of him." And lo, his Satan had warned him of my being there and had awakened him, and then when he was slow [to wake up] (his Satan) spoke to me through (al-Aswad's) tongue; [for] indeed he was looking [at me] and snoring [at the same time]. So I put my two hands forth toward his head, seizing his head with one hand and his beard with the other and then wrenching his neck so that I broke it. Then I went toward my companions, whereupon the woman took hold of my robe, saying, "Your sister! Your advice!" I said, "By God, I have killed him and have given you rest from him."[211] Then I went to my two companions and told them. They said, "Go back and cut off his head and bring it to us." So I entered [again], whereupon he uttered a groan; so I bridled him[212] to cut off his head and took it to the two of them. Then we all went out until we reached our homes. Wabr b. Yuḥannis al-Azdī was with us. He remained with us until we ascended one of the elevated fortresses, whereupon Wabr b. Yuḥannis uttered the call to prayer. Then we said, "Verily God has killed al-Aswad the liar." At this the people gathered to us, so we threw his head. When the people who had been with him saw [this], they saddled up their horses. Then each one of them began to take with him one of our boys, from among the families with whom they were staying; I saw them in the dawn making the boys ride behind them. So I called to

211. Cf. Ibn al-Athīr, *Kāmil*, II, 340; Balansī, 153.
212. I.e., held his head: *aljamtuhu*.

my brother, who was below me with the people, "Hold fast to whomever you can of them; don't you see what they are doing with the children?" So they took hold of them, so that we detained seventy of their men. They took thirty boys from us; then, when they came into open country, lo and behold, they were missing seventy men. When they [realized that] they were missing their companions, they came to us saying, "Send our companions to us." So we said to them, "Send our sons to us!" So they sent our sons to us, and we sent their companions to them.

[1868] The Apostle of God said to his companions, "God has killed al-Aswad al-ʿAnsī the liar; he killed him through the hand of a man who is one of your brethren and of a tribe that embraced Islam and believed [it] to be true." So we were in the same situation we had been in before al-Aswad reached us. The commanders[213] came to feel secure, and gradually returned; and the people made excuses for themselves, as only recently they had been in the *jāhiliyyah*.[214]

According to ʿUbaydallāh—his uncle—Sayf; and according to al-Sarī—Shuʿayb—Sayf—Sahl b. Yūsuf—his father—ʿUbayd b. Ṣakhr: From first to last, (al-Aswad's) rule was three months.

According to al-Sarī—Shuʿayb—Sayf, and according to ʿUbaydallāh—his uncle—Sayf—Jābir b. Yazīd—ʿUrwah b. Ghaziyyah—al-Ḍaḥḥāk b. Fayrūz:[215] Between his emergence at the cave of Khubbān and his murder there were about four months; he had been concealing his affair before that, until it came out openly afterward.

According to ʿUmar b. Shabbah—ʿAlī b. Muḥammad—Abū Maʿshar, Yazīd b. ʿIyāḍ b. Juʿdubah, Ghassān b. ʿAbd al-Ḥamīd, and Juwayriyyah b. Asmāʾ—their teachers:[216] Abū Bakr sent out the army of Usāmah b. Zayd at the end of Rabīʿ I, and [the news of] the murder of al-ʿAnsī came at the end of Rabīʿ I, after the departure of Usāmah. That was the first conquest, [news of] which came to Abū Bakr while he was in Medina.

---

213. *Umarāʾ*; i.e., the Prophet's governors.
214. I.e., the age of pre-Islamic heathenism.
215. Cf. Nuwayrī, 59; Caetani, 685.
216. Cf. Nuwayrī, 59; Caetani, 685.

According to al-Wāqidī: In this year, that is, year 11, in the [first] half of Muḥarram, the deputation of al-Nakhaʿ[217] came [1869] to the Apostle of God; their leader was Zurārah b. ʿAmr. They were the last of the delegations to reach [the Prophet].

In this year the Prophet's daughter Fāṭimah died, on Tuesday, the 3rd of Ramaḍān. At that time she was twenty-nine years old or thereabouts. It is said that this was related on the authority of Abū Bakr b. ʿAbdallāh—Isḥāq b. ʿAbdallāh—Ābān b. Ṣāliḥ. It is alleged that this was related on the authority of Ibn Jurayj—ʿAmr b. Dīnār—Abū Jaʿfar, who said: Fāṭimah died three months after the Prophet.

According to Ibn Jurayj—al-Zuhrī—ʿUrwah: Fāṭimah died six months after the Prophet. (According to al-Wāqidī, this is the more correct [version].) ʿAlī and Asmāʾ bt. ʿUmays[218] washed her [corpse].

According to ʿAbd al-Raḥmān b. ʿAbd al-ʿAzīz b. ʿAbdallāh b. ʿUthmān b. Ḥunayf—ʿAbdallāh b. Abī Bakr b. ʿAmr b. Ḥazm—ʿAmrah bt. ʿAbd al-Raḥmān: Al-ʿAbbās b. ʿAbd al-Muṭṭalib[219] prayed [the funeral prayer] for her.

According to Abū Zayd—ʿAlī—Abū Maʿshar: Al-ʿAbbās and ʿAlī and al-Faḍl b. al-ʿAbbās[220] entered her grave.

In this year ʿAbdallāh b. Abū Bakr b. Abū Quḥāfah died. An arrow had hit him [when he was] at al-Ṭāʾif with the Prophet; it had been shot by Abū Miḥjan.[221] The wound healed up until Shawwāl, when it became bad again; subsequently he died.

According to Abū Zayd—ʿAlī—Abū Maʿshar, Muḥammad b. Isḥāq, and Juwayriyyah b. Asmāʾ, in the chain of informants

---

217. Al-Nakhaʿ b. ʿAmr, a clan of the tribe of Madhḥij in southern Yemen. (Caskel, II, 444).

218. An early convert to Islam of the Khathʿam tribe, married successively to the Prophet's uncle Ḥamzah, to his cousin Jaʿfar b. Abī Ṭālib, to Abū Bakr, and to ʿAlī b. Abī Ṭālib; sister of the Prophet's wife Maymūnah bt. al-Ḥārith. (Ibn al-Athīr, *Usd*, V, 395).

219. One of the Prophet's uncles, eponym of the Abbasid dynasty.

220. Oldest son of al-ʿAbbās and hence a cousin of the Prophet; his mother was a sister of the Prophet's wife Maymūnah bt. al-Ḥārith. (Ibn al-Athīr, *Usd*, IV, 183).

221. A renowned poet of the Thaqīf tribe of al-Ṭāʾif, who embraced Islam only when his town submitted. (Ibn al-Athīr, *Usd*, V, 290).

that I mentioned above:[222] In the year in which the oath of allegiance was sworn to Abū Bakr, the people of Fārs made Yazdagard[223] king over them.

[1870] Abū Ja'far said: In this year occurred the battle between Abū Bakr and Khārijah b. Ḥiṣn al-Fazārī.[224]

According to Abū Zayd—'Alī b. Muḥammad in their chain of authorities, which I mentioned above:[225] Abū Bakr remained in Medina after the death of the Apostle of God and after he sent Usāmah at the head of his army to where his father, Zayd b. Ḥārithah,[226] had been killed in Syria. As it was the place to which the Apostle of God had ordered him to march, (Abū Bakr) made no innovation [in doing this]. There had come to him delegations of apostate Arabs, who confirmed [the observance of] prayer but held back [payment of] the alms tax (*zakāt*). But Abū Bakr did not accept this from them and sent them back. He remained [in Medina] until Usāmah b. Zayd b. Ḥārithah arrived forty days after his marching off (some say after seventy days). Then, when Usāmah b. Zayd had come, he left him in charge of Medina and marched out (some say that he left Sinān al-Ḍamrī[227] in charge of Medina). So he marched and encamped at Dhū al-Qaṣṣah[228] in Jumādah I (some say Jumādah II). Now the Apostle of God had sent Nawfal b. Mu'āwiyah al-Dīlī;[229] then

---

222. Cf. p. 38, above; Caetani, 715.

223. The last king of the Sasanian dynasty.

224. Leader of the delegation from the Fazārah tribe of the Najd that came to the Prophet shortly after his campaign to Tabūk. Cf. Ibn Sa'd, I/1, 42; Ibn al-Athīr, *Usd*, II, 71–72; and Nuwayrī, 61ff. ("Khārijah b. Ḥuṣayn"). On Fazārah, a tribe of the Ghaṭafān group, see *EI*², s.v. "Fazāra" (W. M. Watt); cf. note 233, below.

225. Cf. Nuwayrī, 61, and p. 38, above; Caetani, 592.

226. The Prophet's freedman and an early convert; originally of the Kalb tribe of Syria, he was sent as leader of a raid on southern Syria toward the end of the Prophet's life. Cf. Ibn al-Athīr, *Usd*, II, 224–27.

227. Ibn al-Athīr, *Usd*, II, 359, adds nothing to what we learn here. Ḍamrah b. Bakr was a tribe of Kinānah; cf. Caskel, II, 241.

228. It lies about twenty miles east of Medina on the way to al-Rabadhah, according to al-Mas'ūdī, *Tanbīh* (BGA VIII), 252. (Al-Rabadhah is 175 km east of Medina; see note 271 below.) Yāqūt gives conflicting accounts of Dhū al-Qaṣṣah's location. Cf. Hamdani, 143 l. 21, who lists a "Dhū al-Qiḍḍah" in the vicinity of al-Sharabbah and Zarūd on the road to Iraq.

229. Chieftain of the clan al-Dīl of Kinānah, who, after long resisting the Prophet, joined him late: Caskel, II, 447, and Ibn al-Athīr, *Usd*, V, 47. On the

Khārijah b. Ḥiṣn had lit upon him at al-Sharabbah,[230] taking what he had,[231] and subsequently returned it to the Banū Fazārah. So Nawfal returned to Abū Bakr in Medina, in advance of Usāmah's arrival before Abū Bakr.

The first war in the *riddah* after the death of the Prophet was the war of al-ʿAnsī. The war of al-ʿAnsī was in the Yemen. [Next] was the war of Khārijah b. Ḥiṣn, and [that of] Manẓūr b. Zabbān b. Sayyār[232] at the head of Ghaṭafān[233] while the Muslims were unaware. So Abū Bakr repaired to a forest and hid himself in it; then God routed the unbelievers.

According to ʿUbaydallāh—his uncle—Sayf; and according to al-Sarī—Shuʿayb—Sayf—al-Mujālid b. Saʿīd: After Usāmah [1871] had gone away, the land sank into disbelief, and from every tribe either a small group or the whole showed disobedience[234] and apostatized, except for Quraysh and Thaqīf.[235]

According to ʿUbaydallāh—his uncle—Sayf; and according to al-Sarī—Shuʿayb—Sayf—Hishām b. ʿUrwah—his father:[236] After the Apostle of God had died and Usāmah had departed, the Arabs apostatized, in large or small groups;[237] and Musaylimah and Ṭulayḥah[238] feigned [divine] inspiration, so that the situation

form of the clan name (al-Dīl, later al-Du'il), see Caskel, II, 234, s.v. "al-Du'il b. Bakr."

230. A place between al-Rabadhah and al-Salīlah in the Ghaṭafān country (Yāqūt, s.v.).

231. Wellhausen, *Skizzen*, VI, 147, observes that this means the tribute in livestock that Nawfal had gathered.

232. Another chief of Fazārah; he embraced Islam and had marriage ties to close associates of the Prophet before his rebellion. Cf. Ibn al-Athīr, *Usd*, IV, 420; Caskel, II, 398.

233. Ghaṭafan was a group of tribes east of Medina, including ʿAbdallāh b. Ghaṭafān, ʿAbs, Ashjaʿ, and Dhubyān; Dhubyān included the tribes of Fazārah, Murrah, and Thaʿlabah. Cf. Caskel, II, 274; *EI*², s.v. "Ghaṭafān" (J. W. Fück).

234. *Taṣammarat*, lit., "became avaricious, refused what is demanded." Ibn al-Athīr, *Kāmil*, II, 342, has *taḍarramat al-arḍ nāran*, "the land burned fiercely with fire."

235. The main tribe of al-Ṭā'if. Cf. Caetani, 583.

236. Cf. Ibn al-Athīr, *Kāmil*, II, 342–43; cf. Caetani, 583.

237. *ʿAwāmma aw khawāṣṣa*. Similarly, in other passages on p. 42 *ʿāmma* and *khāṣṣa* are rendered as "the bulk of" and "a few of," or "large and small groups of." Caetani, 583, understands *ʿawāmma* as "all of [Ṭayyi' and Asad]."

238. According to Muslim tradition, the "false prophets" in al-Yamāmah and the Najd respectively.

regarding the two of them became serious. The common people of Ṭayyi' and Asad[239] gathered to Ṭulayḥa, and Ghaṭafān apostatized (except for those from Ashja' and the leaders of groups of mixed origins), and they rendered the oath of allegiance to him. Hawāzin[240] remained ambivalent;[241] they withheld [payment of] the *ṣadaqah* tax,[242] except for those from Thaqīf and its party.[243] The bulk of Jadīlah[244] and the weak groups were guided by them. A few of of Banū Sulaym[245] apostatized, and likewise the rest of the people in every place.

The envoys[246] of the Prophet arrived [in Medina] from Yemen and Yamāmah and the territory of Banū Asad, [along with] delegations of those with whom the Prophet had corresponded. His business regarding al-Aswad and Musaylimah and Ṭulayḥah had been carried out by means of reports and letters; so they presented their letters to Abū Bakr, and informed him of the news. At this Abū Bakr said to them, "You will not leave before messengers come from your commanders and from others, with [news of] more cunning and more bitter [things?] than that which you have described, and [reports of] the unraveling of affairs." It was not long before there came to them from every place the letters of the Prophet's commanders, with [news of] the rebellion[247] of some [group], large or small, and of their

239. Ṭayyi' and Asad were neighboring, largely nomadic tribes whose territory was near the "mountains of Ṭayyi'" ('Ajā' and Salmā) in the Najd. Cf. *EI*², s.v. "Asad, Banū" (H. Kindermann); Caskel, II, 194, 555; Landau-Tasseron, "Asad from Jāhiliyya to Islām"; idem, "The Participation of Ṭayyī in the *Ridda*."

240. A large confederation of tribes in northern and west-central Arabia that included 'Āmir b. Ṣa'ṣa'ah and Thaqīf, although the latter, who were townsmen, often went their own way, as here. Cf. *EI*², s.v. "Hawāzin" (W. M. Watt).

241. Lit., "put one foot forward and held one foot back."

242. Although in later jurisprudence *ṣadaqah* tax came to mean voluntary alms, and thus was little different from *zakāt*, at the time of the *riddah* it meant tribute paid by nomads to the Islamic state. See Simonson, 32–33; Donner, *Conquests*, 251–52, 265, and index.

243. *Liffi-hā*. cf. Ibn Manẓūr, IX, 318.

244. Jadīlah and al-Ghawth were the two main divisions of Ṭayyi', Cf. Caskel, II, 252.

245. A tribe living northeast of Mecca. Cf. Watt, *Medina*, 95–97; Michael Lecker, *The Banū Sulaym* (Jerusalem: The Hebrew University, 1989), infra.

246. Cf. Nuwayrī, 62.

247. Lit., "unraveling, coming undone of what had been done," i.e., renunciation of their agreements.

boldly committing aggression against the Muslims. So Abū Bakr combated them with that which the Apostle of God had combated them—with envoys; hence he sent their messengers back with his orders, and sent [further] envoys after the [original] messengers. And he awaited the arrival of Usāmah [before] [1872] clashing with them.[248] The first who clashed were ʿAbs and Dhubyān;[249] they hastened to [clash with] him, so that he fought them before the return of Usāmah.[250]

According to ʿUbaydallāh—his uncle—Sayf; and according to al-Sarī—Shuʿayb—Sayf—Abū ʿAmr—Zayd b. Aslam:[251] The Apostle of God died while his tax collectors were among the Quḍāʿah. Over the Kalb was Imru' al-Qays b. al-Aṣbagh al-Kalbī of the Banū ʿAbdallāh; and over al-Qayn was ʿAmr b. al-Ḥakam; and over the Saʿd Ḥudhaym was Muʿāwiyah b. Fulān al-Wā'ilī[252]

According to al-Sarī al-Wālibī:[253] Wadīʿah al-Kalbī apostatized with those of Kalb who helped him, whereas Imru' al-Qays remained obedient,[254] and Zumayl b. Quṭbah al-Qaynī rebelled with those of Banū al-Qayn who helped him, whereas ʿAmr remained [obedient]; and Muʿāwiyah apostatized with those of Saʿd Hudhaym who helped him. So Abū Bakr wrote to Imru' al-Qays b. Fulān[255]—he was the grandfather of Sukaynah, daughter of Ḥusayn[256]—to march to[257] Wadīʿah,

---

248. Lit., "He awaited in their clashing the arrival of Usāmah."

249. Tribes of Ghaṭafān; cf. note 233, above.

250. The reading of manuscript C is in some ways more coherent: "They made haste in order to fight him before the arrival of Usāmah," i.e., they wished to move quickly so as to attack Abū Bakr before he could consolidate his position.

251. Cf. Ibn al-Athīr, *Kāmil*, II, 343; Caetani, 583.

252. Kos has "al-Wābilī"; Ibn al-Athīr, *Kāmil*, II, 343, "al-Wālibī." Both are incorrect; cf. Caskel, II, 585, under "Wā'il b. Saʿd Hudhaym."

253. Cf. Ibn al-Athīr, *Kāmil*, II, 343; Caetani, 583–84, 591, a continuation of the preceding account.

254. *ʿAlā dīnihi.*

255. There is some confusion regarding the name. Manuscript C has Imru'al-Qays b. Bilād; Ibn Ḥajar, *Iṣābah*, s.v., has Imru'al-Qays b. ʿAdī b. Aws. . . . Perhaps "b. Fulān" is a dittography from the name of Muʿāwiyah b. Fulān in the preceding line (cf. preceding account).

256. Ḥusayn b. ʿAlī b. Abī Ṭālib, the Prophet's grandson.

257. I.e., against, reading *li-* with the Cairo edition, rather than *bi-* in the text. The sentence is obscure.

and [he wrote to] ʿAmr to take a stand against Zumayl and against Muʿāwiyah al-ʿUdhrī. So when Usāmah found himself in the midst of the Quḍāʿah country, he deployed the cavalry among them and ordered them to make those who had stood firmly by Islam rise up against those who had turned back from it, so that they fled until they took refuge in Dūmah[258] and gathered round Wadīʿah. Usāmah's cavalry returned to him, whereupon he decamped with them until he raided al-Ḥamqatayn,[259] striking among the Banū al-Ḍubayb of Judhām[260]
[1873] and among the Banū Khaylīl of Lakhm[261] and their party[262] of the two factions.[263] He drove them out of Ābil[264] and returned unharmed and bearing spoil.

According to al-Sarī—Shuʿayb—Sayf—Sahl b. Yūsuf—al-Qāsim b. Muḥammad:[265] The Apostle of God died, and Asad and Ghaṭafān and Ṭayyi' gathered around Ṭulayḥah, except for the principal leaders of some groups in the three tribes. Asad gathered at Samīrā',[266] and Fazārah and those who follow them[267] of Ghaṭafān to the south of Ṭībah,[268] and Ṭayyi'[269] on

---

258. Dūmat al-Jandal, an important oasis in northern Arabia, modern al-Jawf. Cf. *EI*², s.v. "Dūmat al-Djandal" (L. Veccia Vaglieri).

259. A place on the fringes of the Syrian steppe (Yāqūt, s.v.).

260. The tribe of Judhām lived in the northern Hijāz and Transjordan; al-Ḍubayb b. Qurṭ was one of their main clans. Cf. *EI*², s.v. "Djudhām" (C. E. Bosworth); Caskel, II, 243, 263.

261. Text has "Khalīl." Lakhm was a tribe of southern Iraq and southern Syria, absorbed in Syria by Judhām; Khaylīl was a branch of Ghassān associated with the tribe of Lakhm. Cf. Caskel, II, 339; Wellhausen, *Skizzen*, VI, 147; *Emendanda*; *EI*², s.v. "Lakhm" (H. Lammens–Irfan Shahid).

262. Cf. note 243, above.

263. *Al-qabīlayn*.

264. Manuscript C has '.y.l; Kos has Ubnā. See note 96, above.

265. Cf. Ibn al-Athīr, *Kāmil*, II, 344–45 (extending as far as p. 52, below); Caetani, 596–99.

266. Ibn al-Athīr, *Kāmil*, II, 344, has "Sumayrā'," probably owing to confusion with Sumayrah, another place near Mecca; cf. Yāqūt, s.v.v. Samīrā' was in the Asad country on the pilgrimage road to Iraq northeast of Mecca.

267. Kos has "those who come to them."

268. Yāqūt identifies this as a village near Zarūd, which was on the Kūfah-Mecca pilgrimage road in the Shaqīq sands. Perhaps it is identical with Ṭābah, a village on the southeast flank of Mt. Salmā in the Asad/Ṭayyi' country; cf. the shift of ā to ī in other names, such as Jāzān/Jīzān. On Ṭābah, see Thilo, s.v. and map B.

269. Kos has Ẓaby.

the borders of their territory. Thaʿlabah b. Saʿd and those who followed them of Murrah and ʿAbs[270] gathered at al-Abraq of al-Rabadhah,[271] and people from the Banū Kinānah[272] crowded around them[273] to the point that the country could not sustain them; so they divided into two groups, one group remaining in al-Abraq while the other went to Dhū al-Qaṣṣah. Ṭulayḥah reinforced them with [his brother] Ḥibāl.[274] Ḥibāl was in charge of the people of Dhū al-Qaṣṣah from Banū Asad and those of Layth and al-Dīl and Mudlij[275] who crowded around; and over Murrah in al-Abraq was ʿAwf b. Fulān b. Sinān; and over Thaʿlabah and ʿAbs was al-Ḥārith b. Fulān, one of the Banū Subayʿ. They[276] had sent delegations that came to Medina and stayed with the chiefs of the people; so (the Medinan chiefs), except for ʿAbbās,[277] put them up and interceded for them before Abū Bakr, on condition that (the petitioning tribes) should perform prayer but not pay the alms tax. But God strengthened Abū Bakr's resolution in the truth, and he said: "If they refuse me [even] a hobble, I shall fight them for it."[278] Now, the hobbles of the *ṣadaqah* camels were required with the [camels paid as] *ṣadaqah* from the people who paid *ṣadaqah*; so he refused [their request], whereupon the delegation of those apostates who were near Medina returned to their tribes, [1874]
telling them how few the people of Medina were and making them covetous of it. After Abū Bakr had expelled the delegation,

---

270. All three tribes were part of Ghaṭafān; cf. note 233, above.
271. Al-Rabadhah was 175 km east of Medina. The epithet "al-Abraq," meaning rough terrain with rock, sand, and clay, is common in composite toponyms; presumably here it refers to a specific spot near al-Rabadhah. Cf. al-Rāshid, *Al-Rabadhah*.
272. Kinānah was a tribe related to Asad, living from near Mecca northeastward to Asad territory. Cf. *EI*², s.v. "Kināna" (W. M. Watt).
273. Manuscript C has "lived" (?) (*nashaʾat*).
274. Manuscript C has *amara-hum . . . bi-khibālin*.
275. Layth b. Bakr, al-Dīl b. Bakr, and Mudlij b. Murrah were branches of Kinānah; cf. Caskel, II, 376, 416, and note 229, above.
276. Cf. p. 69, below; Diyārbakrī, II, 202 top; Ibn Ḥubaysh, 9, 12 middle.
277. One of the Prophet's uncles and eponymous ancestor of the Abbasid dynasty of caliphs.
278. The rope hobble (*ʿiqāl*) worn by the camels given in payment of the *ṣadaqa* tax. The word also came to mean, by extension, a year's *ṣadaqa* tax itself; cf. Lane, *Arabic-English Lexicon*, part 5, p. 2115, s.v. *ʿiqāl*.

he placed some people on the mountain passes[279] of Medina—'Alī al-Zubayr,[280] Ṭalḥah,[281] and 'Abdallāh b. Mas'ūd[282]—and enjoined[283] the people of Medina to go to the mosque. And he said to them: "The land has sunk into disbelief, and their delegation has seen that you are few and that you would be unaware whether you were approached by day or by night. The nearest of them is [only] a stage[284] from you. The people were hoping that we would accept them and be reconciled with them, but we refused them[285] and dissolved their treaty. So get ready." Consequently they made preparations, and it wasn't three [days] before they came raiding Medina by night, leaving some[286] of their [number] behind in Dhū Ḥusā[287] to serve as reserves for them. The mounted raiders[288] reached the mountain passes by night, while the fighting men were in them; there were people on foot in front of them, so they alerted them and sent news to Abū Bakr. Abū Bakr sent back to them that they should hold their positions; so they did so, while [Abū Bakr] came out to them leading the people of the mosque [mounted] on their water-hauling camels. At this the enemy lost their will;[289] so the Muslims pursued them on their camels until they reached Dhū Ḥusā,[290] whereupon the reserves came out against them

279. *Anqāb*. Kos: *anṣāb*, "boundary markers" (?); Ibn al-Athīr, *anṣār*, "helpers." Cf. *Glossary*.

280. Al-Zubayr b. al-'Awwām, early convert from Asad clan of Quraysh, maternal cousin of the Prophet. Cf. Ibn Sa'd, III/1, 70ff.

281. Talḥah b. 'Ubaydallāh, early convert from the Taym clan of Quraysh. Cf. Ibn Sa'd, III/1, 152ff.

282. Early convert and close associate of the Prophet from the Hudhayl tribe. Cf. Ibn Sa'd, III/1, 106ff.

283. IK and Ibn al-Athir, *Kāmil*: "required."

284. *Barīd*, the distance between courier stops, six to twelve miles; cf. Lane, *Arabic-English Lexicon*, s.v.

285. Kos and Manuscript C: "We came to them."

286. IK: "half."

287. A valley near al-Sharabbah in the territory of 'Abs and the rest of Ghaṭafān; cf. Yāqūt, s.v.; Thilo, s.v. and map C, places it *circa* 160 km east of Medina, just west of al-Rabadhah. Nuwayrī, 63, has "Ḥusā."

288. Reading *al-ghārah*, "horsemen making a raid," for the text's *ghiwār*, "raiding" (rare), as proposed by *Glossary*.

289. IK: "turned back."

290. Manuscript C: Dhū Khushub.

with churning skins that they had inflated and on which they had placed ropes. Then they rolled them with their feet in the faces of the camels, so that each skin rolled in its tether. At this the Muslims' camels took fright while they were [mounted] on them—they do not shy at anything the way they did from those skins—and steered (the Muslims) out of their control until they brought them into Medina; but no Muslim was thrown or wounded, so al-Khuṭayl b. Aws, brother of al-Ḥuṭayʾah b. Aws,[291] [1875]
said about that:[292]

My saddle and she-camel are a ransom for Banū Dhubyān,
on the evening when Abū Bakr is stabbed[293] with lances.
But [something] was rolled by the feet so that they feared it,
to a certain degree, no more and no less.[294]
[Even] God has troops who are given a taste of it;[295]
verily they are reckoned in that which is counted among the wonders of the age.

(Al-Zuhrī recited [the end of the last line] as: "among the memorable deeds of the age." According to ʿAbdallāh al-Laythī: Banū ʿAbd Manāt were among the apostates—they and[296] Banū Dhubyān were involved in that affair at Dhū al-Qaṣṣah and Dhū Ḥusā.)[297]

We obeyed the Apostle of God as long as he was[298] among us,[299]
So, oh worshipers of God, what [is so great about] Abū Bakr?

---

291. A famous poet who claimed to be from the ʿAbs tribe; cf. *EI*², s.v. "al-Ḥuṭayʾah" (I. Goldziher–C. Pellat); Ibn al-Athīr, *Usd*, II, 30.

292. Poem text has numerous variant readings not noted here.

293. Reading *yuḥdhā* with the Cairo edition, against *yuḥdā* and other variants in the text.

294. Reading *in yazīdu wa lā yaḥrī* with the Cairo edition, against *in tuqīmu wa lā tasrī* in the text.

295. Literally, "who are made to taste His tasting," perhaps an allusion to Qurʾān 3:185; "every soul tastes death."

296. Reading *hum wa* as proposed by Wellhausen, *Skizzen*, VI, 147, and *Emendanda*, rather than *wa hum*, "and they were," as found in text, for ʿAbd Manāt was part of Kinānah, not of Dhubyān.

297. The verses following this parenthetical aside are a continuation of those before it, sharing the same meter (*ṭawīl*) and rhyme letter (r).

298. Ibn Ḥubaysh, 8: "lived."

299. IK: "in our midst."

[1876] Will he bequeath [leadership of] us to a young camel (*bakr*)[300]
after him, if he should die?
That would be, in God's name,[301] a disaster.[302]
Why won't you return our delegation in time?
Have you no fear of the blast of braying young camels?[303]
Indeed, the thing they requested of you, and that you denied,
is like dates, or sweeter to me than dates.[304]

So the enemy (*qawm*) thought (the Muslims) weak and sent news to the people of Dhū al-Qaṣṣah, whereupon they advanced against them, relying on those who had brought them the news, they being [still] unaware of God's work, which He wished and desired to be communicated among them. At this Abū Bakr passed the night getting ready by putting the army[305] in order; then he went out in battle order in the last part of that night, marching with al-Nuʿmān b. Muqarrin[306] on his right flank, and ʿAbdallāh b. Muqarrin on his left flank, and Suwayd b. Muqarrin with the riders at the rear. No sooner had the dawn broken than they found themselves and the enemy on the same plain. They heard neither a footfall nor a voice from the Muslims until (the Muslims) fell on them with the sword, slaying [them] at the end of that night so that, before the upper limb of the sun arose, they had turned their backs to (the Muslims). (The Muslims) plundered them of all their riding camels,[307] and Ḥibāl[308] was killed. Abū Bakr[309] pursued them until he camped

300. Cairo ed: "Will he bequeath it . . . ?" The verse is clearly a satiric comment on Abū Bakr's name, which means "father of the young camel."

301. Ibn Ḥubaysh: "by God's house."

302. Lit., "the one who breaks the back," *qāsimatu al-ẓahri.*

303. Reading *rāghiyat al-bakri* with Cairo, against *rāʿiyat al-bakri,* "herders of young camels," in the text.

304. I.e., it would have been better had you complied with the delegation's requests.

305. *Al-nās,* lit., "the people." For a very different account of this episode, see Diyārbakrī, II, 204.

306. He and his brothers ʿAbdallāh and Suwayd were warriors of the tribe of Muzaynah who had led large groups of their tribe to the Prophet. Cf. Ibn al-Athīr, *Usd,* V, 30–31.

307. *Ghalabū-hum ʿalā ʿāmmati ẓahri-him. . . .*

308. Kos and Ibn al-Athīr, *Kāmil,* II, 345, have "men." Cf. Ibn al-Athīr, II, 347; and pp. 62–63, below. Diyārbakrī, II, 206 bottom, says that he was captured and asked to be executed.

309. Cf. Nuwayrī, 62.

at Dhū al-Qaṣṣah; it was the first conquest. He put in (Dhū al-Qaṣṣah) al-Nuʿmān b. Muqarrin at the head of a number [of troops] and returned to Medina. The polytheists were humiliated [1877]
by (this victory), so the Banū Dhubyān and ʿAbs fell upon those Muslims who were among them and slaughtered them; and those who backed them did as they did. Meanwhile, the [other] Muslims grew stronger through Abū Bakr's battle. Abū Bakr swore that he would certainly make slaughter among the polytheists [in vengeance for] every killing [of a Muslim], and would kill in every tribe [someone] for each of the Muslims whom they had killed, and more. Ziyād b. Ḥanẓalah al-Tamīmī[310] said about that:

By early morn Abū Bakr hastened to them
just as most of them[311] strove toward their death.
He rejoiced supremely at their braying
while Ḥibāl[312] drooled out his life to them.

He also said:

We set up for them on the left side; then they gathered together in a jumble,[313]
like the troop of warriors who make their camels kneel on well-watered pastures.
They had no endurance for war, when it arose
on the morning when Abū Bakr rose up with [his] men.
We approached the Banū ʿAbs by night, at their nearer Nibāj,[314]
and Dhubyān we scared away with back-breaking losses.

Then they continued that [policy][315] until the Muslims in every tribe were more firm in their religion for it, and [until] the

310. According to Ibn al-Athīr, *Usd*, II, 213, he had been sent by the Prophet to help the Tamīmī chieftain Qays b. ʿĀṣim resist the "false prophet" Musaylimah.

311. Reading, with Cairo, *julāl*, rather than *ḥalāl* as in the text.

312. IK has "mountains."

313. *Fa-kubkibū*; cf. *kabkaba*, "troop," in the next line, presumably an allusion to Qur ʾān 26:94.

314. The nearer of the "two Nibajes" (al-Nibājān) was near Mt. Salmā, about 400 km northeast of Medina; cf. Ibn Manẓūr, II, 372; Yāqūt, s.v. "Nibājān"; Thilo, 76 and Map B.

315. I.e., of severe retaliations; lit., "they did nothing but that."

[1878] fortunes (*amr*) of the polytheists were reversed in every tribe. The *ṣadaqah* tax[316] of [various] people came to Medina by night, [brought by] Ṣafwān and then al-Zibriqān and then ʿAdī[317]—Ṣafwān [arriving] at the beginning of the night, and the second [installment] in the middle of it, and the third at the end of it. The one who announced the good news of [the arrival of] Ṣafwān was Saʿd b. Abī Waqqāṣ,[318] and the one who announced al-Zibriqān was ʿAbd al-Raḥmān b. ʿAwf,[319] and the one who announced ʿAdī was ʿAbdallāh b. Masʿūd—or, according to other [traditionists], Abū Qatādah.[320] As each one of them appeared, the people said, "[He is] bringing a warning [about the enemy]!"[321] But Abū Bakr said, "This is a bearer of good tidings, this is a protector, not [someone] worn out [from urgency]." Then, after he had divulged the good news, they said, "Long live[322] the good news you announce!"

That was sixty days after Usāmah's departure; a few days after that, Usāmah[323] came [back to Medina], two months and some days [after his departure]. Thereupon Abū Bakr left him in charge of Medina, saying to him and his army, "Rest, and rest your riding camels." Then he went out, leading those who had gone out to Dhū al-Qaṣṣah and those who had been in the passes

---

316. Cf. Diyārbakrī, II, 203–4.

317. Cf. Balansī, 12, 17–18, Nuwayrī, 62–63. Ṣafwān is probably Ṣafwān b. Ṣafwān, the Prophet's tax agent over the ʿAmr clan of Tamīm; cf. Ibn al-Athīr, *Usd*, III, 23, and p. 85, below. Al-Zibriqān b. Badr, chief of Saʿd-Tamīm, had come to the Prophet with his tribe's delegation and was appointed collector of *ṣadaqah* tax upon his clan of Banū ʿAwf; cf. Ibn al-Athīr, *Usd*, II, 194. ʿAdī b. Ḥātim, a chief of Tayyiʾ, had been appointed by the Prophet as tax collector over parts of the tribes of Asad and Tayyiʾ; cf. *EI*², s.v. "ʿAdī b. Ḥāṭim" (A. Schaade); Landau-Tasseron, "Asad from Jāhiliyya to Islam," 19–20; Landau-Tasseron, "The Participation of Tayyi" in the *Ridda, infra*.

318. Important early convert from the Zuhrah clan of Quraysh, sometimes said to have been the third male to embrace Islam. Cf. Ibn Saʿd, III/1, 97–105; Watt, *Mecca*, 89–90.

319. Another early convert from Banū Zuhrah of Quraysh. Cf. *EI*², s.v. "ʿAbd al-Raḥmān b. ʿAwf" (M. Th. Houtsma–W. M. Watt); Watt, *Mecca*, 89–90.

320. Abū Qatādah al-Ḥārith b. Ribʿī al-Salmī al-Anṣārī, of the Khazraj tribe, an early Medinan follower of the Prophet; cf. Ibn al-Athīr, *Usd*, V, 273–75.

321. Text simply has *nadhīr*, "a warner," but the term is used in the military context in the sense of one bringing news of the enemy.

322. Lit., "may it be long."

323. Cf. Nuwayrī, 63.

on that side [of the city]. But the Muslims said to him, "Oh Caliph of the Apostle of God, we beg you by God not to expose yourself [to battle], for if you were to be struck down there would be no order among the people. It would be harder on the enemy if you were to remain [here]. So send a man [in your place]; then if he is struck down you can put another in command." But [Abū Bakr] said, "No, by God, I won't do it; indeed, I will set an example for you myself." Then he marched out in battle order to Dhū Ḥusā and Dhū al-Qaṣṣah, with ʿAbdallāh and Suwayd in their accustomed positions,[324] until they descended upon the people of al-Rabadhah at al-Abraq. They fought, God destroying al-Ḥārith and ʿAwf;[325] al-Ḥuṭay'ah[326] was taken prisoner, and ʿAbs and Banū Bakr[327] fled. Abū Bakr remained a few days at al-Abraq. Banū Dhubyān had dominated the country, but he said, "It is [henceforth] forbidden for Banū Dhubyān to control this country, since God has given it to us [1879]
as spoil," and removed it [from their control].[328] Now, when the apostates had been overcome, and entered [once again] the gate [by] which they had [formerly] gone out, and [Abū Bakr] had treated the people leniently,[329] the Banū Thaʿlabah came to encamp in [this country]—it had been their camping grounds—but were kept from it; so they came to Medina, saying, "Why have we been kept from camping in our country?" Whereupon (Abū Bakr) said, "You lie; it is no land of yours, but a gift restored to me [after having been stolen]," and granted them no favor. He reserved al-Abraq for the horses of the Muslims and made the rest of the country of al-Rabadhah a pasture for the people, the Banū Thaʿlabah notwithstanding. Then he reserved all of it for the [camels paid as] *ṣadaqah* tax [to] the Muslims,

---

324. Lit., "over what they had been over"; ʿAbdallāh and Suwayd b. Muqarrin, described on p. 48, above, as commanding the left flank and rear, respectively. The third brother, al-Nuʿmān, had been left at Dhū al-Qaṣṣah.

325. On al-Ḥārith and ʿAwf, see p. 45, above.

326. Kos and Ibn al-Athīr, *Kāmil*, II, 345: al-Khaṭbah.

327. Probably Bakr b. ʿAbdmanāt b. Kinānah, a main segment of this tribe that included many important clans. Cf. Caskel, I, Tables 36ff. and II, 222.

328. *Ajlā-hā*; i.e., Abū Bakr deported the Banū Dhubyān from this territory.

329. The text of this phrase is at best elliptical, perhaps corrupt. Kos has "and damage had become widespread." Here and several lines below "the people" [*al-nās*] refers to the former rebels.

because of a fight that occurred between the people and the collectors of the *ṣadaqah* taxes.[330] So he barred on that account one from the other. After ʿAbs and Dhubyān were broken up, they took refuge with Ṭulayḥah. Ṭulayḥah had encamped at Buzākhah,[331] having traveled to it from Samīrāʾ, and stayed there.

About the battle of al-Abraq, Ziyād b. Ḥanẓalah said:

How many a battle have we witnessed at al-Abraq
 [victorious] against Dhubyān ablaze in fury?
We brought them an onerous disaster
 with the Veracious One[332] when he stopped remonstrating.

According to al-Sarī—Shuʿayb—Sayf—ʿAbdallāh b. Saʿīd b. Thābit b. al-Jidhʿ and Ḥarām b. ʿUthmān—ʿAbd al-Raḥmān b. Kaʿb b. Mālik: When Usāmah b. Zayd arrived, Abū Bakr went out, leaving him in charge of Medina. He proceeded until he came to al-Rabadhah, [and] met Banū ʿAbs and Dhubyān
[1880] and a group of Banū ʿAbd Manāt b. Kinānah. Then he met them at al-Abraq, whereupon he fought them so that God put them to flight and routed them. Then he returned to Medina. Now, when the army of Usāmah collected and those around Medina returned to obedience,[333] (Abū Bakr) went out to Dhū al-Qaṣṣah and encamped with them, one stage from Medina in the direction of Najd. Then he divided the army there and tied the banners;[334] he tied eleven banners over eleven armies and ordered the commander of each army to convoke those armed Muslims who had passed by him, leaving some of the armed men to defend their country.

According to al-Sarī—Shuʿayb—Sayf—Sahl b. Yūsuf—al-Qāsim b. Muḥammad:[335] When Usāmah and his army had

330. Or perhaps "recipients of the *ṣadaqāh* taxes": *aṣḥāb al-ṣadaqāt*.

331. A well in the Najd, in Asad or Tayyiʾ country. Cf. *EI*², s.v. "Buzākha" (C. E. Bosworth).

332. *Al-Ṣiddīq*, the epithet of Abū Bakr.

333. Or "collected, gathered in numbers," *thāba*.

334. The phrase "to tie a banner [for someone]," used here and in the following sentences, is an idiom also meaning "to appoint [someone] the commander of an army."

335. Cf. Ibn al-Athīr, *Kāmil*, II, 345–46; Nuwayrī, 64–65; Caetani, 601–3.

rested their riding camels and had assembled, and more *ṣadaqah* taxes than they needed had come in, Abū Bakr deployed the expeditionary forces and tied the banners,[336] eleven banners [in all]. He tied a banner for Khālid b. al-Walīd,[337] ordering him [to fight] Tulayḥah b. Khuwaylid, and then when he finished to march against Mālik b. Nuwayrah[338] at al-Buṭāḥ,[339] if he resisted him. [He also tied a banner] for ʿIkrimah b. Abī Jahl,[340] ordering him [to fight] Musaylimah; and for al-Muhājir b. Abī Umayyah, ordering him [to fight] the armies of [al-Aswad] al-ʿAnsī and to help the Abnāʾ against Qays b. Makshūḥ and those people of Yemen who supported him against them. Then (al-Muhājir) was supposed to pass on to Kindah in Ḥaḍramawt. [He tied a banner] for Khālid b. Saʿīd b. al-ʿAṣ, who had come at that time from the Yemen and left his governorship, and sent him to al-Ḥamqatayn in the Syrian heights; and for ʿAmr b. al-ʿĀṣ[341] [to go] to the combined [tribes of] Quḍāʿah and [to] Wadīʿah (al-Kalbī)[342] and al-Ḥārith (al-Subayʿī).[343] And [he tied a banner also] for Ḥudhayfah b. Miḥṣan al-Ghalfānī[344] and [1881]

---

336. I.e., appointed the commanders of various forces.

337. Prominent military commander of the Makhzūm clan of Quraysh and a relatively late convert. Cf. *EI*², s.v. "Khālid b. al-Walīd" (P. Crone).

338. Chief of the Yarbūʿ branch of Tamīm, appointed by the Prophet as tax collector over part of Tamīm but said in some (but not all) accounts to have withheld tax after the Prophet's death. Cf. Ibn al-Athīr, *Usd*, IV, 295–96; Shoufani 82–83; *EI*², s.v. "Mālik b. Nuwayra" (E. Landau-Tasseron).

339. A well in the Najd, in Asad country ca. 400 km east-northeast of Medina. Cf. Yāqūt, s.v.; Thilo, s.v. and map C; *TAVO* B, VII, 1.

340. Fierce opponent of the Prophet from Makhzūm of Quraysh; he fled after conquest of Mecca by the Prophet to avoid execution; later he was pardoned by the Prophet and given important posts. Cf. Ibn al-Athīr, *Usd*, IV, 4–7.

341. Late convert from the Sahm clan of Quraysh, sent by the Prophet to be tax agent in ʿUmān. Cf. *EI*², s.v. "ʿAmr b. al-ʿĀṣ" (A. J. Wensinck); Ibn al-Athīr, *Usd*, IV, 115–18.

342. Cf. p. 43, above. Ibn al-Athīr, *Kāmil*, II, 346 omits this name.

343. Cf. p. 45, above. Ibn al-Athīr, *Kāmil*, II, 346 omits this name.

344. According to Ṭabarī, he was of Ḥimyar; he later served as ʿUmar's governor of ʿUmān and al-Yamāma and participated in the conquest of Iraq (p. 152, below; Ṭabarī I, 2207, 2212). However, Ibn al-Kalbī considers him the same as ʿUyaynah b. Ḥiṣn al-Fazārī (see note 403, below); cf. Caskel, II, 328 ("Ḥudhayfah b. Ḥiṣn") and 580 ("ʿUyayna b. Ḥiṣn"). Tabarī considers them two separate individuals, but the possibility of some confusion should be noted. Ḥudhayfah's *nisbah* "al-Ghalfānī" is otherwise unknown, and is sometimes given in another form (e.g., "al-Qalʿānī"; Ibn al-Athīr, *Usd*, I, 390); moreover, the

ordered him to Dabā;[345] and for ʿArfajah b. Harthamah[346] and ordered him to Mahrah,[347] and commanded the two of them to join, each one of them having in his own province priority over his companion. He sent Shuraḥbīl b. Ḥasanah[348] on the heels of ʿIkrimah b. Abī Jahl, saying that when he was finished with al-Yamāmah[349] he should betake himself to Quḍāʿah and fight the apostates with his cavalry. And [he tied a banner] for Ṭurayfah b. Ḥājiz[350] and commanded him to [attack] Banū Sulaym and those who backed them of Hawāzin; and [he tied a banner] for Suwayd b. Muqarrin and ordered him to the coastal district of Yemen, and for al-ʿAlāʾ b. al-Ḥaḍramī[351] and ordered him to Baḥrayn. So the commanders set out from Dhū al-Qaṣṣah and encamped on their course [of march], whereupon each commander's army overtook him, he having charged them with his instructions.[352] (Abū Bakr) [also] wrote to all the apostates to whom [a force] had been sent.

---

word al-Ghalfānī/al-Qalʿānī could have resulted from misreading the word al-Ghaṭafānī—an appropriate *nisbah* for someone (like ʿUyaynah) from Fazārah, as Fazārah was a section of Ghaṭafān.

345. Market town and former capital of ʿUmān. Cf. Yāqūt, s.v.; Muqaddasī (BGA 3), 53.

346. A chief of the Bāriq clan of Khuzāʿah. Cf. Ibn al-Athīr, *Usd*, III, 401; Caskel, II, 192.

347. A tribe of southern Arabia between Ḥaḍramawt and ʿUmān. Cf. Yāqūt, s.v.; Caskel, II, 382.

348. An ally of the Zuhrah or Jumaḥ clan of Quraysh, of uncertain tribal origin; he was an early convert to Islam. Cf. Ibn al-Athīr, *Usd*, II, 391.

349. An oasis district in central eastern Arabia, about 750 km east of Medina, just west of the Dahnāʾ sands; its main oases were Ḥajr (not to be confused with Hajar) and Jaww. Cf. *TAVO* B, VII, 1, and Thilo, s.v., and Map D, warning against misunderstandings in Yāqūt and other medieval geographers.

350. Ibn al-Athīr, *Kāmil*, II, 346, has "Maʿn b. Ḥājiz." Ṭurayfah is said to have been a companion of the Prophet by Ibn al-Athīr, *Usd*, II, 51–52 ("Ṭurayfah b. Ḥajir"), but little information on him survives. Nuwayrī, 65, has "Maʿn b. Ḥājiz—but some say Ṭurayfah b. Ḥājiz. . . ."

351. Al-ʿAlāʾ, of the South Arabian tribe of al-Ṣadif, had been the Prophet's governor over Baḥrayn; cf. Ibn al-Athīr, *Usd*, IV, 7–8.

352. The text leaves ambiguous whether this phrase refers to the commanders instructing the troops or to Abū Bakr's instructing the commanders.

[*Abū Bakr's Letter to the Apostates*][353]

According to al-Sarī—Sayf—ʿAbdallāh b. Saʿīd—ʿAbd al-Raḥmān b. Kaʿb b. Mālik: Qaḥdham[354] participated with him in commissioning [the armies] and in writing [the letter to the apostates], so that the letters to the apostate tribes of the Arabs were identical:

> In the name of God, the Compassionate, the Merciful. From Abū Bakr, caliph of the Apostle of God, to whomever this letter of mine may reach among the commoners and notables who has stood fast in his Islām or who has turned back from it: Peace upon those who follow the [true] guidance and who have not turned back to error and blindness after [having received] the [true] guidance. Verily I praise to you God, other than Whom there is no god. I bear witness that there is no god but God alone, Who has no associate, and that Muḥammad is His Servant and His Apostle; we affirm that which he brought, and that which he denied we declare to be unbelief and strive against it. Now then: Verily God, may He be exalted, sent Muḥammad with His truth to His creation [1882]
> as a bearer of good tidings and as a warner[355] and as one calling [others] to God, with His permission, and as a light-bringing lamp,[356] so that he might warn [all] who live, and so that the saying against the unbelievers might be fulfilled.[357] So God guided with the truth[358] whoever responded to Him, and the Apostle of God, with His permission, struck whoever turned his back to Him until he came to Islām, willingly or grudgingly. Then God took His Apostle to Him, he having carried out God's com-

353. This material is omitted by Ibn al-Athīr, *Kāmil*; cf. Balansī, 27–29; Nuwayrī, 65–69.

354. He is identified in the index to the Cairo edition as the scribe of Yūsuf b. ʿUmar, but, as the latter was a governor of the late Umayyad period, he cannot be meant here; cf. Ṭabarī, I, 2388, and II, 1739.

355. Cf. Qur'ān 2:119.

356. Qur'ān 33:46.

357. Qur'ān 36:70.

358. Nuwayrī, 66: "to the truth."

mand, and counseled His community, and carried out [the duty] that was upon him; for God had made that clear to him and to the people of Islam in the book that was sent down. Thus He said,[359] "You are dead, and they are dead"; and he said,[360] "We have not made any man before you immortal; so, if you die, should they then be immortal?" And to the believers He said,[361] "Muḥammad is only an apostle. The apostles before him have passed away; so, if he dies or is killed, will you turn on your heels? For he who may turn on his heels will not harm God one whit, but God will reward the grateful." So whoever worshiped Muḥammad, indeed Muḥammad has died; but whoever worshiped God alone, Who has no associate, indeed God is always with you,[362] Living, Eternal. He does not die,[363] nor do slumber or sleep take Him; He guards His cause, takes vengeance on His enemy, and punishes him.

I recommend to you the fear of God and your right share and portion of God[364] and of that which your Prophet brought you; and that you let yourselves be guided by His guidance, and cleave to the religion[365] of God. For indeed, whomever God has not guided is astray,[366] and whomever He has not made safe is afflicted, and whomever God has not helped is forsaken. Whomever God guides is on the right way, and whom-
[1883] ever He allows to go astray is lost. God said,[367] "Whomever God guides is on the right way, but whomever He lets get lost, you will find no friend to guide him";

359. Qur'ān 39:30.
360. Qur'ān 21:34.
361. Qur'ān 3:144.
362. Lit., "God lies in wait for you," meaning that He is everywhere and cannot be evaded—a reference to Qur'ān 89:14.
363. Cf. Qur'ān 2:255.
364. Balansī, 28: ". . . and I urge you to your right share. . . ."
365. Or, possibly, "obedience": *dīn*.
366. Balansī, 28: "lost," with greater divergence through the remainder of the paragraph.
367. Qur'ān 18:17.

nor will any work of his in the world be accepted until he acknowledges Him; and neither repentance nor ransom[368] will be accepted from him in the afterlife.

I have learned that some of you have turned back from your religion after you had acknowledged Islam and labored in it, out of negligence of God and ignorance of His command, and in compliance with the devil. God said,[369] "When We said to the angels, 'Bow down before Adam,' they bowed down except for Iblīs. He was one of the *jinn*; so he strayed from the command of his Lord. Do you then wish to take him and his offspring as friends to the exclusion of Me, even though they are your enemy? How bad an exchange [that is] for the transgressors!" And He said,[370] "The devil is an enemy to you, so take him for an enemy. He only calls his party that they may be among the people of the flame." I have sent to you someone[371] at the head of an army of the *Muhājirūn* and the *Anṣār* and those who follow [them] in good works. I ordered him not to fight anyone or to kill anyone until he has called him to the cause of God; so that[372] those who respond to him and acknowledge [Him] and renounce [unbelief] and do good works, [my envoy] shall accept him and help him to [do right], but I have ordered him to fight those who deny [Him] for that reason. So he will not spare any one of them he can gain mastery over, [but may] burn them with fire, slaughter them by any means, and take women and children captive; nor shall he accept from anyone anything except Islam. So whoever follows him, it is better for him; but whoever leaves him, will not weaken God.[373] I have

368. *Ṣarf wa'adl*. For different possible meanings of this phrase, see Lane, *Arabic-English Lexicon*, 1682, col. 1 top.

369. Qur'ān 18:50.

370. Qur'ān 35:6.

371. Balansī, 28: "Khālid b. al-Walīd."

372. The text in Balansī, 28–29, differs considerably for the remainder of this sentence, although the general import is the same.

373. Or perhaps "God will not be incapable [of dealing with him]."

[1884] ordered my messenger to read my letter to you in all gathering places.[374] The invitation [to God's cause] shall be the call to prayer. If, when the Muslims make the call to prayer, they do likewise [in response], leave them alone; but, if they do not make the call to prayer [with the Muslims], then grant them no respite. And, if they do make the call to prayer [with the Muslims], ask them what has come over them; then, if they deny [God], grant them no respite, but, if they acknowledge [God], He will accept them and bring them to what they should do.

So the messengers put the letters through before the armies, and the commanders went out, taking with them the treaties:[375]

> In the name of God, the Compassionate, the Merciful. This is a treaty from Abū Bakr, caliph of the Apostle of God, to so-and-so, sent [by Abū Bakr] when he dispatched [people] to fight whoever had repudiated Islam. He requires him to fear God to the utmost of his ability in all his affairs, whether they be secret or public; and he orders him to take God's command seriously, and to strive against those who turn away from Him and turn back from Islām to the desires of the devil,[376] [only] after he has explained to them [why they are to be attacked][377] and called them to the cause of Islam. Then, if they respond, he should restrain himself from them; but if they do not respond, he should launch his attack against them until they acknowledge Him. Then he

374. Or perhaps ". . . to read my letter in all gathering places of yours." Here it is not clear whether the text refers to the gathering places of the tribes being contacted or to those of the messengers; in the latter instance the party addressed would have shifted from the tribes to the messengers. This shift has already been completed in the next sentence. The parallel version in Balansī, 29, ends with this sentence.

375. Cf. Nuwayrī, 68–69; Ibn Ḥubaysh, 16 l. 18ff., a loose parallel written from Abū Bakr to Khālid b. al-Walīd.

376. Ibn Ḥubaysh: "to error and *jāhiliyya* and the desires (*amānī*) of the devil. . . ." The editor of Nuwayrī suggests "his refuge" or "place of refuge." The rest of the sentence is missing in Ibn Ḥubaysh and in Nuwayrī.

377. *Baʿda an yughdira ilayhim*, lit., "after he has apologized to them."

should inform them of [the duties] that are incumbent upon them and [the advantages] that accrue to them, and should take what is [imposed] on them and give them what they are due. He should not give [those that do not respond] a respite; nor should the Muslims turn back from fighting their enemy. Whoever does respond to God's command and acknowledges Him, he will accept that from him and help him [to accomplish] it in kindness. He should only fight whoever denies God [so as to make him] acknowledge that which has come from [1885] God. So if [someone] has responded to the call, [the Muslim] has no cause to get at him; God shall be his reckoner thereafter in whatever he seeks to conceal.[378] Whoever does not respond to the cause of God shall be killed and fought wherever he may be and wherever he may have come to, as an enemy.[379] [God] shall not accept from [such a] one anything that he may give, except Islam; but whoever responds to Him and acknowledges [Him], He shall accept [it] from him and instruct him. (The Muslim) should fight whoever denies [God]; so, if God lets him prevail over (the unbeliever), he should make slaughter among them by any means, with weapons and fire; then he should divide that which God bestowed as spoil upon him, except for the fifth part, which he should convey to us. And [he should take care] to prevent his companions from rash acts[380] and evil [deeds], and not to introduce into them auxiliary troops[381] until he can get to know them and learn what[382] they are, [making sure that] they should not be

---

378. Ibn Ḥubaysh, 16: "in his actions."

379. Nuwayrī and Cairo read *ḥaythu balagha murāghima-hu* for the text's *ḥaythu balagha murāghamatan*. Cf. Ibn Ḥubaysh, 16, last line: "wherever he learned of their call [to Islam]," *ḥaythu balagha bi-duʿāʾi-him*.

380. Lit., "haste," "precipitancy" (*al-ʿajalah*).

381. Text has *ḥashw*; Ibn Ḥubaysh, 17, has "a kind of people" (*jins min al-nās*). But cf. Ibn Ḥubaysh, 43, 4 lines from end, where in another context he speaks of *ḥashw kathīr min al-ʿarab*, "many Arab (i.e., nomad?) auxiliaries."

382. Ibn Ḥubaysh, 17: "who."

spies,[383] and that the Muslims may not be undermined because of them. And [he should] treat the Muslims justly and deal gently with them in marching and encamping, and should seek them out. And none of (the Muslims) should try to outdo another [in reaching a place]. [The commander] should follow [my] counsel regarding good companionship and gentle speech, as far as the Muslims are concerned.

The Remainder of the Account about Ghaṭafān at the Time of Their Joining with Ṭulayḥah and Other Things Relating to the Affair of Ṭulayḥah

According to ʿUbaydallāh b. Saʿd—his uncle—Sayf; and accord-
[1886] ing to al-Sarī—Shuʿayb—Sayf—Sahl b. Yūsuf—al-Qāsim b. Muḥammad and Badr b. al-Khalīl and Hishām b. ʿUrwah:[384] After ʿAbs and Dhubyān and those attached to them took refuge at al-Buzākhah, Tulayḥah sent to Jadīlah and al-Ghawth [proposing that they] unite with him; so people from the two clans hurried to him, having ordered their tribe to join them, and came before Ṭulayḥah. Meanwhile Abū Bakr sent ʿAdī [b. Ḥātim of Ṭayyiʾ] to his tribe, before sending Khālid out from Dhū al-Qaṣṣah, saying, "Overtake them [so that] they will not be destroyed." So he went out to them and cajoled them.[385] Khālid went out on (ʿAdī's) heels, and Abū Bakr ordered him to begin with Ṭayyiʾ on the flanks [of the mountains],[386] then to head for al-Buzākhah, and then in third place for al-Buṭāḥ, and not to leave [a place] when he finished with a group until he had spoken to (Abū Bakr) and he had ordered him to do so. Abū Bakr let it be known[387]

383. *ʿUyūn*. Manuscript C has "aid" (*ʿawn*); Kos has "a wealthy person" [*ghanī*].

384. Balansī, 31; Ibn al-Athīr, *Kāmil*, II, 346–47; Nuwayrī, 70; Diyārbakrī, II, 205–6 (to p. 62, below); Caetani, 608.

385. Lit., "he twirled [the hair] of the upper parts of the camel's back" (*fatala-hum fī al-dhirwah wa al-ghārib*); on the idiom, see Ibn Manẓūr, XIV, 284, left col., s.v. *al-dhirwah*.

386. *ʿAlā al-ʾaknāf*, that is, on the sides of the "mountains of Ṭayyiʾ" (see note 388, below). Al-Aknāf may be a place name, but more probably it was simply a descriptive term; cf. Yāqūt, s.v.

387. I.e., as a ruse. Cf. p. 63, below.

that he was going out to Khaybar and from it would be going down to gather with him so that he would meet him on the flanks of Salmā.[388] So[389] Khālid went out, skirting al-Buzākhah, and inclined toward Aja', letting it be known that he would be going out to Khaybar[390] and then gathering with them. That made the Ṭayyi' hold back and be slow [in joining] Ṭulayḥah; meanwhile, 'Adī reached them and invited them [to Islam]. At this they said, "We will never render the oath of allegiance to Abū al-Faṣīl." So he said: "There has come to you a group who would violate your womenfolk. Indeed, you will [have to] nickname him 'the Greatest Stud.'[391] So it is your business." At this they said to him, "Then meet the army [of Khālid] and protect us from it so that we can extricate those of us who went to al-Buzākhah [to join Ṭulayḥah]; for, if we break with Ṭulayḥah while they are in his hands, he will kill them or take them hostage."

So[392] 'Adī met Khālid while he was in al-Sunḥ,[393] saying "Oh [1887]
Khālid, hold back from me[394] for three days; there should gather to you five hundred warriors with whom you may strike your enemy. That is better than that you should hasten them to the Fire and be distracted by them." So (Khālid) did that, whereupon 'Adī returned to (the tribe of Ṭayyi'). They had sent their tribes-

---

388. *Bi-al-'aknāf, 'aknāf Salmā.* Salmā and Aja' (next line) were the "two mountains of Ṭayyi'" (modern Jabal Shammar) in the Najd, about 400 km northeast of Medina. Cf. *EI*², s.vv. "Adja' and Salmā" (W. Caskel); Thilo, s.v.v. and maps A and B. Cf. Balansī, 21.

389. Cf. Nuwayrī, 71 (—Ibn al-Kalbī).

390. An important oasis town in the northern Ḥijāz. Cf. *EI*², s.v. "Khaybar" (L. Veccia Vaglieri).

391. The account turns around a play on words. Abū Bakr literally means "father of the lively young he-camel"; a *bakr* is young and strong, perhaps several years old, and the word is commonly used as a name. The Ṭayyi' refer to him pejoratively as "Abū al-Faṣīl"; Faṣīl, never used as a name, means "newly weaned camel," presumably implying inexperience, weakness, and helplessness. The *faḥl* or stallion (here translated "stud") is a byword for strength and vigor; hence the use of the word to designate the most highly esteemed poets as "*fuḥūl al-shu'arā',*" etc. Cf. p. 53.

392. Ibn Ḥubaysh, 18, citing Wāqidī, has an interesting variant version of this section. Cf. Nuwayrī, 71.

393. Yāqūt knows this as a place in the Najd, but his localization is clearly derived from this account. Cf. Wellhausen, *Skizzen*, VI, 148; *Emendanda*.

394. I.e., from his tribe, Ṭayyi'. Kos has "from us."

men[395] to (those of them who had joined Ṭulayḥah), so that they reached them as reinforcements from Buzākhah. But for that, they would not have been left alone.[396] Then ʿAdī returned to Khālid with [news of] their Islām,[397] and Khālid set out toward al-Ansur,[398] intending [to confront] Jadīlah. At this ʿAdī said to him, "Ṭayyi' is like a bird, and Jadīlah is one of the wings of Ṭayyi'. So give me a few days' time; perhaps God will recover Jadīlah just as he recovered al-Ghawth." So (Khālid) did so. ʿAdī went to them and kept after them until they rendered the oath of allegiance to him, whereupon he brought (Khālid) [news of] their Islam. A thousand of their mounted warriors joined the Muslims. So (ʿAdī) was the best person born in the country of Ṭayyi' and the greatest of [the tribe], with regard to the blessing he brought upon them.

As for Hishām b. Muḥammad al-Kalbī,[399] he alleged that, when Usāmah and those of the army who had been with him returned, Abū Bakr became earnest about fighting the apostates and went out with the men. He [remained] with them until he encamped at Dhū al-Qaṣṣah, one stage from Medina toward the Najd. There he put his armies in battle order, and then sent Khālid b. al-Walīd [to be] over the men. He put Thābit b. Qays[400] over the Anṣār, ordered him to [join] Khālid,[401] and ordered (Khālid) to head for Ṭalḥah[402] and ʿUyaynah b. Ḥiṣn[403] while the two of them were at Buzākhah, one of the wells of Banū

395. Lit., "their brothers" [*ikhwāna-hum*].

396. I.e., Ṭulayḥah would not have let them go.

397. Perhaps here and several lines farther on we should translate "their submission."

398. According to Yāqūt, a well of Ṭayyi' this side of the sands (i.e., west of the sands of Nafūd and Shaqīq).

399. Cf. Baladhuri, *Futūḥ*, 95–96; Nuwayrī, 71–72; Caetani, 608–9.

400. Thābit b. Qays b. Shammās, orator of the Anṣār and of the Prophet; cf. Ibn al-Athīr, *Usd*, I, 229–30.

401. I.e., to join Khālid's army as a subordinate commander.

402. I.e., Ṭulayḥah, here given in its regular form, rather than in the usual pejorative diminutive.

403. A chief of Fazārah; he opposed the Prophet at the Battle of the Ditch (Khandaq), later embraced Islam, then joined Ṭulayḥa in apostasy. According to Ibn al-Kalbī, ʿUyaynah was a by-name of Ḥudhayfah b. Miḥṣan al-Ghalfānī (see note 344, above); Caskel, II, 580. Ṭabarī and Ibn al-Athīr, *Usd*, I, 390, IV, 166–67, clearly consider them different people.

Asad. (Abū Bakr)[404] let it be known that he would go with those who were with him to meet (Khālid), [coming] from the direction of Khaybar; that was a ruse, as he had sent all the army with Khālid, but he wished to let the enemy know that in order to frighten them; then he returned to Medina. Khālid[405] b. al-Walīd marched until, when he came near the enemy, he sent out as scouts ʿUkkāshah b. Miḥṣan[406] and Thābit b. Aqram, one of the Banū al-ʿAjlān and an ally of the Anṣār.[407] When the two of them got near the enemy, Ṭulayḥah and his brother Salamah came out to take a look.[408] As for Salamah, it was not long before he killed Thābit. Ṭulayḥah called to his brother when he saw that he had finished off his opponent, [saying], "Help me with [my] man, for he is getting the better [of me].[409] So they teamed up against (ʿUkkāshah) until they killed him; then they went back. Khālid advanced with the men until they passed the slain Thābit b. Aqram, unaware of him until the riding camels stepped on him with their feet. That distressed the Muslims greatly; then they looked, and lo, there prostrate before them was ʿUkkāshah b. Miḥṣan. So the Muslims were overcome with grief at that, and said, "Two of the leaders of the Muslims and two of their horsemen have been killed." So Khālid turned toward Ṭayyi'. [1888]

According to Hishām—Abū Mikhnaf—Saʿd b. Mujāhid—al-

404. The narrative shifts to direct speech (of Abū Bakr) for the first part of this sentence, but it has been converted to indirect speech in the translation to make it fit more smoothly with the rest of the account.

405. Here begins a parallel with Ibn al-Athīr, *Kāmil*, II, 347; cf. Baladhurī, *Futūḥ*, 96; Diyarbakrī, II, 207 (< Ibn Isḥāq); Balansī, 38–39; Ibn Ḥubaysh, 21 bottom (< Ibn Isḥāq); Ibn Ḥubaysh, 21–22 (Wāqidī).

406. An Asadite, ally of ʿAbd Shams (Umayyah clan of Quraysh) before Islam, an early settler in Medina, and one of the most prominent early companions of the Prophet, who promised him entry into paradise. Cf. Ibn al-Athīr, *Usd*, IV, 1–2.

407. Banū ʿAjlān was a branch of the Ḥijāz section of the Balī tribe. Thābit was an early convert in Medina; cf. Ibn al-Athīr, *Usd*, I, 220; Caskel, II, 546.

408. Lit. "to see and to ask." At this point Nuwayrī, 72, inserts the following passage: "The two of them [Khālid and Salamah] met them both [ʿUkkāshah and Thābit], whereupon Salamah challenged Thābit to single combat, and ʿUkkāshah challenged Ṭulayḥah."

409. *'Ākil*, "devouring." See *Glossary*, s.v. Balansī, 39; Diyārbakrī, II, 207; and Ibn Ḥubaysh, 21–22 have "for he is killing me."

Muḥill b. Khalīfah—ʿAdī b. Ḥātim: I sent to Khālid b. al-Walīd, [saying]: "March to me and remain with me a few days, so that I might send to the tribes of Ṭayyi' and gather for you from them more [men] than you have with you. Then I will accompany you to your enemy." So he marched to me.

According to Hishām—Abū Mikhnaf—ʿAbd al-Salām b. Suwayd—one of the Anṣār: When Khālid saw how grief-stricken his companions were over the killing of Thābit and ʿUkkāshah, he said to them, "Would you like me to repair with you to one of the tribes of the Arabs, whose numbers are great, whose [1889] might[410] is strong, and among whom no one has apostatized from Islam?" To which the men replied, "And what tribe do you mean, what an excellent tribe it is, by God?" He said, "Ṭayyi'." At this they said, "May God give you success, what a good idea you have had!" So he went with them and stayed with the army among Ṭayyi'.

According to Hishām—Judayl b. Khabbāb[411] al-Nabhānī of Banū ʿAmr b. Ubayy: Khālid advanced until he encamped at Uruk,[412] the city of Salmā.

According to Hishām—Abū Mikhnaf—Isḥāq: He encamped at Aja', whereupon he put [the army] in order for war; then he marched until the two [forces] met at Buzākhah, while Banū ʿĀmir,[413] under their chiefs and leaders, were nearby listening and waiting expectantly [to see] who would be defeated.[414]

According to Hishām—Abū Mikhnaf—Saʿd b. Mujāhid—elders of his tribe:[415] We asked Khālid that we [be allowed to] protect

---

410. Or perhaps "weapons" or "valor": *shawkah*.

411. Kos has Judayl b. Jāb (?). Nabhān was a branch of the Ghawth clan of Ṭayyi', but no lineage of ʿAmr b. Ubayy is listed in it; cf. Caskel, I, table 257, II, 439.

412. Yāqūt, s.v. "Uruk," confirms that Uruk is the city of Salmā (perhaps deriving his information from this account) and claims that it was in Ghaṭafān country.

413. Banū ʿĀmir b. Ṣaʿṣaʿah, a large tribal group of central Arabia that included such tribes as Kilāb, Kaʿb, ʿĀmir b. Rabīʿah, Hilāl, and Numayr, among others. Cf. *EI*², s.v. "ʿĀmir b. Ṣaʿṣaʿa" (W. Caskel).

414. Cf. Balansī, 6.

415. His tribe was Ṭayyi'. Cf. Ibn al-Athīr, *Kāmil*, II, 347; Caetani, 609.

him against Qays,[416] for Banū Asad were our allies, so he said, "By God, Qays is not the weaker of the two powers; direct yourself at whichever of the two tribes you wish." Then 'Adī said: "If [even] the closest of my family and the closest of my tribe left this religion,[417] I would fight them because of it; so should I abstain from fighting Banū Asad because of their [former] alliance [with my tribe]? No, by the Eternal God, I will not!" At this, Khālid said to him: "Fighting against either of the two parties is [still] holy war (*jihād*). Do not oppose the opinion of your companions; [rather], proceed to one of the two parties and conduct (your companions) to the enemy they are most enthusiastic to fight." [1890]

Hishām—Abū Mikhnaf—'Abd al-Salām b. Suwayd: The horsemen of Ṭayyi' used to meet the horsemen of Banū Asad and Fazārah before the arrival of Khālid among them, and they would exchange words without fighting. Asad and Fazārah would say, "No, by God, we will never render the oath of allegiance to Abū al-Faṣīl," whereupon the horsemen of Ṭayyi' would say to them, "I bear witness that [Abū Bakr] will fight you until you [will be willing to] call him "father of the greatest stud."[418]

Ibn Ḥumayd—Salamah—Muḥammad b. Isḥāq—Muḥammad b. Ṭalḥah b. Yazīd b. Rukānah—'Ubaydallāh b. 'Abdallāh b. 'Utbah:[419] When the men fought, 'Uyaynah fought energetically on the side of Ṭulayḥah at the head of seven hundred of Banū Fazārah. Ṭulayḥah was wrapped up in a cloak of his in the courtyard of one of his hair tents, pretending to prophesy for

---

416. Qays 'Aylān (or Qays b. 'Aylān) was a broad genealogical grouping that included the tribes of Ghaṭafān, Sulaym, Hawāzin, 'Āmir b. Ṣa'ṣa'ah, and others. Cf. Caskel, II, 462, s.v. "Qays b. al-Nās"; *EI*², s.v. "Ḳays 'Aylān" (W. M. Watt). Presumably in the present context it is meant as a reference to Fazārah, as suggested by Landau-Tasseron, "The Participation of Ṭayyi' in the Ridda," 63. In this account the Ṭayyi' ask Khālid not to line them up against Asad, their former allies, when the battle is closed, but rather against Fazārah (E. Landau-Tasseron, personal communication).

417. Kos and Ibn al-Athīr, *Kāmil*, II, 347, have "If this came down on those who are the closest of my family . . . ."

418. Cf. p. 61 and note 391, above, for an explanation of the plays on words.

419. Cf. Ibn al-Athīr, *Kāmil*, II, 347–48; Baladhuri, *Futūh*, 96; Balansī, 35–36; Diyārbakrī, II, 207 top; Ibn Ḥubaysh, 20 middle; Ibn Ḥubaysh, 21; Nuwayrī, 72–73; Caetani, 614–15.

them while the men were fighting. After the warfare had shaken ʿUyaynah and the fighting had become severe, he returned to Ṭulayḥah and said to him, "Has Gabriel come to you yet?" He replied that he had not, so (ʿUyaynah) returned to fight until, when the fighting became severe and the warfare shook him [again], he returned to him and said: "You bastard![420] Has Gabriel come to you yet?" (Ṭulayḥah) replied, "No, by God." ʿUyaynah was uttering an oath:[421] "How long will it be, by God? It has worn us out!"[422] Then he returned to fight, until, when [the revelation] came, he returned to him and said, "Has Gabriel come to you yet?" (Ṭulayḥah) said that he had, so he asked, "So what did he say to you?" He replied, "He told me that I have a millstone[423] like his millstone, and a story[424]
[1891] that you shall not forget." ʿUyaynah said, "I think God knew that there would be a story you would not forget, Oh Banū Fazārah, in this way; so turn away, for by God this one is a liar."[425] So they turned away, and the men were routed. Whereupon they came to Ṭulayḥah, saying, "What do you order us [to do]?" Now he had made his horse ready near him, and prepared a camel for his wife al-Nawār, so when they came to him and asked him what he ordered them to do, he stood up, jumped on his horse, and carried his wife to save her. [Then] he said, "Whoever of you can do as I have done and save his family, let him do so." Then he traveled by al-Jūshiyyah[426] until he

---

420. Lit., "May you have no father!"

421. *Yaqūlu . . . ḥilfan.* E. Landau-Tasseron suggests that the text should perhaps be emended to *yaqūlu . . . jalafan,* "he said rudely." (personal communication).

422. *Qad balagha minnā.*

423. *Raḥā.* The word has many significations—mill, molar tooth, high rugged ground, breast, tribe, chief, or any of several other meanings; see Ibn Manẓūr, XIV, 314.

424. Baladhuri, *Futūh,* 96: "a day"; Balansi, 36: "an effect"; Diyarbakri, II, 207 and Ibn Ḥubaysh, 21: "a matter."

425. Diyarbakri, II, 297, and Ibn Ḥubaysh, 21, have: "'. . . a matter you will not forget, Oh Fazārah, in this way'—and he pointed to them [standing] under the sun. 'This one, by God, is a liar . . .'." Ibn Ḥubaysh, 20, has "By God, I think we will have a story we won't forget."

426. Reading with Nuwayrī, 73; text has "al-Ḥawshiyyah." Al-Jūshiyyah was, according to Yāqūt (s.v. "Jūsiyyah," second half of article), a town between Najd and Syria.

reached Syria. His gathering scattered, and God killed some of them. Banū ʿĀmir had been near them with their leaders and chiefs, and those tribes of Sulaym and Hawāzin were [also] in that state, but when God inflicted upon Ṭulayḥah and Fazārah that which befell them, those [tribes] came, saying, "We enter into that which we had left, and we believe in God and His Apostle, and we accept His sovereignty over our property and ourselves."

Abū Jaʿfar said, the reason for the apostasy of ʿUyaynah and Ghaṭafān and those who apostatized of Ṭayyi' was [as follows]:

According to ʿUbaydallāh b. Saʿd—his uncle—Sayf, and according to al-Sarī—Shuʿayb—Sayf—Ṭalḥah b. al-Aʿlam—Ḥabīb b. Rabīʿah al-Asadī—ʿUmārah b. Fulān al-Asadī:[427] Ṭulayḥah [1892] had apostatized in the lifetime of the Apostle of God, and had asserted a claim to prophecy, so the Prophet sent Ḍirār b. al-Azwar[428] to his tax agents[429] over the Banū Asad [to find out] about that, and ordered them to stand firm in that [matter] against all who apostatized. So they perturbed Ṭulayḥah and made him afraid. The Muslims encamped at Wāridāt,[430] while the unbelievers encamped at Samīrā', and the Muslims continued growing [in numbers] and the unbelievers decreasing until al-Ḍirār determined to march on Ṭulayḥah, so that he took everyone[431] who remained peaceably, except for a blow that he struck [at Ṭulayḥah] with the cutting sword. But [the sword] shrank from him,[432] at which [news of this] spread among the army. Then, while they were in that state, the Muslims received the news of the death of their Prophet. People in the army said

427. Diyarbakri, II, 260; Nuwayrī, 69–70; Caetani, 606–607.

428. A warrior and poet of Asad; the Prophet appointed him tax agent over the Banū al-Ṣaydā' of Asad and Banū al-Dīl. Cf. Ibn al-Athīr, *Usd*, III, 39–40.

429. *ʿUmmāl*; sometimes the word seems to mean "governor" in a more general sense.

430. A place northeast of Samīrā'; cf. Yāqūt, s.v. and Thilo, s.v.

431. Reading with Kos and Cairo edition. The sentences that follow are confused; Nuwayrī, 70, evidently in an attempt to smooth them out, has the following: "... so that he took everyone by surrender. Then he agreed to deliver a blow with a sword, so he shrank from him. [News of] that blow spread among the army, but they said, 'The weapons will not affect Ṭulayḥah.' So while the army was in that state, the news of the Prophet's death reached them. ..."

432. I.e., the sword miraculously did not harm Ṭulayḥah.

about that blow, "Weapons will not affect Ṭulayḥah." So from that day forth the Muslims knew decreasing [of numbers], and people scattered to Ṭulayḥah and his situation was in the ascendant.[433] Dhū al-Khimārayn ʿAwf al-Jadhamī[434] approached so that he encamped opposite us. Thumāmah b. Aws b. Lām al-Ṭāʾī[435] sent to him, "With me are 500 of Jadīlah, so, if something should happen to you unexpectedly, we are at al-Qurdūdah[436] and al-Ansur just this side of the sands. And Muhalhil b. Zayd sent to him, "With me are the army (*ḥadd*) of al-Ghawth, so if
[1893] something should happen to you unexpectedly, we are on the flanks [of the mountains] facing Fayd.[437] Ṭayyiʾ showed nothing but benevolence toward Dhū al-Khimārayn ʿAwf because there had been an alliance in the *jāhiliyyah* among Asad and Ghaṭafān and Ṭayyiʾ; then, some time before the sending of the Prophet, Ghaṭafān and Asad gathered against Ṭayyiʾ and forced them to leave the territory they had had in the *jāhiliyyah*, [both] Jadīlah and Ghawth. ʿAwf disliked that, so he broke with Ghaṭafān. The two tribes followed one another in emigration. ʿAwf sent to these two tribes of Ṭayyiʾ, renewing their alliance, and undertook to help them, so that they [were able to] return to their territories. That distressed Ghaṭafān; but, when the Apostle of God died, ʿUyaynah b. Ḥiṣn stood up among Ghaṭafān saying, "I no longer recognize the boundaries of Ghaṭafān since the termination of what was between us and Banū Asad, so I will renew the alliance that was between us of old and follow Ṭulayḥah. By God,[438] it is preferable for us to follow a prophet from our two allies than to follow a prophet from Quraysh. [In any

---

433. Diyarbakri, II, 160, and Nuwayrī, 70, gloss this passage, but the idea there also is clearly that the death of the Prophet strengthened Ṭulayḥah and weakened the Muslims.

434. Jadhīmah was a clan of Asad. Little information is available on Dhū al-Khimārayn, "the one with two veils"; cf. Wellhausen, *Skizzen* VI, 148; Landau-Tasseron, "The Participation of Ṭayyiʾ," 58–59; Landau-Tasseron, "Asad," 21.

435. Lām b. ʿAmr was a branch of the Jadīlah clan of Ṭayyiʾ; cf. Caskel, II, 376.

436. Yāqūt, s.v. "al-Qurdūdah" offers a variation of this sentence but provides no further information on its location.

437. Or "at Al-Aknāf facing Fayd." Fayd is a well-known oasis on the Mecca-Kūfa road, just east of Mt. Salmā. Cf. Yāqūt, s.v.; Thilo, s.v. and Map B.

438. Ibn al-Athīr, *Kāmil*, II, 342.

case] Muḥammad has died, whereas Ṭulayḥah remains." Then they agreed with his opinion, so he did [as he had proposed], and so did they. So when Ghaṭafān gathered to assist Ṭulayḥah, Ḍirār and Quḍāʿī and Sinān[439] and whoever [else] had undertaken some of the Prophet's work among Banū Asad fled to Abū Bakr. Those who had been with them were scattered, so they gave Abū Bakr the news and told him to exercise caution.[440] Then Ḍirār b. al-Azwar said, "I have seen no one, other than the Apostle of God,[441] who is more likely[442] to carry out widespread war than Abū Bakr; for [when] we began to tell him [of it], it was as if we had informed him of something to his advantage, [1894]
not [something] detrimental to him."

The delegations of Banū Asad and Ghaṭafān and Hawāzin and Ṭayyi'[443] came to him, and the delegations of Quḍāʿah encountered Usāmah b. Zayd, whereupon he led them to Abū Bakr; so they gathered in Medina, staying with the chiefs of the Muslims on the tenth [day] after the death of the Apostle of God. Then they proposed to do the ritual prayer, provided that they be exempted from the *zakāt*. A council of those who were lodging them agreed to accept that, so that they might attain what they desired. Every one of the chiefs of the Muslims lodged someone of them, except al-ʿAbbās. Then they came to Abū Bakr to inform him of their tidings and of what their council had agreed on. But Abū Bakr did not [agree],[444] for he refused [to accept] anything except what the Apostle of God had accepted. They refused [these terms], so he sent them back, giving them respite of a day and a night [to leave], whereupon they dispersed to their tribes.

---

439. Quḍāʿī b. ʿAmr was the Prophet's tax agent over the Banū al-Ḥārith of Asad, cf. Ṭabarī I, 1798; Ibn al-Athīr, *Usd*, IV, 305. Sinān b. Abī Sinān b. Miḥsan al-Asadī was an ally of ʿAbd Shams (Umayyah—Quraysh) and an early convert to Islam; he was the Prophet's tax agent over the Banū Mālik of Asad; cf. Ibn al-Athīr, *Usd*, II, 358. On Quḍāʿī and Sinān, cf. Landau-Tasseron, "Asad," 19.

440. Or "vigilant." Kos and Manuscript B omit the phrase.

441. Kos omits this phrase.

442. *Amlaʾa* "fuller," hence "more suitable, more capable, more inclined to," as suggested by *Glossary*.

443. Cf. pp. 44–45, and notes.

444. *Illā mā kāna min Abī Bakr.*

According to al-Sarī—Shuʿayb—Sayf—al-Ḥajjāj—ʿAmr b. Shu-
ʿayb:[445] The Apostle of God had sent ʿAmr b. al-ʿĀṣ to Jayfar[446]
upon his return from the farewell pilgrimage.[447] Then the Apostle
of God died, while ʿAmr was in ʿUmān; so he came until, when
he reached al-Baḥrayn, he found al-Mundhir b. Sāwī[448] on the
point of death. Whereupon al-Mundhir said to him, "Advise me
with regard to my wealth in a matter that will be to my benefit
and not to my detriment." He replied, "Give your real property
as an almsgiving (ṣadaqah)[449] that will continue after you." So
he did that. Then (ʿAmr) left him and marched among the Banū
Tamīm;[450] then he went from them to the territory of Banū
ʿĀmir and stayed with Qurrah b. Hubayrah,[451] while Qurrah
[1895] was playing for time,[452] and all the Banū ʿĀmir likewise, except
for a few.[453] Then (ʿAmr) marched until he came to Medina; at
this Quraysh gathered about him and asked him [for informa-
tion]. So he informed them that armies were gathered together
from Dabā to where he had reached them. At this they dispersed
and formed circles.[454] ʿUmar b. al-Khaṭṭāb came to greet ʿAmr,
and passed by a circle while they were [talking] about what they

---

445. Cf. Ibn al-Athīr, Kāmil, II, 352–53; Balansi, 43; Dıyarbakri, II, 208;
Caetani, 584.

446. Jayfar b. al-Julandā of the Azd tribe and his brother ʿAbd were corulers in
ʿUmān who embraced Islam upon receiving a letter from the Prophet; cf. Caskel,
II, 104, 256 (s.v. "ʿAbd b. al-Julandā"); Ibn al-Athīr, Usd, I, 313, Shoufani, 36–37.
Their father, al-Julandā b. al-Mustakir, had founded the dynasty at Ṣuḥār; cf.
Caskel, II, 264; J. C. Wilkinson, "The Julandā."

447. The Prophet's final pilgrimage to Mecca, A H 10. Cf. note 104, above.

448. A chief of the Dārım clan of Tamīm, he was the Prophet's tax agent over
al-Baḥrayn; cf. Ibn al-Athīr, Usd, IV, 417; Caskel, II, 430.

449. Reading the verb as taṣaddaq instead of the text's ṣaddiq. The term
ṣadaqah is here used in the later sense as alms, rather than as a tax imposed on
nomads; cf. note 242, above.

450. Tamīm b. Murr was a powerful tribe of central and northeastern Arabia;
they had close ties to Mecca on the eve of Islam. Cf. Watt, Medına, 137–40;
Caskel, II, 544; M. J. Kıster, "Mecca and Tamīm," JESHO 8 (1965), 113–63.

451. Chieftain of Banū Qushayr, a part of ʿĀmir b. Ṣaʿṣaʿah; he embraced Islam
late in the Prophet's life, and was sent by him as tax agent over his tribe. Cf.
Caskel, II, 473; Ibn Ḥajar, Iṣābah, s.v.

452. Lit., "putting a foot forward and holding a foot back."

453. Al-khawāṣṣ. Kos, manuscript C, and Ibn al-Athīr, Kāmil, omit the clause
of exception.

454. I.e., circles formed to discuss the news.

had heard from ʿAmr. In that circle were ʿUthmān [b. ʿAffān], ʿAlī [b. Abī Ṭālib], Ṭalḥah [b. ʿUbaydallāh], al-Zubayr [b. al-ʿAwwām], ʿAbd al-Raḥmān [b. ʿAwf], and Saʿd [b. Abī Waqqāṣ].[455] When ʿUmar drew near them, they fell silent; so he said, "What are you [talking] about?" But they did not answer him, so he said, "How well I know what you are meeting secretly about!" At this Ṭalḥah grew angry and said, "By God, oh Ibn al-Khaṭṭāb, then tell us about the unseen!" He replied, "No one knows the unseen except God; but I think you were saying how much you fear for Quraysh because of the Arabs, and how likely (the Arabs) are not to affirm this cause." [When] they said that he was right, he continued, "Do not fear this situation. By God, I am more afraid of what you might do to the Arabs than I am of what the Arabs might do to you! If you were to go into a hole in the ground, oh company of Quraysh, the Arabs would enter it after you. So be God-fearing in regard to them." He passed on to ʿAmr and greeted him, and then returned to Abū Bakr.

According to al-Sarī—Shuʿayb—Sayf—Hishām b. ʿUrwah—his father:[456] Upon his return from ʿUmān after the death of the Apostle of God, ʿAmr b. al-ʿĀṣ stayed with Qurrah b. Hubayrah b. Salamah b. Qushayr. Around him was an army of obscure groups (*afnāʾ*) of Banū ʿĀmir. (Qurrah) slaughtered for him[457] and honored his dwelling, and then, when (ʿAmr) wished [to resume] traveling, Qurrah met with him privately and said to him, "Hey you, the Arabs will not be pleased with you by the [demand for] tribute (*al-itāwah*). If you spare them the taking of their wealth, [1896] they will listen to you and obey, but if you deny [that] I do not think they would gather to you." At this ʿAmr replied, "Have you become an unbeliever, Oh Qurrah?" Now around (Qurrah) were the Banū ʿĀmir, and (Qurrah) hated to make the fact that they were following [him] known, lest they should deny following him, with the result that he would end up in a

455. All leading early converts to Islam, and later the six members of the council that selected ʿUthmān to be the third caliph.

456. Cf. Balansī, 44–45; Ibn al-Athīr, *Kāmil*, II, 352–53.

457. I.e., slaughtered animals for a feast.

disastrous [situation]. So he said, "We shall send you back to your old ways (he had been a Muslim). Let's set a date between us and you [to do battle]." Whereupon 'Amr said, "Do you threaten us[458] with the Arabs and [try to] frighten us with them? Your alliance is [no better than] your mother's knick-knacks![459] By God, I shall make the cavalry trample you!"[460] And he came to Abū Bakr and the Muslims and gave them the news.

According to Ibn Ḥumayd—Salamah—Ibn Isḥāq: When Khālid was done with the matter of Banū 'Āmir and their taking the oath of allegiance accepting [the conditions] that he imposed on them,[461] he bound 'Uyaynah b. Ḥiṣn and Qurrah b. Hubayrah to send them to Abū Bakr. When they came before him,[462] Qurrah said to him, "Oh Caliph of the Apostle of God, I had been a Muslim, and I have a witness to that—to my Islam—in 'Amr b. al-'Āṣ, [for] he passed by me, whereupon I honored him and showed favor to him and protected him." So Abū Bakr summoned 'Amr b. al-'Āṣ, saying, "What do you know about the affairs of this [man]?" Thereupon ('Amr) told him the story until he got to what (Qurrah) had said to him regarding the *ṣadaqah* tax,[463] [at which] Qurrah said to him, "Let that be enough for you, may God have mercy on you!" [But] ('Amr) said, "By God, not until I have informed him of everything that you said." So he related [it] to him, but Abū Bakr pardoned (Qurrah) and spared his life.

[1897] According to Ibn Ḥumayd—Salamah—Muḥammad b. Isḥāq—Muḥammad b. Ṭalḥah b. Yazīd b. Rukānah—'Ubaydallāh b. 'Abdallāh b. 'Utbah:[464] Those who saw 'Uyaynah b. Ḥiṣn with

---

458. Reading *a-tū'idunā* with Cairo ed. and manuscript B for *a-tuwā'idunā* in the text.

459. Text: *ḥifsh*; Cairo: *ḥafsh*, meaning "your mother's lowly hut," or "incense box" or "box for spindles," etc., in any case, intended as a denigration of Qurrah's promise.

460. Reading with the Cairo edition.

461. Cf. pp. 66–67, above, on 'Āmir's oath of allegiance; Caetani, 621–22.

462. Cf. Ibn al-Athīr, *Kāmil*, II, 353; Baladhuri, *Futūh*, 97; Balansı, 47–48; Ibn Ḥubaysh, 26–27.

463. Ibn al-Athīr, *Kāmil*: *zakāt*.

464. Cf. Ibn al-Athīr, *Kāmil*, II, 348; Balansı, 47; Diyarbakrı, II, 208; Ibn Ḥubaysh, 25; Ibn al-Athīr, *Usd*, IV, 167; Nuwayrī, 74; Caetani, 622.

his hands bound to his neck with a rope informed me that the boys of Medina used to prick him with palm branches, saying, "Oh enemy of God, have you become an unbeliever after [acknowledging] your faith?" Whereupon he would say, "By God, I never believed in God." But Abū Bakr pardoned him and spared his life.

According to al-Sarī—Shuʿayb—Sayf—Sahl b. Yūsuf:[465] The Muslims took a man of Banū Asad, so he was brought to Khālid at al-Ghamr.[466] He was knowledgeable about the affairs of Ṭulayḥah, so Khālid said to him, "Tell us about him and about what he says to you." Whereupon he alleged that among the things he brought [as revelation] was: "By the doves and the wild pigeons, by the famished sparrow hawk, they fasted[467] before you by years, may our kingship reach Iraq and Syria."[468]

According to al-Sarī—Shuʿayb—Sayf—Abū Yaʿqūb Saʿīd b. ʿUbaydah:[469] When the people of al-Ghamr took refuge at al-Buzākhah, Ṭulayḥah stood up among them. Then he said, "I order you to make a millstone with handles,[470] with which God can grind up[471] those whom He will, and upon which He may throw down those whom He will." Then he put his armies in battle order. After that he said,[472] "Send two horsemen on two dark horses of Banū Naṣr b. Quʿayn,[473] bringing you a spy." So they sent out two horsemen of Banū Quʿayn, whereupon he and [his brother] Salamah went out as two lookouts.

According to al-Sarī—Shuʿayb—Sayf—ʿAbdallāh b. Saʿīd b. [1898]
Thābit b. al-Jidhʿ—ʿAbd al-Raḥmān b. Kaʿb[474]—those of the

465. Cf. Ibn al-Athīr, *Kāmil*, II, 348–49; Nuwayrī, 70; Caetani, 605.

466. A well of Asad, evidently just south of Mt. Ajaʾ; cf. Yāqūt, s.v.; Thilo, s.v. and Map B.

467. Text and Nuwayrī, 70: "stood surety" (?); we read with Cairo edition.

468. This passage, like the one at the end of the next paragraph, is couched in rhymed prose reminiscent of the Qurʾān; unlike the Qurʾān, however, the doggerel attributed to Ṭulayḥah has a ludicrous or comic effect.

469. Cf. Balansi, 33, from third sentence onwards; Caetani, 605–6.

470. *Raḥan dhātu ʿuran.*

471. Lit., "strike, smite": *aṣāba*.

472. Cf. Ibn Ḥubaysh, 19, l. 16f.

473. A clan of Asad, closely related to Ṭulayḥah's clan. Cf. Caskel, II, 446 and Table 50; Landau-Tasseron, "Asad," 2.

474. Cf. Ibn al-Athīr, *Kāmil*, II, 349 top; Caetani, 617–18.

Anṣār who witnessed Buzākhah: At Buzākhah Khālid did not capture a single family; the families of Banū Asad were guarded. (According to Abū Ya'qūb: [the families of Asad were] between Mithqab and Falj,[475] and the families of Qays were between Falj and Wāsiṭ.[476]) So no sooner were they defeated than they all recognized Islām out of fear for [their] off-spring, and protected themselves from Khālid by honoring his demands,[477] and claimed [assurances of] safety. Ṭulayḥah[478] went on until he descended among Kalb at al-Naq';[479] then he embraced Islām and remained staying among Kalb until Abū Bakr died. He embraced Islām there when he had learned that Asad and Ghaṭafān and 'Āmir had embraced Islām. Then he went out toward Mecca to make the *'umrah*[480] during the reign of Abū Bakr, and passed by Medina. At this Abū Bakr was told that this was Ṭulayḥah; but he said, "What should I do to him? Leave him alone; for God has guided him to Islam." Ṭulayḥah continued toward Mecca and performed his *'umrah*. Then he came to 'Umar to render the oath of allegiance when he assumed the caliphate. So 'Umar said to him, "You are the murderer of 'Ukkāshah and Thābit; by God, I do not like you at all." To which he replied, "Oh Commander of the Faithful, why are you troubled by two men whom God ennobled by my hand,[481] when He did not disgrace me through their hands?" So 'Umar accepted the oath of allegiance from him; then he said to him, "You imposter, what is left of your soothsaying?" He replied, "A puff or two in the bellows." Then he returned to the territory of his tribe and remained in it until he left for Iraq.

---

475. Yāqūt is vague on Mithqab, there being several places with the name. Falj (or Baṭn Falj) is a wide valley in northeast Arabia, stretching toward Baṣrah in Iraq; cf. Yāqūt, s.v., Thilo, s.v. and Map B.

476. Wāsiṭ is, again, difficult to localize, since many places bore this name.

477. *Ittaqaw Khālidan bi-ṭalabatihi*. Cf. Wellhausen, *Skizzen*, VI, 148.

478. Cf. Ibn al-Athīr, *Kāmil*, II, 348; Baladhuri, *Futūḥ*, 96; Nuwayrī, 74–75.

479. Kalb b. Wabarah was a strong tribe of the Quḍā'ah confederation in northern Arabia and the Syrian steppe. Cf. Caskel, II, 368; *EI*², s.v. "Kalb b. Wabara" (J. W. Fück). No information on the location of al-Naq' is listed in the standard geographical sources.

480. The "lesser pilgrimage" to Mecca.

481. I.e., by making them martyrs.

The Apostasy of Hawāzin, Sulaym, and ʿĀmir [1899]

According to al-Sarī—Shuʿayb—Sayf—Sahl and ʿAbdallāh:[482] As for Banū ʿĀmir, they played for time while they looked to see what Asad and Ghaṭafān would do. So when they were surrounded while Banū ʿĀmir was under their leaders and chiefs, Qurrah b. Hubayrah was among Kaʿb[483] and their allies, and ʿAlqamah b. ʿUlāthah among Kilāb[484] and their allies. Now ʿAlqamah had embraced Islam and then apostatized in the time of the Prophet; then he went out after the [Prophet's] conquest of al-Ṭā'if until he reached Syria. So when the Prophet died, (ʿAlqamah) came back hurriedly so that he encamped among the Banū Kaʿb, playing for time. Abū Bakr learned of that, so he sent a raiding party to him, putting al-Qaʿqāʿ b. ʿAmr[485] in command of it. He said, "Oh Qaʿqāʿ, march until you raid ʿAlqamah b. ʿUlāthah. Perhaps you will take him [captive] for me or kill him; [but] know that the [only] remedy for a tear is to stitch it up, so do what you must." So he went out at the head of this raiding party until he raided the spring where ʿAlqamah was. (ʿAlqamah) was still holding back, so he made an effort to outdistance them on his horse and escaped them.[486] His family[487] and his children embraced Islām, so (al-Qaʿqāʿ) carried off his wife and his daughters and his [other] womenfolk and those men who stood fast, who protected themselves from him through submission (*islām*). Then he brought them before Abū Bakr, whereupon ʿAlqamah's children and his wife denied that they had assisted him while they were staying in [his] household. That was all (Abū Bakr) learned;[488] and

---

482. Cf. Ibn al-Athīr, *Kāmil*, II, 349; Caetani, 603–4, 619–20.
483. Kaʿb b. Rabīʿah was the subsection of ʿĀmir b. Ṣaʿṣaʿah to which Qurrah's tribe, Qushayr, belonged.
484. Kilāb b. Rabīʿah was a tribe of the ʿĀmir b. Ṣaʿṣaʿah group residing in west central Arabia, east of Medina. ʿUlāthah was a chief of Kilāb, whom the Prophet made a special effort to win over following the conquest of Mecca in AH 8.
485. A poet and warrior of the ʿAmr clan of Tamīm, he later occupies a prominent role in Sayf's accounts of the Islamic conquests. Cf. Ella Landau-Tasseron, "Sayf Ibn ʿUmar in Medieval and Modern Scholarship," 16.
486. Cf. Wellhausen, *Skizzen*, VI, 148.
487. Cf. Balansi, 48; Ibn Ḥubaysh, 27 top.
488. I.e., he learned no incriminating information about them.

[1900] they said, "What is our fault in what ʿAlqamah did in this [situation]?" So (Abū Bakr) set them free. Afterward (ʿAlqamah) submitted,[489] so (Abū Bakr) accepted that from him.

According to al-Sarī—Shuʿayb—Sayf—Abū ʿAmr and Abū Ḍamrah—Ibn Sīrīn: A similar account.[490] After the defeat of the people of Buzākhah, Banū ʿĀmir came, saying, "Let us enter that which we had left," so he[491] made an agreement with them on [the same terms] that the people of Buzākhah from Asad and Ghaṭafān and Ṭayyiʾ had agreed to before them. They gave him their hands[492] to Islam. The only thing he would accept from anyone of Asad or Ghaṭafān or Hawāzin[493] or Sulaym or Ṭayyiʾ was that they bring him those who during their apostasy had burned the people of Islām and mutilated them[494] and waged aggression against them; so they brought them to him, whereupon he accepted that from them [as atonement] except for Qurrah b. Hubayrah[495] and some people with him whom he fettered. He mutilated those who had waged aggression against Islām by burning them with fire, smashing them with rocks, throwing them down from mountains, casting them headlong into wells, and piercing them with arrows; and he sent Qurrah and the [other] prisoners[496] and wrote to Abū Bakr, "Banū ʿĀmir has come forward after being reluctant, and entered Islām after awaiting [the outcome of things]. I have accepted nothing from anyone, whether he fought me or made peace with me, until he brought me whoever waged aggression against the Muslims; those I have killed by every means of slaughter. And I have sent you Qurrah and his companions."

According to al-Sarī—Shuʿayb—Sayf—Abū ʿAmr—Nāfiʿ: Abū Bakr wrote to Khālid, "May that which God has granted you by way of blessings increase for you! Fear God in your affairs, for

489. Or: embraced Islām.

490. Cf. Ibn al-Athīr, *Kāmil*, II, 350; Caetani, 620–21.

491. Ibn al-Athīr, *Kāmil*, says "Khālid."

492. This refers to the traditional hand clasp symbolizing the *bayʿah*, or oath of allegiance.

493. Ibn al-Athīr, *Kāmil*, has ʿĀmir.

494. Here and below, *maththala*, "to mutilate" or "to punish severely."

495. Cf. Wathīma, 7/46.

496. Ibn al-Athīr, *Kāmil*, adds: "and Zuhayr."

verily God is with those who are pious and who do good works. [1901] Take seriously the command of God and be not remiss; for you shall not be victorious over anyone who fought the Muslims unless you fight him and, by punishing him as an example, warn another. So kill whomever you like of those who showed enmity to God or who opposed Him, [if] you think there will be some benefit in doing so." Hence (Khālid) remained in al-Buzākhah for a month, going 'round about it[497] and returning to it in pursuit of those [evildoers]; so that some of them were burned and some cut to pieces and some smashed with rocks and some thrown from mountaintops. He brought Qurrah and his companions, but they did not encamp, nor was there said to them what had been said to ʿUyaynah and his companions,[498] because they were not in the same situation and had not done the things [the companions] had done.

According to al-Sarī—Shuʿayb—Sayf—Sahl and Abū Yaʿqūb:[499] The shattered remnants of Ghaṭafān[500] gathered at Ẓafar.[501] With them was Umm Ziml Salmā, daughter of Mālik b. Ḥudhayfah b. Badr; she resembled her mother Umm Qirfah, daughter of Rabīʿah b. Fulān b. Badr.[502] Now Umm Qirfah had been [married] to Mālik b. Ḥudhayfah and bore him Qirfah, Ḥakamah, Jurāshah,[503] Ziml, Ḥuṣayn, Sharīk, ʿAbd, Zufar, Muʿāwiyah, Ḥamalah, Qays, and Laʾy. As for Ḥakamah, the Apostle of God killed him on the day ʿUyaynah b. Ḥiṣn raided the livestock of Medina; Abū Qatādah [actually] killed him. So those shattered remnants rallied around Salmā; she was as renowned as her mother [had been], and she had Umm Qirfah's [1902] camel, so (Ghaṭafān) encamped with her. Then she stirred them

497. Lit., "ascending and descending from it."

498. Cf. p. 73, above.

499. Cf. Ibn al-Athīr, *Kāmil*, II, 350; Caetani, 623–24.

500. Ibn al-Athīr, *Kāmil*, has "Ghaṭafān and Ṭayyiʾ and Sulaym and Hawāzin and others." Cf. list on p. 78, below.

501. Yāqūt, s.v., places this near Ḥawʾab on the Baṣrah-Mecca road, but the localization is probably derived from this account; cf. p. 78 and note 505, below.

502. Her name was Fāṭimah bt. Rabīʿah b. Badr; a paternal cousin of Mālik b. Ḥudhayfah. Cf. Caskel, I, Table 130; II, 246 and 477; Ibn al-Athīr, *Kāmil*.

503. Caskel, I, Table 130, has "Khurāshah."

up and commanded them to make war, and marched about at the head of them summoning them to make war on Khālid, until they [all] gathered about her. They became encouraged on that account, and solitary remnants congregated to them from every side. ([Back] in the days of Umm Qirfah, (Salmā) had been taken captive and had fallen to 'Ā'ishah, who then set her free, so that [Salmā] used to be with her. Subsequently [Salmā] returned to her own tribe. Now one day[504] the Prophet called on them and said, "Verily, one of you [women] will make the dogs of Ḥaw'ab[505] bark." Salmā caused that to happen when she apostatized and demanded that vengeance.) Then she marched about between Ẓafar and al-Ḥaw'ab to gather [followers] to herself, whereupon every company of vanquished warriors and every oppressed person from those clans of Ghaṭafān and Hawāzin and Sulaym and Asad and Ṭayyi' rallied to her. So when Khālid learned of that, while he was engaged in exacting vengeance and taking *ṣadaqah* tax and calling people [to Islām] and calming them down, he marched to the woman. Her situation had grown grave and her case was serious, so he fell upon her and her followers; then they fought intensely while she was standing on her mother's camel with the same bravery as [her mother]. People began to say, "Whoever goads her camel shall have one hundred camels because of her fame." [Many] noble families of Khāsi'[506] and Hāribah[507] and Ghanm[508] perished on that day, (Abū Ja'far [al-Ṭabarī] said: Khāsi' is a clan of Ghanm.) and

504. That is, one day when she was still in 'Ā'ishah's household.

505. Ḥaw'ab was a well on the Baṣrah road in the territory of Banū Abū Bakr b. Kilāb, south of Ḥimā Ḍariyyah, 325 km east of Medina. Cf. Yāqūt, s.v. and Thilo, s.v.

506. Cairo has Jās; *Emendanda* proposes Jalas; Wellhausen, *Skizzen*, VI, 148 suggests Jāsī, a branch of Dhubyān, and says that Ṭabarī's note equating them with Ghanm is not right. Ibn al-Athīr, *Lubāb*, relates "al-Jāsī" to a branch of Fazārah—Lawdhān, but no one else knows of it. Perhaps we should read Jassās [b. 'Amr], the name of a family of Fazārah; cf. Caskel, II, 260 and Ibn Ḥazm, *Jamharat ansāb al-'Arab* (Cairo 1971), 256.

507. Hāribah b. Dhubyān was a declining branch of Dhubyān (Caskel, II, 279).

508. Possibly Ghanm b. 'Abdallāh of Ghaṭafān. The Cairo edition (index) identifies it as Ghanm of Banū Ḥadas, but according to Ibn al-Kalbī, Ḥadas was a clan of Lakhm from Transjordan, and seems to have included no subclan named Ghanm. (Caskel, II, 290).

among the people [many] were struck down of Kāhil.[509] Their fighting was intense until some horsemen gathered around [Salmā's] camel, wounding it and killing her. Around her camel were slain a hundred men. (Khālid) sent [news of] the victory, so that it arrived about twenty days after [the arrival of] Qurrah. [1903]

According to al-Sarī—Shuʿayb—Sayf—Sahl and Abū Yaʿqūb:[510] The story of al-Jiwā' and Nāʿir[511] was that al-Fujā'ah Iyās b. ʿAbd Yālīl[512] came to Abū Bakr saying, "Assist me with weapons and order me [to fight] whomever you wish of the apostates." So (Abū Bakr) gave him weapons and gave him his command. But he disobeyed his command with regard to the Muslims, going out until he camped at al-Jiwā', and he sent Najabah[513] b. Abū al-Maythā' from the Banū al-Sharīd[514] and ordered him against the Muslims. So he launched them in a raid against every Muslim amongst Sulaym, ʿĀmir and Hawāzin. Abū Bakr learned of that, so he sent to Ṭurayfah b. Ḥājiz[515] ordering him to gather [men] to himself and to march against (al-Fujā'ah); and he sent ʿAbdallāh b. Qays al-Jāsī[516] to him by way of reinforcement, so he [went]. Then the two of them rose up against (al-Fujā'ah) and pursued him, so he began to seek shelter from the two of them until they caught up with him at al-Jiwā', whereupon they fought. Najabah was killed and Fujā'ah fled, so Ṭurayfah followed him and took him captive, sending him to Abū Bakr. [When] he was brought to Abū Bakr he

---

509. Presumably Kāhil b. Asad; cf. Caskel, II, 368. However, *kāhil* may have a more general sense, meaning "those upon whom [people] relied."

510. Cf. Ibn al-Athīr, *Kāmil*, II, 350–51; Balādhurī, *Futūḥ*, 98; Caetani, 624–25; Balansi, 130ff. Balansī links al-Jiwā' to the story of Abū Shajarah; see pp. 81ff., below.

511. According to Yāqūt, al-Jiwā' was a well in the Ḥimā Ḍariyyah, ca. 325 km east of Medina. Yāqūt's localization of Nāʿir is derived from this account.

512. Balādhurī, *Futūḥ*, 98: "al-Fujā'ah, who was Bujayr b. Iyās b. ʿAbdallāh al-Sulamī." Caskel, II, 228–29 and 247: Bujayrah b. Iyās of Banū ʿĀmirah of Sulaym, noting that the manuscript of Ibn al-Kalbī has "Baḥīrah."

513. Ibn al-Athīr, *Kāmil*, II, 350: Nukhbah.

514. Sharīd b. Riyāḥ was a branch of Sulaym (Caskel, II, 527).

515. Of Sulaym; cf. Shoufani, 138. Ibn al-Athīr, *Usd*, III, 51 ("Ṭurayfah b. Ḥājir") adds nothing to Ṭabarī's account.

516. Ibn al-Athīr, *Kāmil*, II, 351: al-Jāshī. Manuscript B: no points. Manuscript C: Jāsī of Qays. Cf. note 506, above.

ordered a fire to be kindled with much firewood in the prayer yard (*muṣallā*) of Medina and threw him, with arms and legs bound, into it.

According to Abū Ja'far—Ibn Ḥumayd—Salamah—Muḥammad b. Isḥāq—'Abdallāh b. Abī Bakr, regarding the affair of al-Fujā'ah:[517] A man of Banū Sulaym came to Abū Bakr. He was Iyās b. 'Abdallāh b. 'Abd Yālīl b. 'Umayrah b. Khufāf, called al-
[1904] Fujā'ah. He said to Abū Bakr, "I am a Muslim, and I want to fight[518] those unbelievers who have apostatized; so give me a mount and help me." So Abū Bakr mounted him upon camels and gave him weapons, whereupon he went forth indiscriminately against the people, Muslim and apostate [alike], taking their property and striking whoever of them tried to resist. With him was a man of Banū al-Sharīd named Najabah b. Abī al-Maythā'. So when Abū Bakr received news of him, he wrote to Ṭurayfah b. Ḥājiz: "The enemy of God al-Fujā'ah came to me, alleging that he was a Muslin, and asked me to empower him over those who apostatized from Islām, so I mounted him and armed him. Then absolutely certain information reached me that the enemy of God has gone forth indiscriminately against the people, the Muslim and the apostate [alike], taking their property and killing whoever of them opposes him. So march against him with whatever Muslims are with you until you kill him or take him [captive] to bring to me." Ṭurayfah b. Ḥājiz duly marched against (al-Fujā'ah). Then when the people met they shot arrows back and forth, whereupon Najabah b. Abī al-Maythā' was killed by an arrow shot at him. So when al-Fujā'ah saw the earnestness of the Muslims, he said to Ṭurayfah, "By God, you are no more entitled to command than I am; you are a commander of Abū Bakr, and I [likewise] am his commander." At this Ṭurayfah said to him, "If you are telling the truth, then lay down your weapons and depart with me to Abū Bakr." So he went out with him. Then when the two of them approached Abū Bakr, he ordered Ṭurayfah b. Ḥājiz to take him out to this clearing[519] and burn him in it with fire. So Ṭurayfah took him

---

517. Balansī, 126–28; Caetani, 625.
518. *Jihād*, lit. "to strive against."
519. *Al-baqī'*; perhaps a reference to Baqī' al-Gharqad, the famous Muslim cemetery in Medina.

out to the prayer yard and kindled a fire for him and threw him into it.

Khufāf b. Nudbah (Khufāf b. ʿUmayr)[520] said, in reference to al-Fujā'ah and what he did:

Why did they take his weapons to fight him [1905]
even though those are sins in the eyes of God?
Their religion [*dīn*] is not my religion,[521] but I am not one causing error,[522]
until Shamām[523] marches to al-Ṭarāt.[524]

According to Ibn Ḥumayd—Salamah—Ibn Isḥāq—ʿAbdallāh b. Abī Bakr:[525] Some of Sulaym b. Manṣūr had rebelled and returned [to being] unbelievers, while others had stood fast in Islām with a commander of Abū Bakr's over them named Maʿn b. Ḥājiz, one of the Banū Ḥāritha.[526] So when Khālid b. al-Walīd marched against Ṭulayḥah and his companions, he wrote to Maʿn b. Ḥājiz to march with those of Banū Sulaym who had stood fast with him in Islām, [so that they might join] with Khālid. So (Maʿn) marched, leaving in charge of his duties[527] his brother Ṭurayfah b. Ḥājiz. Abū Shajarah b. ʿAbd al-ʿUzzā[528] had joined the apostates at the head of those of Sulaym who did so. He was the son of al-Khansā',[529] and said:[530]

---

520. A black poet and warrior of Banū Sharīd; he fought on the Prophet's side at Ḥunayn and did not defect from Islam. Nudbah was his mother's name, ʿUmayr his father's. Cf. Ibn al-Athīr, *Usd*, II, 118–19; Caskel, II, 348.

521. An allusion to Qur'ān 109:6.

522. Cairo: "I am not [one] of them." Cairo notes that the Aṣmaʿiyyat has "I am not an unbeliever."

523. A mountain of Bāhilah, ca. 200 km west of al-Yamāmah. Cf. Yāqūt, s.v.; Ibn Manẓūr, XII, 327; Thilo, s.v. and Map D.

524. A well-known mountain in Najd, according to Yāqūt, s.v. The sense of the verse is that the speaker would never cause error, not until one mountain moved to another.

525. Cf. Ibn al-Athīr, *Kāmil*, II, 351; Balādhurī, *Futūh*, 97–98; Balansī, 126; Caetani, 579.

526. A brother of Ṭurayfah b. Ḥajīz of Sulaym, and one of the Prophet's tax agents over part of his tribe. Cf. Shoufani, 138–39.

527. *ʿAmal*, i.e., collection of tax.

528. Cf. Wathīmah, 10/49–50; Caskel, II, 168, s.v. "ʿAmr b. ʿAbdalʿuzzā" poet of Sulaym.

529. A famous poetess of Sulaym and early convert to Islam, proper name Tumāḍir bt. ʿAmr; cf. Caskel, II, 546.

530. Cf. Ibn Ḥajar, *Iṣābah*, IV, 101 (no. 609), s.v. "Abū Shajarah al-Sulamī."

So if she asked about us on the morning of Murāmir[531]
As I would have asked about her if I had been distant from her,
The encounter of Banū Fihr[532]—their encounter[533]
on the morning of al-Jiwā' was a necessity, so I fulfilled it.
I restrained for them my soul, and steered my filly
into the melée until the dark bay in her reddened.
When she shied away from some courageous armed man I wanted,
I turned her chest toward him and guided her on.

When he apostatized from Islām, Abū Shajarah said:[534]

[1906] The heart has given up youthful folly and amorousness by ridding itself of its love for Mayyah and has held back,
and agreed with those who found fault with her; then it [was able] to see [the truth].
The yearning to be close [to her] of [that] boyish foolishness has become,
like her love of us, estranged.
And the yearning for joining with them,
just like her ties with us, has been severed.
Oh, you who brag about the numerousness of his tribe,
[what good is that] when it is your fate [as part?] of them to be humiliated and conquered?
Ask the people about us on every day of calamity
whenever we met [in battle], clad in mail or unprotected.
Did we not give the disobedient horse his bit,
and make stabs in the battle when death has spread [its] desolation?

531. Cf. *Emendanda* and Wellhausen, *Skizzen*, VI, 148. Balādhurī, *Futūh*, 97 has Khālid meeting Sulaym at "Jaww Qurāqir" or al-Nuqrah, but De Goeje notes that the text should probably read "Jaww Murāmir." On this basis Wellhausen suggested that Murāmir/Jaww Murāmir should probably be identified with al-Jiwā' (see following lines). For this line, Ibn Ḥajar has "If Salmā asked on the morning about a man."

532. Banū Fihr b. Mālik, that is, Quraysh. Cf. Caskel, II, 246.

533. Ibn Ḥajar has "The melée (*ṭi'ān*) among the Lu'ayy b. Ghālib." Lu'ayy is another way of referring to most of Quraysh, specifically the "Quraysh al-Biṭāḥ" or "inner Quraysh" of the city of Mecca; cf. Caskel, II, 246, and Watt, *Mecca*, 5ff.

534. Cf. Ibn al-Athīr, *Kāmil*, II, 351.

When opposing him [was] a great and well-armed troop that
shakes its lance,
you see the black mixed with white, and the coats of mail,
[glinting] in their ranks.
So I quenched the thirst of my lance from Khālid's squadron,
and I hope after it that I may live long.

Then Abū Shajarah embraced Islam, and entered into that which the people had entered. He came to Medina in the time of ʿUmar b. al-Khaṭṭāb.

According to Ibn Ḥumayd—Salamah—Muḥammad b. Isḥāq—ʿAbd al-Raḥmān b. Anas al-Sulamī—men of his tribe, and according to al-Sarī—Shuʿayb—Sayf—Sahl and Abū Yaʿqūb and Muḥammad b. Marzūq, and according to Hishām—Abū Mikhnaf—ʿAbd al-Raḥmān b. Qays al-Sulamī:[535] (Abū Shajarah) made his camel kneel in the high ground of the Banū Qurayẓah. Then he came to ʿUmar while he was giving the destitute some *ṣadaqah* tax and dividing it among the poor of the Arabs, so he said, "Oh commander of the believers, give [some to] me, for I [1907]
am needy." (ʿUmar) said, "And who are you?" [When] he said that he was Abū Shajarah b. ʿAbd al-ʿUzzā al-Sulamī, (ʿUmar) replied, "Abū Shajarah! Oh enemy of God, are you not the one who said: 'So I quenched the thirst of my lance from Khālid's squadron, and I hope after it that I may live long'?" Then he began to strike (Abū Shajarah) on the head with the whip, until he outran him, returned to his she-camel, and rode off on her. Then he made her go at an easy pace[536] in the Ḥarrat Shawrān[537] on his way back to the territory of Banū Sulaym, and said:

Abū Ḥafṣ[538] was stingy to us with his favor,
though everyone who shakes a tree some day gets leaves.[539]

---

535. Cf. Ibn al-Athīr, *Kāmil*, II, 351–52; Balādhurī, *Futūḥ*, 98; Balansı, 131–32; Caetani, 579–80.

536. *Asnada-hā*, cf. Ibn Manẓūr, III, 221, left col.

537. According to Yāqūt, s.v. "Shawrān," a valley in Sulaym country 3 miles from Medina; also a mountain on the left when leaving Medina for Mecca. Cf. Lecker, *Banū Sulaym*, 5f.

538. I.e., ʿUmar b. al-Khaṭṭāb.

539. *Waraq*, "leaves," also means "silver" or "silver coins."

He continued to oppress me until I abased myself to him
and fear kept [me] from some covetousness.[540]
When I dreaded[541] Abū Ḥafṣ and his police[542]—
for an old man sometimes is consumed with fear[543] and loses his judgment—
Then I turned to her while she was charging ahead,[544]
[running] like the flushed-out prey for which no leaf [of cover] grows.[545]
[1908] I steered her forward to the path of Shawrān;
indeed, I scolded her [to go faster] as she went.
Flint of the mountains of Abānī[546] flies from her soles,[547]
as silver is selected out[548] by the money changer.
When confronted by an open desert, she contends with it
rashly; if you ask her to be quick, her soles[549] hardly touch the ground.
Her hindquarters are impatient with her forequarters [when running];
she is fleet of foot, thrusting her neck [forward].

Banū Tamīm and the Affair of Sajāḥ bt. al-Ḥārith b. Suwayd

According to al-Sarī—Shuʿayb—Sayf—al-Ṣaʿb b. ʿAṭiyyah b. Bilāl—his father and Sahm b. Minjāb:[550] The situation among Banū

540. Balansī, 132, has "and wearisome distance kept [me] from some goal" (*wa ḥāla min dūna baʿḍ al-bughyati al-shuqaqu*).

541. Balansī, 133, has "met."

542. *Shurṭah.*

543. Balansī, 133, has "sometimes strikes."

544. *Jāniḥah*; i.e., he turned to his she-camel to escape. Cf. Ibn Manẓūr, II, 429.

545. Numerous divergent readings of this half-line exist, none of which is entirely satisfactory, as noted by the editor.

546. Two mountains in Fazārah country northeast of Medina. Cf. Yāqūt, s.v. "Abān" and "Abānān."

547. Balansī, 133: "She flies, vehemently driving (? *mardā*) her paces from her soles."

548. Balansī, 133: "scrutinized." Balansī ends with this verse.

549. Cf. Ibn Manẓūr, X, 75, s.v. "khuruq."

550. Cf. Nuwayrī, 75–77 (as far as p. 90, below); Ibn al-Athīr, *Kāmil*, III, 353–55, who adds Sahm b. Minjāb to the list of tax collectors (as far as p. 94,

Tamīm was that the Apostle of God died, having sent among them his tax collectors (*ʿummāl*), such that al-Zibriqān b. Badr was [placed] over al-Ribāb[551] and ʿAwf and the Abnāʾ,[552] and Qays b. ʿĀṣim[553] was over Muqāʿis[554] and the Buṭūn clans, and [1909] Ṣafwān b. Ṣafwān and Sabrah b. ʿAmr[555] were over Banū ʿAmr, the former over Bahdā and the latter over Khaḍḍam,[556] two tribes of Banū Tamīm; and Wakīʿ b. Mālik[557] and Mālik b. Nuwayrah over Banū Ḥanẓalah,[558] the former over Banū Mālik and the latter over Banū Yarbūʿ. When the news of the death of the Prophet came to Ṣafwān, he struck out for Abū Bakr with the *ṣadaqah* taxes of Banū ʿAmr, of which he was in charge, and with that of which Sabrah had charge. Sabrah remained among his tribe in case some misfortune should overcome the tribe.[559] Qays had remained silent [waiting] to see what al-Zibriqān might do, while al-Zibriqān was reproving him; and scarcely did

---

with much poetry and most difficult spots omitted); Caetani, 628–35, 646–47; cf. also pp. 139–40, below.

551. A group of tribes, most of them closely allied to Tamīm, including Banū Ḍabbah b. ʾUdd and ʿAdī, Taym, ʿUkl, and Thawr b. ʿAbd Manāt b. ʾUdd; cf. Caskel, II, 8 and 486.

552. ʿAwf b. Kaʿb was the section of Saʿd b. Zaydmanāt b. Tamīm to which Zibriqān belonged. The Abnāʾ ("sons") was the collective term for eight other lineages of Saʿd b. Zaydmanāt b. Tamīm, not including Kaʿb and ʿAmr, who together were known as "al-Buṭūn" (Caskel, I, Tables 75 and 77, and II, 230).

553. Renowned as a man of tact and good judgment; of Muqāʿis/Tamīm, he came in the Tamīm delegation to the Prophet, who praised him as "lord of the nomads" (Ibn al-Athīr, *Usd*, IV, 219).

554. Muqāʿis was probably a lineage of Saʿd/Tamīm, although Sayf presents it as an alliance of Tamīm clans; cf. Caskel, II, 431.

555. He had been in the Tamīm delegation to the Prophet, according to Ibn Isḥāq (Ibn al-Athīr, *Usd*, II, 259–60).

556. ʿAmr b. Tamīm was one of the main nomadic sections of the tribe; Cf. Caskel, II, 8 and 184–85. Ibn al-Kalbī knows neither Bahdā nor Khaḍḍam; the former may be Bahdalah b. ʿAwf, a lineage of the Saʿd/Tamīm (Caskel, II, 220). ʿUmar Riḍā Kaḥḥālah, *Muʿjam qabāʾil al-ʿarab* (Beirut, 1968) I, 247, identifies a Khaḍḍam b. al-ʿAfīr b. Tamīm.

557. Ibn Ḥajar, *Iṣābah*, s.v., citing Sayf b. ʿUmar and Ṭabarī, says he was of the Dārim clan of Tamīm.

558. Ḥanẓalah b. Mālik was a group of Tamīm clans including Mālik and Yarbūʿ (Caskel, II, 298).

559. Reading *li-ḥadathin ʾin nāba al-qawma*, along with Cairo, instead of Leiden's *li-ḥadathi arbābin*, which generated problematic "solutions" from both Wellhausen (*Skizzen*, VI, 148) and De Goeje (*Emendanda*). Cairo's reading seems to derive from Nuwayrī, 75 bottom.

(Qays) flatter him before al-Zibriqān impugned him for his good fortune and high standing.[560] Qays said while he was waiting to see what he would do to oppose him when he was stalling on him, "Woe to us from the son of the "Uklī woman![561] By God, he has slandered me so that I do not know what to do. If I had followed Abū Bakr and brought the *ṣadaqah* tax to him, (al-Zibriqān) would have slaughtered (the camels)[562] [I had collected as tax] among the Banū Sa'd and blackened my name[563] among them; [on the other hand,] if I had slaughtered them among the Banū Sa'd, (al-Zibriqān) would have come to Abū Bakr and blackened my name with him." So Qays determined to divide it among the Muqā'is and the Buṭūn, and did so; while al-Zibriqān determined on full payment, so he followed Ṣafwān with the
[1910] *ṣadaqah* taxes of al-Ribāb and 'Awf and al-Abnā' until he brought them to Medina, saying in reference to Qays:

I paid in full the several camels[564] [due to] the Apostle, when the
collectors [of *ṣadaqah* tax] had refused,
and not a camel had been paid [to him] by its trustee.[565]

The clans dispersed, and evil flared up [among them] and they kept each other busy, one occupying another; then Qays repented after that, so when al-'Alā' b. al-Ḥaḍramī drew near him he sent out its *ṣadaqah* tax[566] and received (al-'Alā') with it. Then (Qays) went out with him, and said about that:

Indeed! Send Quraysh news of me by letter,
since evidence of the deposits [of tax] has come to them.

---

560. Reading *ḥaẓwah*, "high standing," along with Cairo, instead of *khaṭwah* in the text.

561. Presumably al-Zibriqān's mother was of the tribe of 'Ukl, a part of the confederation of al-Ribāb. The antecedents of the many pronouns in this sentence are uncertain; presumably Qays was waiting to see what al-Zibriqān would do.

562. The *ṣadaqah* tax or tribute was paid in camels or other livestock.

563. Reading *yusawwidu-nī*, with text and Wellhausen, *Skizzen*, VI, 148, rather than *Emendanda*'s *yasūdu-nī*, "conquered/overcame me."

564. *Adhwād*. The singular (*dhawd*) is defined variously as a number of camels between two and nine, or between three and thirty, etc.

565. Cf. p. 140, below for a more complete version of this poem.

566. I.e., presumably the *ṣadaqah* camels Qays had once collected among the Muqā'is and Buṭūn clans of Tamīm, but had redivided among them.

In this circumstance ʿAwf and the Abnāʾ were kept busy by the Buṭūn, and al-Ribāb by Muqāʿis; and Khaḍḍam were occupied by Mālik, and Bahdā by Yarbūʿ. Sabrah b. ʿAmr was in charge of Khaḍḍam; that was what he had been appointed over as successor for Ṣafwān.[567] Al-Ḥuṣayn b. Niyār[568] was in charge of Bahdā and al-Ribāb.[569] ʿAbdallāh b. Ṣafwān[570] was in charge of Ḍabbah, and ʿIṣmah b. Ubayr[571] was in charge of ʿAbd Manāt. In charge of ʿAwf and the Abnāʾ was ʿAwf b. al-Bilād b. Khālid of Banū Ghanm al-Jushamī,[572] and over the Buṭūn was Siʿr b. Khufāf. Reinforcements from Banū Tamīm used to come to Thumāmah b. Uthāl,[573] but when this situation arose among [1911] them, they returned to their tribes; but that put Thumāmah b. Uthāl at a disadvantage until ʿIkrimah [b. Abī Jahl] came to him and stirred him up, so he did not do anything [before ʿIkrimah arrived].[574] Then while people in the country of Banū Tamīm were in that [state], some of them having busied themselves with others so that [each] Muslim [among] them was face to face with those who played for time and waited [to see what would happen] and face to face with those who doubted, Sajāḥ bt. al-Ḥārith came upon them by suprise, having arrived from the

---

567. I.e., when Ṣafwān left to see Abū Bakr (cf. p. 85, above).

568. Traceable only in Ibn Ḥajar, *Iṣābah*, s.v., which adds no new information.

569. Wellhausen (*Skizzen*, VI, 148) noted that al-Ribāb should probably be struck from the text here, as al-Ribāb consisted of Ḍabbah and ʿAbd Manāt, mentioned in the following sentence (see *Emendanda*); but all manuscripts seem to have the word. Perhaps we should assume that the original intent was "*bi-l-Ribāb*" and that the *waw* was missing before the name of ʿAbdallāh b. Ṣafwān, as it actually is in the Cairo edition; this would yield the translation, "Among al-Ribāb, ʿAbdallāh ... was in charge of Ḍabbah ...," etc. For Bahdā, read, probably, Bahdalah; cf. note 556 above.

570. A Tamīmī who came to the Prophet with his father, probably Ṣafwān b. Ṣafwān; cf. Ibn al-Athīr, *Usd*, III, 186 and note 317, above.

571. A delegate to the Prophet from his tribe, Banū Taym b. ʿAbd Manāt of al-Ribāb; cf. Ibn al-Athīr, *Usd*, III, 408–9.

572. Jusham b. Awf was a clan of Saʿd/Tamim; cf. Caskel, I, Table 77 and II, 268.

573. Of the Ḥanīfah tribe of eastern Arabia, he was captured by the Muslims; later he embraced Islam and was pardoned. He then seems to have been involved in cutting off Mecca's supply of grain from eastern Arabia on behalf of the Prophet. Cf. Ibn al-Athīr, *Usd*, I, 246–48; F. M. Donner, "Mecca's Food Supplies and Muḥammad's Boycott," 262.

574. Cf. p. 53, above on ʿIkrimah being sent against Musaylimah.

Jazīrah. She and her clan had been among Banū Taghlib.[575] She was leading splinter groups of Rabī'ah, among them al-Hudhayl b. 'Imrān[576] at the head of Banū Taghlib and 'Aqqah b. Hilāl at the head of al-Namir[577] and Wattād b. Fulān[578] at the head of Iyād[579] and al-Salīl b. Qays at the head of Banū Shaybān.[580] So a grave matter faced them, more serious than what the people were [already] involved in, because of Sajāḥ's attack upon them and because of their disagreements and squabbles over what divided them. About this 'Afīf b. al-Mundhir[581] said:

Did he not come to you by night with the news
of that which the chiefs of Banū Tamīm encountered?
From their chiefs men called on each other,
and they were among the noblest and best.
They forced them out, after they had had [their own] territory,
into empty quarters and retreat.[582]

Sajāḥ bt. al-Ḥarith b. Suwayd b. 'Uqfān and the offspring of her father 'Uqfān were among the Banū Taghlib. Then, after the death of the Apostle of God she pretended to be a prophetess in the Jazīrah among the Banū Taghlib, whereupon al-Hudhayl complied with her and left Christianity, and [also complied]

575. A major tribe of the Rabī'ah group, living between eastern Arabia northward into southern Iraq and the Euphrates fringes. Cf. Caskel, II, 27–28 and 541–42.

576. I have not been able to trace further any of these three leaders of Rabī'ah—al-Hudhayl, 'Aqqah, and Wattād.

577. Al-Namir b. Qāsiṭ was a minor tribe of Rabī'ah, closely affiliated with Taghlib. Cf. Caskel, II, 444.

578. Nuwayrī, 76: Ziyād b. Fulān.

579. A Christian tribe of eastern Arabia, southern and central Iraq. Cf. Caskel, II, 359–60; *EI²*, s.v. "Iyād" (J. W. Fück).

580. Bishr "al-Salīl" b. Qays was brother of the more famous Bisṭām, chief of the Hammām b. Murrah clan of Shaybān. Shaybān was the most powerful tribe of the Bakr b. Wā'il confederation (part of Rabī'ah), occupying the lower Euphrates steppe region. Cf. Caskel, II, 507 and 524; F. M. Donner, "The Bakr b. Wā'il Tribes . . . ," 22ff. Cf. pp. 90–91, below, where 'Aqqah is called maternal uncle of Bishr.

581. A poet of 'Amr b. Tamīm; cf. Balansī, 141, 143, and 146. I am grateful to Dr. Landau-Tasseron for these references. Cf. Landau-Tasseron, "Sayf ibn 'Umar," 20.

582. Because of the requirements of rhyme, the poem has *khīm* for *khaym*, "retreat, withdrawal."

with those chiefs who advanced with her to raid Abū Bakr. When she got as far as al-Ḥazn,[583] she sent letters to Mālik [1912] b. Nuwayrah and called him to an alliance; whereupon he answered her, turned her back from her raiding, and incited her against clans of Banū Tamīm. She said, "Yes, so pursue your business with whomever you think [right]; for I am only a woman from Banū Yarbūʿ, so if there is to be [any] sovereignty, it shall be yours."[584] Then she sent to Banū Mālik b. Ḥanẓalah inviting them to an alliance; whereupon ʿUṭārid b. Ḥājib[585] and the chiefs of Banū Mālik went out as fugitives until they came as guests among the Banū al-ʿAnbar,[586] [staying] with Sabrah b. ʿAmr. They had disliked what Wakīʿ [b. Mālik] had done, and those like them of Banū Yarbūʿ, having disliked what Mālik [b. Nuwayrah] had done, went out until they came as guests to al-Ḥuṣayn b. Niyār among the Banū Māzin.[587] Then when her messengers came to the Banū Mālik demanding alliance, Wakīʿ agreed to that; so Wakīʿ and Mālik and Sajāḥ joined, having made an alliance one with another, and agreed to fight the people. They said, "With whom should we begin? With Khaḍḍam or Bahdā[588] or with ʿAwf and the Abnāʾ or with al-Ribāb?" They held back from Qays [b. ʿAṣim] because of what they saw of his indecision, hoping earnestly for him.[589] Then she said, "Prepare your mounts, and get ready for booty, then raid al-Ribāb, for there is no veil before them."[590] Sajāḥ headed for the wells[591] until she encamped there and said to them, "The Dahnāʾ[592] is the barrier of Banū Tamīm, and when [1913]

583. A high plateau in northeastern Arabia, near the fringes of Iraq. Cf. Yāqūt, s.v. and Thilo, s.v.

584. Both Mālik and Sajāḥ were originally from Yarbūʿ.

585. Of the Dārim clan of Tamīm, led a delegation or Dārim to the Prophet (Caskel, II, 580).

586. ʿAnbar b. Yarbūʿ was Sajāḥ's clan of Tamīm (Caskel, II, 189).

587. Probably Māzin b. Mālik, a clan of Banū ʿAmr b. Tamīm. Cf. Caskel, I, Table 82, and II, 406.

588. Probably Bahdalah; cf. note 556, above.

589. I.e., hoping that he would join their cause.

590. Sajāḥ's statement is couched in rhymed prose.

591. Or "for al-Aḥfār"; Yāqūt mentions a place with this name, but gives no precise location.

592. An extensive tract of waterless sand desert in the Najd; at the time of the

casualties press them, al-Ribāb will not delay in taking refuge in al-Dajānī[593] and sand deserts (*al-dahānī*); so let some of you encamp there."[594] At this, "al-Jafūl," that is, Mālik b. Nuwayrah,[595] headed for al-Dajānī and encamped in it. Al-Ribāb heard of this, so they gathered to it, [both] their Ḍabbah and ʿAbd Manāt [clans]. Now Wakīʿ and Bishr[596] were responsible for [battling] Banū Bakr of Banū Ḍabbah, and ʿAqqah was responsible for [fighting] the Thaʿlabah b. Saʿd b. Ḍabbah, and al-Hudhayl [b. ʿImrān] was responsible [for fighting] the ʿAbd Manāt; so Wakīʿ and Bishr met Banū Bakr of Banū Ḍabbah [in battle], whereupon the two were routed, and Samāʿa[597] and Wakīʿ and Qaʿqāʿ[598] were taken prisoner, and many were killed. So Qays b. ʿĀṣim said regarding that [event]—that being the first that there appeared in him any remorse:[599]

It is as if you never witnessed Samāʿa when he raided
 and Qaʿqāʿ did not rejoice, while Wakīʿ was thwarted.
I saw that you had accompanied Ḍabbah unwillingly,
 [as though] having a painful scab on both sides,
The releaser of prisoners whose march was foolish.
 All of their business is on the rocks.

Then Sajāḥ and al-Hudhayl and ʿAqqah let Banū Bakr go because of the alliance between her and Wakīʿ; ʿAqqah [more-

---

riddah wars, territory of the Tamīm. Cf. Thilo, s.v.; *EI*[2], s.v. "Dahnāʾ" (C. D. Mathews).

593. A place in eastern Arabia; cf. Hamdānī, 168, l. 19.

594. Again, (loosely) rhymed prose.

595. According to Diyarbakri, II, 209 and Balansī, 51, he earned his nickname (meaning "the refunder") because he sent the camels collected as *ṣadaqah* tax back to the tribes after the Prophet's death.

596. Presumably Bishr "al-Salīl" b. Qays; cf. note 580, above.

597. Caskel, II, 510, thinks this may be Samāʿah b. ʿAmr of Dārim/Tamīm.

598. Cairo ed. (index) indentifies him as al-Qaʿqāʿ b. Maʿbad, chief of the Dārim clan of Tamīm; he was in the Dārim delegation to the Prophet, and famed for his generosity. Cf. Caskel, II, 465; Ibn Ḥajar, *Iṣābah*, s.v. It is not clear, however, whether al-Qaʿqāʿ b. Maʿbad played any role in the *riddah*. Landau-Tasseron believes that there were two men of Tamīm named al-Qaʿqāʿ b. ʿAmr, one a kinsman of Sajāḥ's who backed the *riddah*, the other of the ʿAmr-Tamīm who remained loyal to Medina. The latter would be the person mentioned here: cf. Landau-Tasseron, "Sayf ibn ʿUmar," 16.

599. Ibn al-Athīr, *Kāmil*, II, 355 clarifies: "remorse over having held back the *ṣadaqah* tax from Abū Bakr."

over] was the maternal uncle of Bishr. (Sajāḥ) said, "Kill al-Ribāb and they will make a treaty with you and release your [1914] prisoners. You should carry to them their blood prices, and the others will praise the consequence of their decision." So Ḍabbah released the prisoners to them and paid the blood price for the slain, and they went out from them. Then Qays recited [verses] about that, reproaching them for the truce of Ḍabbah, and supporting Ḍabbah and reproving[600] them. No one of ʿAmr or Saʿd or al-Ribāb had joined the affair of Sajāḥ; from all of these [clans], they yearned only [to be aligned with] Qays, until he showed support for Ḍabbah and began to show regret. No one from Ḥanẓalah aided them except Wakīʿ and Mālik, and their assistance was an alliance on [condition] that they help one another and gather together to one another. About this Aṣamm al-Taymī[601] said:

A sister of Taghlib came to us and then considered weak[602]
the armies[603] from among the nobles of our ancestor's tribe.
And she planted a call [to join her] firmly among us, out of stupidity,
although she was one from the great foreign tribes.[604]
We did not accept from them even what an ant could carry in its mouth,[605]
nor would she embrace [Islam] if she came to us.
May your sound judgment be folly and error
the evening you gathered troops together for her!

Then Sajāḥ went out heading the armies of the Jazīrah until she reached al-Nibāj, whereupon Aws b. Khuzaymah al-Hujaymī[606] [1915]

---

600. Reading *ta'nīban* with the Cairo edition and (possibly) the Berlin manuscript, instead of the text's *ta'bīnan* and other manuscript variants. "Supporting" here is *isʿād*, lit., "rendering happy." The verses are omitted from the text.

601. The poet Aṣamm b. Wallād b. Khuzaymah, of Taym al-Ribāb; cf. Caskel, II, 201.

602. *Istahadda*; possibly "threatened," as proposed by *Glossary*.

603. Possibly "flocks." Arabic *jalā'ib*.

604. *ʿAmā'ir 'ākhirīnā*, lit., "great tribes of [people] other than us."

605. I.e., we accepted nothing from them.

606. I have not been able to trace him further. Hujaym was a clan of the B. ʿAmr/Tamīm; cf. Caskel, I, Table 84 and II, 286.

launched a raid against them leading those who crowded to him from Banū ʿAmr, so that al-Hudhayl was taken captive by a nomad of Banū Māzin[607] named Nāshirah. ʿAqqah was taken prisoner by ʿUbdah al-Hujaymī. They stopped fighting on condition that they return the prisoners to one another and that they turn back from them and not pass against the[ir will],[608] so they did that. So they repulsed her and bound her and the two of them to an agreement that they withdraw from them and that they would not cross the[ir territory] except with their permission.[609] Then they fulfilled [their promises] to them, but it continued [to burn] in the soul of al-Hudhayl against the Māzinī until, when ʿUthmān b. ʿAffān was killed, he gathered a troop and launched a raid against Safār[610] while Banū Māzin was there; so Banū Māzin killed him and shot him at Safār.[611]

When[612] al-Hudhayl and ʿAqqah returned to (Sajāḥ) and the chiefs of the people of the Jazīrah had gathered, they said to her, "What do you order us [to do] now that Mālik and Wakīʿ have bound their two tribes to treaties so that they will not help us and will let us do no more than cross their territory, and [now that] we have made a treaty with this[613] tribe?" So she replied, "Al-Yamāmah." At this they said, "The might of the people of al-Yamāmah is great, and the situation of Musaylimah has become rough." But she said, "Betake yourselves to al-Yamāmah, fly in with the flapping of the dove, for it is a gallant raid, no blame shall attach to you after it."[614]

[1916] Then she rushed upon Banū Ḥanīfah. Musaylimah learned

607. *Rajulun min Banī Māzin thumma min banī wabar.* Although this construction is a common way of expressing a man's clan and subclan, I find no "Banū Wabar" among Māzin or anywhere else.

608. [*An*] *lā yajtāzū ʿalayhim*, i.e., that they not pass through the territories of Aws against their will; cf. Ibn al-Athīr, II, 335: *wa lā yaṭiʾu arḍa Awsin*, "and not come to the land of Aws."

609. *Lā yattakhidhū-hum ṭarīqan illā min warāʾihim.*

610. A watering place of Banū Māzin in the desert southeast of al-Baṣrah (Yāqūt, s.v.).

611. We should perhaps read *qātalathu* for *qatalathu*: "Banū Māzin fought him. . . ."

612. Cf. Nuwayrī, 77–78 (to p. 93); Caetani, 646–47.

613. Presumably meaning Banū Māzin.

614. Rhymed prose.

of that and was afraid of her; he feared that, if he busied himself with her, Thumāmah would get the better of him in Ḥajr, or Shuraḥbīl b. Ḥasanah or the tribes that were around them. So he sent gifts to her, and then wrote to her requesting her pledge of security for his life so that he could come to her. At this she made the armies encamp at the wells, granting him permission and offering him security, so he came to her as a delegation at the head of forty people of Banū Ḥanīfah. Now she was knowledgeable about Christianity, having learned from the knowledge of the Christians of Taghlib, so Musaylimah said, "Half of the earth is to us, and half would be to Quraysh if they had acted rightly; but God has returned to you the half which Quraysh rejected, and has given it to you, even though it would have been to (Quraysh) had she accepted." (Sajāḥ) said, "The half is not returned except by those who incline,[615] so carry the half to the cavalry you see as if they were dying of thirst."[616] So Musaylimah said,[617] "God listened to whomever He listened to, and made him yearn for good when he yearned, and His cause is still arranged in everything that delights him. Your Lord saw you and gave you life and preserved you from loneliness, and saved you and gave you life on the day of His religion; for us some prayers of the company of the pious, neither miserable nor licentious, staying up at night and fasting by day; indeed your Lord is great, the Lord of the clouds and the rain."[618] And he said also, "When I saw their faces they were comely, and their complexions were clear, and their hands were soft; I said to
them, 'You shall not come to women, nor drink wine, but [1917]
you are the company of the pious fasting by day and costing a day.' So praise be to God! Verily life came to where you live; ascend to the King of heaven. [Even] if it[619] were only a mustard seed, a witness would take care of it who would know what is [hidden] in the breasts; but most people in it [will meet]

615. *Man ḥanaf*; a pun on the name of Banū Ḥanīfah.
616. Reading, with Nuwayrī, 78 and Cairo, *ka al-sahafi*. Rhymed prose.
617. Cf. Ibn Ḥubaysh, 35, ll. 7ff.
618. Rhymed prose.
619. I.e., one's good (or bad?) deeds.

perdition."[620] Among the laws that Musaylimah prescribed for them was that whoever produced a single son as progeny should not come to a woman unless[621] that son should die; then he should [again] seek [to procreate] children until he produced [another] son, and then forbear [again]. So he had forbidden women to anyone who had a male child.

According to Abū Jaʿfar—authorities other than Sayf:[622] When Sajāḥ descended upon Musaylimah he locked the fortress in front of her, so Sajāḥ asked him to come down. He replied, "Then put your companions away from you"; so she did that. Then Musaylimah said, "Erect a domed tent (qubbah) for her and perfume it, perhaps it will make her think of sex."[623] So they did so; then when she entered the tent, Musaylimah came down and said, "May ten [men] stop here and ten stop there." Then he studied with her,[624] saying, "What has been revealed to you?" But she replied, "Do women usually begin? Rather, you: what has been revealed to you?" He replied, "Do you not see how your Lord has done with the pregnant woman,[625] He has brought forth from her a soul that strives, from between the belly skin and the waist." She said, "What else?" He said, "It was revealed to me, 'Verily God created women as vulvas, and made men for them as husbands, so we insert into them fat cocks,[626] then we withdraw them when we wish, so they may

[1918]

---

620. Reading, with Mss. B and C and Cairo, wa-h-ʾakthar al-nāsı fīhā al-thubūr, as do Emendanda.

621. Lit., "until."

622. Nuwayrī, 78–80, as far as p. 95, below; Ibn al-Athīr, Kāmil, II, 355–57, close parallel until p. 97, with gaps; Caetani, 647–48.

623. Or, possibly, "perhaps she will mention marriage (al-bāh)." Ibn al-Athīr, Kāmıl, II, 355: "he perfumed it so that the sweet scent would make her thınk of intercourse."

624. Diyārbakrī, II, 159, in a loose paraphrase has tadārasā al-nubuwwah, "the two of them studied prophecy together." Balansī, 62 and Ibn Ḥubaysh, 34, top, have Musaylimah say, taʿāli natadārasu al-nubuwwah ayyunā ahaqqu, "come, let us study which of us is more entitled to [claim] prophethood."

625. Diyarbakri, II, 158: "Verily, God has bestowed grace on the pregnant woman."

626. Text has fuʾs, not found in Ibn Manẓūr. We follow Nuwayrī and Caıro, whıch read quʾs, (pl. of aqʿas); Cairo, citing Aghānī, glosses this as gharāmıl, "coarse penises." Cf. Ibn Manẓūr, VI, 177 (s.v. aqʿas), "with chests protrudıng and backs in."

produce for us a kid."[627] She said, "I bear witness that you are a prophet." He said, "Do you want me to marry you, so that I may devour[628] the Arabs with my tribe and your tribe?" She replied that she did. [So] he said,

Why don't you go to fuck,
  as the bed has been prepared for you?
If you wish, in the house,
  or, if you wish, in the closet.
If you wish we shall take you thrown on your back,
  or, if you wish, on [all] fours.
If you wish, with two-thirds of it,
  or, if you wish, with all of it.

She said, "No, rather with all of it." He said, "Revelations came to me about that." So she remained with him three days, and then returned to her tribe, whereupon they said, "What do you think?" She replied, "He was in the right, so I followed him and married him." They said, "And did he give you anything as a dowry?" She said that he had not, so they said, "Go back to him, for it is disgraceful for one like you to return without a dowry." So she returned to him, whereupon when Musaylimah saw her he locked the fortress and said, "What do you want?" She said, "Give me something as dowry." He replied, "Who is your [1919]
muezzin?" She told him it was Shabath b. Ribʿī al-Riyāḥī,[629] so he said, "Bring him to me." So (Shabath) came, whereupon (Musaylimah) said, "Call out among your companions that Musaylimah b. Ḥabīb, the Apostle of God, has unburdened you of two of the prayers that Muḥammad imposed upon you—the last evening prayer and the dawn prayer." Among her companions were al-Zibriqān b. Badr and ʿUṭārid b. Ḥājib and the likes of them.

According to al-Kalbī—informants of Banū Tamīm:[630] Most of Banū Tamīm in the sands did not pray the two [prayers]. Then she went back, and with her were her companions, among them

627. As always with Musaylimah's alleged revelations, rhymed prose.
628. Nuwayrī, 79: "conquer" or "humble" the Arabs.
629. Riyāḥ was another clan of Yarbūʿ, Sajāḥ's subtribe of Tamīm.
630. Cf. Nuwayrī, 80.

al-Zibriqān b. Badr, ʿUṭārid b. Ḥājib, ʿAmr b. al-Ahtam,[631] Ghaylān b. Kharashah,[632] and Shabath b. Ribʿī. So ʿUṭārid b. Ḥājib said,[633]

Our prophetess entered the evening[634] a female whom we visited,[635]
while the prophets of the people entered the morning as males.

And Ḥukaym b. ʿAyyāsh "al-Aʿwar" al-Kalbī[636] said, rebuking Muḍar on account of Sajāḥ and mentioning Rabīʿah:[637]

They brought you a steadfast religion, and you brought
verses copied in a knowing book.

Continuation of the Account of Sayf[638]

(Musaylimah) made a treaty with (Sajāḥ) on condition that he deliver to her half of the revenues of al-Yamāmah; she refused
[1920] [to accept] unless he delivered the [installment of the] first year in advance, so he conceded that to her. He said, "Leave behind someone who can collect the advance payment for you, and go back yourself with half of [this] year['s share]." Then he returned and carried to her the half, so she carried it off and returned to the Jazīrah, leaving al-Hudhayl and ʿAqqah and Wattād[639] so that the remaining half might be paid. Then they were taken

631. ʿAmr b. Sinān "al-Ahtam" ("the toothless") was a poet and member of the Tamīm delegation to the Prophet. He became a follower of Sajāḥ, but later embraced Islam. On him see *EI*², s.v. "ʿAmr b. al-Ahtam" (A. J. Wensinck-Ch. Pellat); Caskel, II, 184.

632. Of Banū Ḍabbah. Cf. Caskel, II, 270.

633. Cf. Ibn Ḥubaysh, 34.

634. Balansi, 62: the morning. Ibn Ḥubaysh, 34: the forenoon.

635. *Nuṭifu bi-hā*; sometimes with prurient intent.

636. Poet of Kinānah b. Awf branch of Kalb; probably lived in the second half of the first century A.H. Cf. Caskel, II, 331.

637. Muḍar and Rabīʿah were the two main genealogical divisions of the "North Arabs," portrayed as two sons of Nizār. The Kalbite (South Arab or Qaḥṭānī) poet reproaches the North Arabs, who included Sajāḥ's tribe of Tamīm and her allies of Ribāb and Ḍabbah.

638. Cf. Nuwayrī, 80; Caetani, 648.

639. Text, Cairo, Nuwayrī, and Ibn al-Athīr, *Kāmil*, have Ziyād; see *Emendanda* and p. 88, note 578, above.

by surprise by Khālid b. al-Walīd's approach to them, so they dispersed.

Sajāḥ remained among Banū Taghlib until Muʿāwiya transferred them in his day, in the "year of union."[640] When the people of Iraq agreed [to recognize] Muʿāwiyah [as caliph] after ʿAlī, Muʿāwiyah took to expelling from al-Kūfah those who had been most vehement in the cause of ʿAlī, and to settle in their homes those people of Syria and al-Baṣrah and the Jazīrah who were most vehement in his own cause; it is they who were called the "transfers"[641] in the garrison towns. So he expelled Qaʿqāʿ b. ʿAmr b. Mālik[642] from al-Kūfah to Īliyāʾ[643] in Palestine, and petitioned him to settle in the residences of his paternal relatives, Banū ʿUqfān,[644] and to transfer them[645] to [the properties of] Banū Tamīm. So he transferred them from the Jazīrah to al-Kūfah and settled them in the residences of al-Qaʿqāʿ and his relatives. [Sajāḥ] came with them and became a good Muslim.

Al-Zibriqān and al-Aqraʿ[646] went out to Abū Bakr and said, "Make over to us the *kharāj*.[647] of al-Baḥrayn and we will guarantee for you that no one from our tribe will repudiate [Islām]." So (Abū Bakr) did that and wrote the document. The one who acted as middleman for them was Ṭalḥah b. ʿUbaydallāh. They called upon witnesses, among them ʿUmar; but when the document was brought to ʿUmar, he looked at it [1921]

---

640. *ʿĀm al-jamāʿah*: the year 40 AH/AD 660–661, so called because the Muslim community came together in recognizing Muʿāwiyah, ending the political division of the first civil war. *Pace* Caetani, 648; see Abū Zurʿah al-Dimashqī, *Taʾrīkh*, 188 (no. 101) and 190 (no. 105).

641. *Al-nawāqil*.

642. Cf. notes 485 and 598, above.

643. I.e., Aelia Capitolina (Jerusalem).

644. ʿUqfān b. Suwayd was a clan of Yarbūʿ residing in al-Kūfah; cf. Caskel, II, 574; Ibn al-Athīr, *Lubāb*, II, 350.

645. Presumably Banū Taghlib.

646. Cf. Nuwayrī, 80–81. Al-Aqraʿ b. Ḥābis, chief of Dārim clan of Tamīm, was the first Tamīmī to go to the Prophet, during the conquest of Mecca; he was put in charge of the *ṣadaqah* of Banū Hanẓalah. Cf. *EI*², s.v. "Al-Akraʿ b. Ḥābis" (M. J. Kister).

647. In classical juristic usage, *kharāj* is a kind of land tax, but such clear-cut systematization of terminology was not yet in force during the *riddah* wars; perhaps "tribute" is a better rendering. For a recent discussion of the development of tax terminology, see Simonsen, *Studies*.

without witnessing it. Then he said, "No, by God, absolutely not!" and tore up the document and erased it. Ṭalḥah became angry at this, so he went to Abū Bakr saying, "Are you the commander or is ʿUmar?" Whereupon (Abū Bakr) replied, "ʿUmar is, except that obedience is owed to me." So he calmed down. The two of them witnessed with Khālid all the battles up to al-Yamāmah;[648] then al-Aqraʿ went to Dūmah with Shuraḥbīl.

Al-Buṭāḥ and Its Story

According to al-Sarī b. Yaḥyā—Shuʿayb—Sayf—al-Ṣaʿb b. ʿAṭiyyah b. Bilāl:[649] When Sajāḥ returned to the Jazīrah, Mālik b. Nuwayrah held back and repented and became perplexed over his situation. Wakīʿ and Samāʿah[650] knew the shamefulness of what they had done, so they returned to the fold and behaved humbly.[651] The two of them extracted the *ṣadaqah* taxes and came out with it to meet Khālid; so Khālid said, "What caused you to make an alliance with these people?" Whereupon they replied, "Some blood vengeance we were in the course of pursuing among the Banū Ḍabbah; they were days of preoccupation and opportunities." About that Wakīʿ said:

Do not reckon me a renegade, for indeed I
was constrained when the fingers were being bent for me.[652]
[1922] But I guarded the bulk of Mālik
and watched until my eyes gave out on me.[653]
So when Khālid came to us with his battle standard
the payments reached him first[654] at Buṭāḥ.

648. Or, perhaps, "even al-Yamāmah."
649. Cf. Ibn al-Athīr, *Kāmil*, II, 357; Nuwayrī, 82; Caetani, 652–53.
650. Cf. p. 90, above.
651. Lit., "returned a good returning and were not haughty," reading *wa-lam yatajabbarā* with text. *Emendanda* proposes *lam yataḥayyarā*, "they were not perplexed."
652. I.e., even as I was being counted among the renegades (by the bending of fingers as a way of counting), I was being held back by others from declaring my allegiance to Islam.
653. Lit., "until the ocular veins grew dark on me."
654. I.e., payment of *ṣadaqah* reached Khālid at Buṭāḥ before the people who paid it themselves arrived? (*takhaṭṭat ilayhi*).

In the country of Banū Ḥanẓalah the only hateful [situation] that remained was that of Mālik b. Nuwayrah and those who surrounded him at al-Buṭāḥ. He was perplexed and worried.

According to al-Sarī—Shuʿayb—Sayf—Sahl—al-Qāsim and ʿAmr b. Shuʿayb:[655] When Khālid wanted to march, he left Ẓafar mopping up[656] Asad, Ghaṭafān, Ṭayyi', and Hawāzin; so he marched heading for al-Buṭāḥ this side of al-Ḥazn, while Mālik b. Nuwayrah was there. His situation became doubtful to him, and the Anṣār hesitated [to join] Khālid and held back from him saying, "These were not the caliph's orders to us; the caliph charged us to stand fast until he wrote to us after we had finished with al-Buzākhah and mopped up [opposition in] the people's territory." Whereupon Khālid said, "He did not charge you with this; rather, he charged me to proceed, and I am the commander and the one to whom communications come. Even if there reached me no letter nor any command of his, I would [1923] seize any opportunity that I perceived before informing him of it, if I thought that by informing him the opportunity would slip away from me.[657] Likewise, if we were tempted by some situation about which we had no instructions from him, we would not fail to consider what was the most desirable option before us and then to act on it. Now this Mālik b. Nuwayrah is right opposite us and I am heading for him with those who are with me of the Muhājirūn and those who follow in good works; I shall not force you." Khālid proceeded and the Anṣār repented and urged one another on, saying, "If the group achieves good [results], it is a good you will be excluded from; and if some misfortune befalls them, the people will shun you for it." So they agreed to join with Khālid, and dispatched messengers to

655. Cf. partial parallel in Diyarbakri, II, 209 top; Ibn al-Athīr, *Kāmil,* II, 357–58; Balansī, 50–51; Ibn Ḥubaysh, 28 (from Wāqidī); Ibn Ḥubaysh, 28 (from Ibn Isḥāq); Nuwayrī, 82–83; Iṣfahānī, XIV, 66–67; Caetani, 650.

656. Here and below, *istabra'a* + direct object. Cf. Ibn Ḥubaysh, 58 (<Ibn Isḥāq).

657. I.e., by causing delay while waiting for the caliph's reply. The syntax is problematic; see the discussion of the sentence in J. Bellamy, "Arabic Yerses from the First/Second Century: The Inscription of ʿEn ʿAvdat," *Journal of Semitic Studies* 35 (1990), 76, note 6, with other references and translations.

him, whereupon he waited for them until they joined him. Then he marched until he reached al-Buṭāḥ, but found no one there.

According to Abū Jaʿfar—al-Sarī b. Yaḥyā—Shuʿayb. b. Ibrāhīm—Sayf b. ʿUmar—Khuzaymah b. Shajarah al-ʿUqfānī—ʿUthmān b. Suwayd—Suwayd b. al-Mathʿabah al-Riyāḥī:[658] Khālid b. al-Walīd arrived in al-Buṭāḥ, whereupon he found no one there;
[1924] he found that Mālik had dispersed them among their flocks[659] and forbidden them to gather when he became perplexed over his situation. [In doing so] he said, "Oh Banū Yarbūʿ, we have disobeyed our commanders, inasmuch as they called us to this religion, whereas the people held us back from it, so that we have neither prospered nor succeeded. I have reconsidered this situation and found it feasible for them without any managing (*siyāsah*). For lo, the situation is one that the people do not manage. Beware of acting in a hostile manner against a group having a mandate [from God to exercise authority];[660] so disperse to your territories and enter into this cause." So they dispersed accordingly to their flocks,[661] and Mālik went out until he returned to his residence. When Khālid reached al-Buṭāḥ, he scattered portions of the army and ordered them to summon [the people] to Islām, and to bring to it whoever had not [yet] responded; and if he resisted, to kill him. [This] was part of that with which Abū Bakr had charged him:[662] "When you encamp someplace, make the call to prayer and the *iqāmah*.[663] Then, if the people make the call to prayer and the *iqāmah*, leave them alone; but if they do not do so, there is no [course] but to raid them. [In that case] kill them by every means, by fire or whatever else. And if they respond to you in the call to Islām, then question them [further]; if they affirm [payment of] the alms tax,

658. Cf. Ibn al-Athīr, *Kāmil*, II, 358, intermittent parallel; Balādhurī, *Futūḥ*, 98–99; Nuwayrī, 83; Iṣfahānī, XIV, 67; Caetani, 653–55.

659. Here and below, *amwāl*, lit., "properties." It can refer to flocks or to real property.

660. *Qawmun ṣuniʿa lahum*.

661. Or, perhaps, "properties, lands" (*amwāl*).

662. Cf. Balansi, 53; Wathīmah, 15/56.

663. The *iqāmah* is the second call to prayer, not broadcast publicly to notify people at large, but made to the faithful gathered in the mosque to indicate that prayer is about to begin.

then accept that from them; but if they deny it, then there is no [course] but to raid them without any word [of warning]."

Then[664] the cavalry brought Mālik b. Nuwayrah to [Khālid], along with some people of Banū Thaʿlabah b. Yarbūʿ, of ʿĀṣim [1925]
and ʿUbayd and ʿArīn and Jaʿfar.[665] The raiding party disagreed about them; among them was Abū Qatādah, who was one of those who testified that they had made the call to prayer and the *iqāmah* and had performed the prayer. So when they disagreed about them, (Khālid) ordered that they be locked up, on a cold night against which nothing was sufficient [for warmth]. [The night] began to get colder, so Khālid ordered a crier to call out, "Keep your captives warm." Now in the Kinānah dialect, when one says, "*adfi'ū al-rajul*," it means "keep him warm" or "wrap him up," but in the dialects of others it means 'kill him."[666] So the people thought, since [the word] meant 'kill" in their dialect, that he wanted them killed, so they did so; Ḍirār b. al-Azwar killed Mālik. Khālid heard the outcry, so he went out after they had finished with them; whereupon he said, "If God desires something, He effects it."

The people disagreed about them.[667] Abū Qatādah said [to Khālid], "This is your doing." At this Khālid countered him with rough speech,[668] whereupon (Abū Qatādah) became angry and proceeded to Abū Bakr. At this Abū Bakr became angry at (Abū Qatādah) until ʿUmar spoke to him on his behalf, but (Abū Bakr) would only be content if (Abū Qatādah) returned to (Khālid); so [Abū Qatādah] returned to [Khālid], so that he came to Medina with him.

Khālid married Umm Tamīm bt. al-Minhāl,[669] and abstained [1926]

---

664. Cf. Balansi, 54–55; Nuwayrī, 83–84; Iṣfahānī, XIV, 67.

665. Subclans of Thaʿlabah b. Yarbūʿ of Tamīm; cf. Caskel, I, Table 69. Banū ʿUbayd genealogically included ʿĀṣim; perhaps ʿUbayd here is used to refer to all clans other than ʿĀṣim.

666. Evidently the crier was a Kinānī. The text is confused here, although the meaning is clear. See *Glossary*; *Emendanda*; Lane, *Arabic-English Lexicon*, s.v. *dafa'a*; Wellhausen, *Skizzen*, VI, 149; Ibn al-Athīr, *Kāmil*, II, 358.

667. I.e., about whether their deaths were reprehensible.

668. Or, perhaps, "pelted him with stones" (*zabara-hu*).

669. The slain Mālik b. Nuwayrah's wife: cf. Ibn Ḥajar, *Iṣābah*, s.v. "Mālik b. Nuwayrah"; Diyarbakri, II, 209, calling her "Umm Mutammim."

from her so that the period between her menstruations should elapse.[670] Now the Arabs used to find [the taking of] women abhorrent in war, and condemn it. ʿUmar said to Abū Bakr, "In the sword of Khālid there really is forbidden behavior; and even if this [story about Mālik's execution] were not true, it is necessary for you to take retaliation on him." He pestered him about that, but Abū Bakr did not take retaliation on [any of] his tax agents or commanders.[671] Then he said, "Tell me, ʿUmar, (Khālid) sought to clear something up but [in the process] made a mistake;[672] so stop berating him. (Abū Bakr) paid the blood price for Mālik and wrote to Khālid to come before him; so he did that to explain his story, whereupon (Abū Bakr) pardoned him and accepted [his explanation]. But (Abū Bakr) did censure him over [his] marriage to[673] one whom the Arabs considered it disgraceful [to marry] in that way.

According to al-Sarī—Shuʿayb—Sayf—Hishām b. ʿUrwah—his father:[674] A group from the raiding party testified that they [themselves] had made the call to prayer and done the *iqāmah* and prayed, whereupon [the people being raided] had done likewise; whereas others testified that nothing like that had occurred, so that [those raided] were killed. [Mālik's] brother,[675] Mutammim b. Nuwayrah, came begging Abū Bakr for [permission to seek vengeance for] his blood and requesting him to make [the guilty parties] captive; but he wrote to him rejecting [their] capture. ʿUmar pressed him to dismiss Khālid, saying, "In his sword there really is forbidden behavior," whereupon he replied, "Oh ʿUmar, I will not sheathe a sword that God has drawn against the unbelievers."

---

670. The idea being to wait until after she had menstruated before consummating the new marriage, thus removing any doubt about the paternity of eventual children; an allusion to the *ʿiddah* or "waiting period" enjoined by Islamic law. Cf. *EI*[2], s.v. "ʿIdda" (Y. Linant de Bellefonds).

671. *kāna . . . ʿlā yuqīdu min ʿummāli-hi wa-lā wazaʿati-hi.*

672. *taʿawwala fa-ʾakhṭaʾa.* Cf. Balansi, 54, Ibn Ḥubaysh, 29: *in kāna Khālidun taʿawwala amran fa-ʾakhṭaʾa-hu.* Hoenerbach translates "er hat eine Erklärung gesucht und sich dabei geirrt." (Wathīmah, 12/53).

673. Cf. Wellhausen, *Skizzen*, VI, 149; *Emendanda.*

674. Cf. Diyarbakrı, II, 209; Iṣfahānī, XIV, 67–68; Caetani, 655.

675. Cf. Ibn al-Athīr, II, 359, different story.

According to al-Sarī—Shuʿayb—Sayf—Khuzaymah—ʿUthmān—Suwayd:[676] Mālik b. Nuwayrah was one of the hairiest of people. Now the men of the army used the heads [of the slain captives] to hold up their cooking-pots, and there was no head among them whose skin the fire did not reach except Mālik's; the pot became well-cooked but his head did not cook because of the amount of hair on it, the hair preventing [the fire's] heat from reaching the skin. Mutammim described him in verse, mentioning his slenderness.[677] ʿUmar had seen him when he came to the Prophet, so he said, "Was he really like that, Oh Mutammim?" He replied, "As for what I said, yes."

According to Ibn Ḥumayd—Salamah—Muḥammad b. Isḥāq—Ṭalḥah b. ʿAbdallāh b. ʿAbd al-Raḥmān b. Abū Bakr al-Ṣiddīq:[678] Among Abū Bakr's instructions to his armies was [this]: "When you come upon one of the peoples' abodes, and then hear the call to prayer in it, desist from its people until you have asked them for what reason they were hostile. But if you do not hear the call to prayer, then launch a raid such that you kill and burn."[679] Among those who testified that Mālik [b. Nuwayrah][had embraced] Islām was Abū Qatādah al-Ḥārith b. Ribʿī, a brother of Banū Salimah. He made a vow to God that he would never witness a war with Khālid b. al-Walīd after [1928] that. He used to relate that when they came upon a group they would watch them under cover of night so that the group took up arms. "Then[680] we would say, 'We are Muslims,' 'whereupon they would say, 'We too are Muslims.' [So] we would say, 'Then what is the meaning of your weapons?' They would say, 'And what is the meaning of your weapons?' whereupon we would say, 'If you are as you say, then put your weapons down.' So they would put them down; then we would pray and they would pray."

676. Cf. Diyarbakrı, II, 209; Balansı, 54; Wathīmah, 12/52; Ibn Ḥubaysh, 29; Iṣfahānī, XIV, 68, which includes a couplet by Mutammim omitted in Ṭabarī.

677. Dr. Landau-Tasseron informs me that in *jāhilī* poetry slenderness is considered a praiseworthy characteristic, since it reveals that the person feeds his neighbor while remaining hungry himself.

678. Ibn Ḥubaysh, 29 top (Ibn Isḥāq); Iṣfahānī, XIV, 68; Caetani, 655–56.

679. Cf. pp. 57, 59, above.

680. Cf Ibn al-Athīr, *Kāmil*, II, 359; Balansi, 51 (both fragmentary).

Khālid used to excuse himself for killing [Mālik] [on the grounds] that [Mālik] had said, when he was interrogating him, "I think your companion[681] was only saying such and such." (Khālid) said, "And why didn't you reckon him a companion of yours?" Then he made him come forward and struck off his head and those of his companions. Then, when ʿUmar b. al-Khaṭṭāb learned of their murder, he spoke of it with Abū Bakr repeatedly, saying, "The enemy of God transgressed against a Muslim man, killing him and then leaping upon his wife." Khālid b. al-Walīd[682] approached [Medina] on his return until he entered the mosque, wearing a robe of his on which was iron rust, and with his head wrapped in a turban of his in which arrows had become planted. So when he entered the mosque, ʿUmar went to him and pulled the arrows from his head and smashed them. Then he said, "What hypocrisy, to kill a Muslim man and then leap upon his wife! By God, I would pelt you with stones."[683] Khālid b. al-Walīd did not speak to him, and thought that Abū Bakr would only have the same opinion about him as ʿUmar, until he entered upon Abū Bakr. When he entered upon him, he told
[1929] him the story and Abū Bakr pardoned him and forgave him without punishment for whatever had happened in his recent campaign. So Khālid went out when Abū Bakr favored him. ʿUmar was seated in the mosque, so he said, "Come to me, you son of the world!"[684] From this, ʿUmar knew that Abū Bakr had favored him, so he did not speak to him and went into his house.

The one who killed Mālik b. Nuwayrah was ʿAbd b. al-Azwar al-Asadī.[685]

According to Ibn al-Kalbī, the one who killed Mālik b. Nuwayrah was Ḍirār b. al-Azwar.[686]

---

681. I.e., the Prophet, as a gloss in Isfahānī, XIV, 68 makes clear.

682. Cf. Ibn al-Athīr, II, 359, fragment; Nuwayrī, 84–85.

683. The punishment for adultery in classical Islamic law. See Joseph Schacht, *Introduction to Islamic Law*, 15–16.

684. Or: "one with the cloak": *b. umm Shamlah*. Ibn al-Athīr, *Kāmil*, II, 359 has "b. Umm Salamah."

685. According to Ibn al-Athīr, *Usd*, III, 334, same as Ḍirār b. al-Azwar; according to Ibn Ḥajar, *Iṣābah*, s.v., Ḍirār's brother.

686. Cf. Wathīmah, 12/52.

Remainder of the Story of Musaylimah the Liar and His Tribe of the People of al-Yamāmah

According to al-Sarī—Shuʿayb—Sayf—Sahl b. Yūsuf—al-Qāsim b. Muḥammad:[687] When Abū Bakr sent ʿIkrimah b. Abī Jahl against Musaylimah and sent Shuraḥbīl after him, ʿIkrimah made haste and strove to precede Shuraḥbīl so that he might secure [for himself] the fame [of having made war.][688] He attacked (Musaylimah's followers), whereupon they defeated him. Shuraḥbīl remained on the road where[689] the news reached him. ʿIkrimah wrote to Abū Bakr about his situation, so Abū Bakr wrote to him, "Oh Ibn Umm ʿIkrimah, let me not see you, nor should you see me in this situation; nor should you turn back, thereby weakening the army. Forge ahead so that you assist Ḥudhayfah and ʿArfajah, fighting along with them the people of ʿUmān and Mahrah. And if the two of them are occupied, proceed yourself; then march with your army mopping up those whom you pass until you meet al-Muhājir b. Abī Umayyah in [1930]
the Yemen and Ḥaḍramawt." And (Abū Bakr) wrote to Shuraḥbīl ordering him to stay put until his [further] order should reach him. Then he wrote to him several days before directing Khālid to al-Yamāmah: "When Khālid reaches you, then you will be unoccupied if God wills, so betake yourself to Quḍāʿah so that you and ʿAmr b. al-ʿĀṣ may be against those of them who have denied and resisted [Islām]." So when Khālid arrived before Abū Bakr from al-Buṭāḥ, Abū Bakr was pleased with Khālid, listened to his excuse, and accepted [it] from him, and believed him and was pleased with him and directed him against Musaylimah. The army went campaigning with him; Thābit b. Qays[690] and al-Barāʾ b. Fulān[691] led the Anṣār, Abū Ḥudhayfah[692] and Zayd[693]

---

687. Cf. Ibn al-Athīr, *Kāmil*, II, 360–61; Nuwayrī, 89–90.
688. Lit., "that he might take away its reputation."
689. Ibn al-Athīr: "When." Kos, Manuscript B, Nuwayrī: "until."
690. Cf. Ibn Ḥubaysh, 39 top, p. 116, below, for different arrangement.
691. Perhaps al-Barāʾ b. Mālik; cf. p. 118, below.
692. Abū Ḥudhayfah b. ʿUtbah was an early convert to Islam from the Umayyah clan of Quraysh and an emigrant to Abyssinia; later killed at al-Yamāmah. Ibn al-Athīr, *Usd*, V, 170.
693. Ibn al-Athīr, *Kāmil* identifies him as Zayd b. al-Khaṭṭāb, who was the older half-brother of the future caliph ʿUmar b. al-Khaṭṭāb and one of the first Muhājirūn. Cf. Ibn al-Athīr, *Usd*, II, 228–29.

led the Muhājirūn, and leading the tribes was a man over each tribe. Khālid hurried to reach the men of the army at al-Buṭāḥ, and awaited the levy that was being raised in Medina; then, when it reached him, he went forth until he came to al-Yamāmah. Banū Ḥanīfah were at that time numerous.

According to al-Sarī—Shuʿayb—Sayf—Abū ʿAmr b. al-ʿAlāʾ—a man:[694] The number of Banū Ḥanīfah in those days were 40,000 fighting men in their villages and adjacent tracts. So Khālid marched until, when he drew near them, he made some cavalry bear down on ʿAqqah and al-Hudhayl and Wattād,[695] who had stayed [behind to take care of] the tribute that Musaylimah had given out to them so that they might take it to Sajāḥ. He [also] wrote to the tribes of Tamīm about (ʿAqqa, al-Hudhayl and Wattād), so that (the Tamīmīs) drove them away
[1931] and expelled them from the Arabian peninsula. Shuraḥbīl b. Ḥasanah hurried and did what ʿIkrimah had done; he tried to precede Khālid by fighting Musaylimah before Khālid could reach him; but he was struck by disaster, so he refrained from fighting. So when Khālid reached him he reproached him. Khālid only relied on those cavalry out of fear that (the enemy) would come upon him from behind while they were on the outskirts of al-Yamāmah.

According to al-Sarī—Shuʿayb—Sayf—ʿAbdallāh b. Saʿīd b. Thābit—someone who informed him—Jābir b. Fulān:[696] Abū Bakr reinforced Khālid with Salīṭ,[697] so that he would support him against anyone who might come upon him from behind. So (Salīṭ) went out; then, when he drew near Khālid, he found those cavalry who had gone repeatedly to[698] that country had scattered and fled. So he stayed close to them, as reinforcement. Abū Bakr used to say, "I do not appoint[699] the people of Badr;[700] [rather] I

694. Cf. Ibn al-Athīr, *Kāmil*, II, 361; Nuwayrī, 90.
695. Reading thus instead of Ziyād in the text, as *Emendanda*: cf. p. 88.
696. Cf. Ibn al-Athīr, *Kāmil*, II, 361; Nuwayrī, 90.
697. Nuwayrī, 90 identifies him as Salīt b. ʿAmr b. ʿAbd Shams al-ʿĀmirī al-Qurashī. According to Ibn al-Athīr, *Usd*, II, 344, Salīt b. ʿAmr, brother of Suhayl b. ʿAmr, was one of the first Muhājirūn, and the Prophet had sent him in A.H. 6 or 7 to Hawdhah b. ʿAlī and Thumāmah b. Uthāl al-Ḥanafī.
698. *Intābat*. Cf. Ibn Manẓūr, I, 775.
699. *Lā astaʿmilu*.
700. One wonders if the text here originally read "nomads" (*ahl al-wabar*); cf. Donner, *Early Islamic Conquests*, 264 and note 44.

leave them to meet God with the best of their works. For truly God delivers more and better [things] through them and through the upright among the nations (*umam*) than He achieves victory through them." [But in his caliphate] ʿUmar b. al-Khaṭṭāb used to say, "By God, I make them [truly] partners; and may I be imitated [in doing this]."

According to al-Sarī—Shuʿayb—Sayf—Ṭalḥah b. al-Aʿlam—ʿUbayd b. ʿUmayr—Uthāl al-Ḥanafī, who was with Thumāmah b. Uthāl: Musaylimah used to treat everyone gently and be amicable with him, and it did not occur to the people to know evil from him. With him was Nahār "al-Rajjāl" b. ʿUnfuwah;[701] [1932] he had emigrated to the Prophet, recited the Qurʾān, and become knowledgeable in religion; so (the Prophet) had sent him as a teacher to the people of al-Yamāmah, and to stir up discord against Musaylimah and strengthen the situation of the Muslims. He was more [a cause of] sedition[702] among the Banū Ḥanīfah than was Musaylimah; he swore to (Musaylimah) that he had heard Muḥammad say that he was made a partner with him. Consequently (people) believed (Musaylimah) and responded to [his call]. They ordered him to write to the Prophet, and promised him that they would support him against (the Prophet) if (the latter) did not accept. Now, Nahār al-Rajjāl b. ʿUnfuwah would not say anything, but only followed him in it, and ending up [doing what he suggested]. [Among Muslims] the call to prayer used to be made [in the name of] the Prophet, and it was declared in the call to prayer that Muḥammad was the Apostle of God. The one who used to make the call to prayer for (Musaylimah) was ʿAbdallāh b. al-Nawwāḥah, and the one who used to make the *iqāmah* for him was Ḥujayr b. ʿUmayr,[703] who [also] made the declaration [of prophethood] to him. [But] when Ḥujayr was about to make the declaration, Musaylimah would

701. Cf. Ibn al-Athīr, *Kāmil*, II, 361; Nuwayrī, 85–86; Caetani, 639. The name is uncertain; cf. p. 117, below, "al-Rahhāl." Diyārbakrī, II, 189 and 211 has "al-Dajjāl." Balansi, 58–59 and Ibn Ḥubaysh, 30 bottom have "al-Rajjāl"; but Ibn Ḥubaysh, 63 bottom, suggests that there were two brothers, named al-Rajjāl and al-Rahhāl or al-Dajjāl, both killed at al-Yamāmah.

702. *Fitnah*.

703. Possibly Ḥujayr b. ʿUmayr, poet of the Usayyid clan of Tamīm: cf. Caskel, II, 329.

say, "Speak clearly, Ḥujayr!" So he would raise his voice and exert himself in declaring himself and Nahār veracious, and in imputing error to those who had embraced Islām.[704] His dignity made a great impression upon them.

(Musaylimah)[705] erected a sacred enclave in al-Yamāmah, restricting it and imposing it upon the people so that it was respected. Now there were situated within that sacred enclave the villages of the Aḥālīf[706]—sections of Banū Usayyid[707] whose abode was in al-Yamāmah; so the place of their abode came to be in the sacred area. (The Aḥālīf are Sayḥān, Numārah, Nimr, and al-Ḥārith, sons of Jurwah).[708] So if (the Yamāmans) had abundant fruits, (Banū Usayyid) raided the orchards[709] of the
[1933] people of al-Yamāmah and defiled the sacred enclave. If (the Yamāmans) got wind that they had entered (the sacred enclave), they withdrew from (Usayyid) in fear; but if they were not aware of them, that was what (Usayyid) wanted.[710] That happened (to the Yamāmans) frequently, until they asked (Musaylimah) for help against them. At this (Musaylimah) said, "I am expecting something to come to me from heaven about you and them." Then he said, "By the darkest night, by the blackest wolf, by the mountain goat, Usayyid has not defiled a sacred thing."[711] So they replied, "Is it not forbidden to desecrate the holy enclave

---

704. The text about the calls to prayer is difficult; either we must assume several unmarked changes of subject, or assume that the sentence relates to Nahār's and Ḥujayr's change of sides. The former assumption has been adopted here. Cf. the version of the story in Ibn Ḥubaysh, 34 bottom and 35 middle: Ḥujayr would say the call to prayer in Muhammad's name, and then say "Musaylimah is..." and stop. So one of Musaylimah's followers would say, "Speak clearly, Ḥujayr!" Whereupon he would say, "Musaylimah is the Apostle of God." Ibn al-Athīr, *Kāmil*, condenses Ṭabarī's version, but also attempts to show Hujayr vacillating in his call to prayer.

705. Cf. Nuwayrī, 86–88 (as far as p. 111, below); Caetani, 639–41.

706. Or "confederates."

707. A section of Banū 'Amr b. Tamīm.

708. Of these only al-Ḥārith b. Jurwah conforms to the information in Caskel I, Table 83, where the other sons of Jurwah are Juwayy, Sahm, and Shurayf. Ibn Ḥazm, 20, has Jurdah b. Usayyid, and the sons are different again. Ibn Durayd, 130, has a Banū al-Ḥārith b. Juhwah. Kos has S.yjān. On Jurwah b. Usayyid, cf. Kister, "Mecca and Tamīm," 146.

709. *Thimār*, lit., "the fruits."

710. I.e., they could raid the oasis undisturbed.

711. Rhymed prose.

and to ruin property?" Then (Usayyid) went back to raiding and (the Yamāmans) went back to complaining, so he said, "I am expecting something [more] to come to me." Then he said, "By the obscure night, by the restless wolf, Usayyid never cut anything, neither succulent nor dry."[712] At this they replied, "Aren't date palms succulent? Yet they cut them off; aren't garden walls dry? Yet they tore them down." So he said (to the Yamāmans), "Go! Return, for you have no claim." Among the things that he recited to them about (Usayyid) was: "Banū Tamīm is a tribe of purity, an independent tribe with nothing reprehensible about them and [who pay] no tribute [to anyone]; let us be allies of protection with them in goodness as long as we live, let us protect them from every person, then when we die their fate will be to the Merciful One (*al-Raḥmān*)." And he [also] used to say, "By the goats, by their kinds, by the most remarkable of them—the black ones and their milk, by the black goat, by the white milk, indeed it is the wonder of pure milk, adulterating milk has been forbidden, so what you have, do not mix milk with dates." And he used to say,[713] "Oh frog, [1934]
daughter of a frog, croak what you croak, your upper part is in the water and your lower part in the mud, do not bar any person drinking, nor make the water turbid." And he used to say, "By the women who scatter seed at planting, by the women reaping at harvest, by the women who winnow wheat, by the women who grind flour, by the women who break bread, by the women who break bread into crumbs, by the women who gobble mouthfuls of grease and fat, you[714] have been favored over the people of the hair [tents],[715] nor shall the settled people[716] take pre-

712. Rhymed prose. Nuwayrī, 87 offers "powerful wolf" as a gloss.

713. Authors wishing to ridicule Musaylimah are fond of quoting this passage from his alleged revelations; cf. p. 133, below; Diyārbakrī, II, 158, 210 bottom; Ibn Ḥubaysh, 32, 34, 61; Ibn at-Athīr, *Kāmil*, II, 361–62; Balansī, 117–18; Nuwayrī, 87.

714. Here and subsequently the verbs and pronouns are masculine plural; i.e., the passage is addressed to Musaylimah's followers in general, not to women in particular.

715. I.e., over the nomads; *ahl al-wabar*.

716. *Ahl al-madar*.

cedence over you, defend your cultivated land,[717] shelter the one seeking favor, and oppose the oppressor."[718]

There[719] came to (Musaylimah) a woman of Banū Ḥanīfah called Umm al-Haytham, saying, "Our date palms are tall[720] and our wells are dried up; so pray to God for our water and our palms as Muḥammad prayed for the people of Hazmān." Whereupon (Musaylimah) said, "Oh Nahār, what is she talking about?" So (Nahār) explained, "The people of Hazmān came to Muḥammad complaining of how far away their water was; and their wells were dried up and their palms very tall. So he prayed for them, so that their wells overflowed and every date palm that was expired leaned over so that its branches, that is its top,
[1935] touched the ground so that it struck roots; then it was cut from below, so that it once again had blooming palm shoots growing upward."[721] (Musaylimah) said, "And what did he do with the wells?" (Nahār) replied, "He called for a bucket full of water and then prayed for them into it. Then he rinsed with a mouthful of it and spat it into it, whereupon they took it away to empty it into those wells; then they watered their palms with it, doing with the aged [palm] what I described to you,[722] whereas the other [palms] remained [as they were] until they aged."[723] So Musaylimah called for a bucket of water and prayed for them into it. Then he rinsed with some of it and spat [it] into it, so they took it and poured it into their wells, whereupon the waters of those wells sank into the ground and their palms became barren;[724] but that only became evident after his defeat.

Nahār said to (Musaylimah), "Ask[725] blessings upon the newborns of Banū Ḥanīfah," at which he said to him, "What is

---

717. *Rīf*; Ibn al-Athīr, *Kāmil*, has *rīq*, "saliva"; Abbott, citing al-Kīlānī, *al-Du'āt*, 56, suggests *rafīq*, "companion."

718. Perhaps "the adulterer": *al-bāghī*.

719. Cf. Ibn al-Athīr, *Kāmil*, II, 362; Caetani, 639.

720. I.e., and therefore hard to harvest.

721. The sentence is awkward; cf. Wellhausen, *Skizzen*, VI, 149.

722. Aged palm = *al-muntahā*; i.e., it was bent over to the ground so that the top struck roots, etc.

723. *Ilā intihā'i-hi*.

724. Cf. Diyārbakrī, II, 158.

725. Cf. Ibn Ḥubaysh, 33, l. 13ff; Ibn al-Athīr, *Kāmil*, II, 362; Nuwayrī, 88.

this 'asking for blessings'?" [Nahār] replied, "Whenever a newborn was born among the people of the Ḥijāz, they used to bring him to Muḥammad, whereupon he would rub his palate with a date pit[726] and anoint his head." No child was brought to Musaylimah for such treatment, however, but that he would gnash the teeth and speak defectively; but that [only] became apparent after his defeat.

They said, "Search out their walled gardens, as Muḥammad used to do, to pray in them." So he entered one of the gardens of al-Yamāmah and washed in it; whereupon Nahār said to the owner of the garden, "Why don't you water your garden with the wash water of al-Raḥmān until it was irrigated and drenched, [1936] just as Banū al-Mahriyyah, a family of Banū Ḥanīfah, did?" (Now a man of al-Mahrīyyah had come to the Prophet, and taken his wash water and carried it with him to al-Yamāmah and poured it into his well. Then he drew it out and used it for irrigation. His land [formerly] used to be parched, but [thereafter] it was quenched and satisfied, so that you would find only tall greenery.) So [the owner] did so, whereupon [his land] became once again wasteland, [and] its pasture would not grow.[727]

A man came to (Musaylimah) saying, "Pray to God for my land, for it is saline, just as Muhammad prayed for a man of Sulaym on behalf of his land." At this (Musaylimah) asked, "What is he talking about, oh Nahār?" So (Nahār) said,[728] "A man of Sulaym whose land exuded salty water came to (Muḥammad), so he prayed for him and gave him a bucket of water and spat into it for him; whereupon he poured it out into his well. Then he drew some, and it had become sweet and good." So (Musaylimah) did the same, whereupon the man left and did with the bucket just as the man of Sulaym had done; but his land drowned, its moisture did not dry up, and its fruit did not ripen.[729]

A woman fetched him to come to some date palms of hers, to

---

726. A ritual used to invoke blessings on newborns; cf. Avner Gil'adi, "Some Notes on *Tahnīk* in Medieval Islam."

727. Cf. Dìyārbakrī, II, 158.

728. Cf. Ibn Ḥubaysh, 33, ll. 22ff.

729. Cf. Balansi, 63.

pray for them on her behalf; then she cut off all their date clusters on the day of ʿAqrabāʾ.[730] They had learned [that Musaylimah was a fraud], and it had become clear to them, but the wretch overcame them.

According to al-Sarī—Shuʿayb—Sayf—Khulayd b. Zufar al-
[1937] Namarī—ʿUmayr b. Ṭalḥah al-Namarī:[731] His father came to al-Yamāmah and said, "Where is Musaylimah?" At this people said, "Careful! [Call him] the Apostle of God!" So he replied, "No, [not] until I have seen him." So when he came to him he said, "You are Musaylimah?" He replied, "Yes." He said, "Who comes to you?" (Musaylimah) replied, "Raḥmān." He asked, "Does [he come] in light or in darkness?" He replied, "In darkness." Whereupon he said, "I bear witness that you are a liar and that Muḥammad tells the truth; but a liar of Rabīʿah is dearer to us than a veracious person of Muḍar." So he was killed with (Musaylimah) at the battle of ʿAqrabāʾ.

According to al-Sarī—Shuʿayb—Sayf—al-Kalbī: the same [account], except that he said, "A liar of Rabīʿah is dearer to me than a veracious person of Muḍar."

According to al-Sarī—Shuʿayb—Sayf—Ṭalḥah b. al-Aʿlam—ʿUbayd b. ʿUmayr—a man of them:[732] When Musaylimah learned of Khālid's approach, he established his army at ʿAqrabāʾ. He called the people together to fight and people began to go out against him. Mujjāʿah b. Murārah[733] went out at the head of a raiding party, seeking blood revenge he had among Banū ʿĀmir and Banū Tamīm.[734] He feared that he might die, and hastened

730. The decisive battle between the Muslims and the followers of Musaylimah; cf. below, pp. 118ff.

731. Cf. Ibn al-Athīr, *Kāmil*, II, 362; Caetani, 641–42.

732. Cf. Ibn al-Athīr, *Kāmil*, II, 362; Diyārbakrī, II, 211; Balansī, 71–72; Ibn Ḥubaysh, 36 middle.

733. Caskel, II, 419 and Ibn al-Athīr, *Usd*, IV, 300–301 have him linked to different clans of the tribe of Ḥanīfah. He is said to have come to the Prophet, who gave him tracts of land (*aqtaʿa-hu*) in al-Yamāmah—perhaps actually only confirming his previous ownership; cf. Balādhurī, *Futūḥ*, 93. Since Khawlah bt. Jaʿfar (see text, below, and note 736) was of al-Dūl, it seems likely that Mujjāʿah was of this clan also. Nuwayrī, 90: Mujjāʿah b. Murārah b. Salmā.

734. Balansī, 71 and 117, and Ibn Ḥubaysh, 36 say Banū Numayr—possibly Numayr b. Usayyid, a clan of ʿAmr b. Tamīm. Cf. Caskel, II, 450.

to the task. As for their[735] blood revenge among Banū ʿĀmir, Khawlah bt. Jaʿfar[736] was among them, so they kept him from her; but he abducted her [anyway]. As for his blood revenge among Banū Tamīm, [it was about] camels they took from him. Khālid received Shuraḥbīl b. Ḥasanah and then sent him ahead, and ordered Khālid b. Fulān al-Makhzūmī[737] over the vanguard; and he put over the two wings Zayd[738] and Abū Ḥudhayfah. Musaylimah put over his two wings al-Muḥakkam[739] and al-Rajjāl; then Khālid marched, along with Shuraḥbīl, until, when [1938] he was a day's march[740] from the army of Musaylimah, he attacked Jubaylah Hujūʿ[741] with forty [men]—according to those who diminish [the numbers]—or sixty [men]—according to those who augment [them]. Lo and behold, there was Mujjāʿah and his companions; sleep had overcome them while they were returning from the Banū ʿĀmir country, having passed by them and extricated Khawlah bt. Jaʿfar, who was with them. They stopped for a brief rest this side of the lowest part of the pass[742]—the pass of al-Yamāmah; whereupon they found them asleep, with the leads of their horses in their hands under their cheeks, unaware that the army was near them. So they woke them up and said, "Who are you?" They said, "This is Mujjāʿah and these are Ḥanīfah." They replied, "And who are you, may God not give you life?" Then they tied them up and waited until Khālid b. al-Walīd came to them, and brought them to him. Khālid thought that they were coming to him to meet him and to take

---

735. Cairo: "his."

736. Khawlah bt. Jaʿfar, the "Ḥanifite woman" (*al-hanafiyya*), became the wife of ʿAlī b. Abī Ṭālib after the death of his first wife, the Prophet's daughter Fāṭimah. Cf. Ibn Saʿd, III/1, 11, l. 24.

737. Possibly Khālid b. al-ʿĀṣ b. Hishām b. al-Mughīrah, who later served as governor of Mecca for ʿUmar and ʿUthmān. Cf. Caskel, I, Table 23 and Ibn al-Athīr, *Usd*, II, 85–86.

738. Cairo index identifies him as Zayd b. Ḥārithah; but possibly Zayd b. al-Khaṭṭāb; cf. p. 105, above. Diyārbakrī, II, 211 has Zayd b. al-Khaṭṭāb, Abū Ḥudhayfah b. ʿUtbah b. Rabīʿah, with other individuals and posts listed being different from version in the text.

739. Al-Muḥakkam b. al-Ṭufayl, a Ḥanafī: cf. Caskel, II, 421; Wathīmah, 19/60.

740. Lit., "the march of a night."

741. Manuscript B, Cairo: "Jubaylah Hujūm."

742. *Thaniyyah*, "mountain pass" or possibly "mountain."

precautions against him in his business.[743] So he said, "When did you hear about us?" They replied. "We weren't aware of you; we were only returning from a [raid for] blood vengeance of ours among those around us of Banū ʿĀmir and Tamīm." (If they had been wise, they would have said, "We [wished to] receive you when we heard of you.") So (Khālid) ordered that they be killed. They were all ready to give their lives protecting Mujjāʿah b. Murārah; so they said, "If you wish good or evil with the people of al-Yamāmah tomorrow, spare this one and do not kill him." So Khālid killed them and kept Mujjāʿa imprisoned with himself, as a hostage.

According to al-Sarī—Shuʿayb—Sayf—Ṭalḥah—ʿIkrimah—Abū Hurayrah and ʿAbdallāh b. Saʿīd—Abū Saʿīd—Abū Huray-
[1939] rah: Abū Bakr had sent to al-Rajjāl to come to him and receive his charge; then he sent him to the people of al-Yamāmah, being of the opinion that he was being truthful when he responded to him. According to Abū Hurayrah:[744] I was sitting with the Prophet in a group of us among whom was al-Rajjāl b. ʿUnfuwah, when (the Prophet) said: "Truly there is among you a man whose molar tooth, [when he is] in the fire, will be larger than [Mount] Uḥud."[745] [Eventually] the group passed away, and only al-Rajjāl and I remained [alive], so I was afraid because of this until al-Rajjāl rebelled with Musaylimah and testified that he was a prophet.[746] The dissension[747] of al-Rajjāl was more serious than the dissension of Musaylimah. Abū Bakr[748] sent Khālid

---

743. I.e., he thought they were coming to conclude a truce with him.

744. Cf. Ibn Ḥajar, *Iṣābah*, s.v. "al-Rajjāl."

745. Cf. p. 118. The *ḥadīth* occurs in Ibn Mājah, *Sunan*, II, 1445 (no. 4322). The meaning is that the body of the unbeliever who has gone to hell will be enlarged so that it will suffer more; the molar tooth will be larger than Mt. Uhud, by Medina, and the rest of the body enlarged proportionately. Many variants are listed in Wensinck, *Concordance*, III, 508. I thank Dr. Iftikhar Zaman for clarifying this *ḥadīth* for me.

746. Although the text does not indicate as much, it seems likely that the account of Abū Hurayrah ends here, and that the following paragraph is transmitted not by him but by ʿIkrimah and Abū Saʿīd.

747. *Fitnah*. E. Landau-Tasseron notes that the word here is close to "its original meaning, i.e., an error caused by Satan's temptation" (personal communication). For a clearer sense of what the sentence means, see p. 120, below.

748. Cf. Diyārbakrī, II, 211 top.

against them, so he marched until, when he reached the pass of al-Yamāmah, he encountered Mujjā'ah b. Murārah, a chief of Banū Ḥanīfah, with a company from his tribe, intending to raid the Banū 'Āmir[749] in search of blood vengeance. They were twenty-three horsemen and cameleers. They had stopped for a brief rest; but Khālid took them by surprise at night in their camp, whereupon he asked, "Whence did you hear about us?" To which they replied, "We had not heard about you, we had only gone out to exact a blood vengeance due to us from the Banū 'Āmir." So Khālid ordered that their heads be cut off, sparing Mujjā'ah. Then he marched to al-Yamāmah, but Musaylimah and the Banū Ḥanīfah went out when they heard of [the approach of] Khālid and encamped at 'Aqrabā', whereupon he alighted there with them. Now ('Aqrabā') was on the outskirts of al-Yamāmah this side of the flocks[750] with the cultivated land of al-Yamāmah at their backs. Shuraḥbīl b. Musaylimah said,[751] "Oh Banū Ḥanīfah, today is the day of vigilance; today, if you are defeated, [your] womenfolk will be carried off on horseback as captives, and will be taken as wives without being demanded in marriage.[752] So fight for your reputations and defend your women." So they fought at 'Aqrabā'. The standard[753] of the [1940]
Muhājirūn was with Sālim,[754] the *mawlā* of Abū Ḥudhayfah, but (the Muhājirūn) said, "Do we have anything to fear from you for our own sake?"[755] At this he replied, "What a bad bearer of

749. Ibn Ḥubaysh, 36 middle: Banū Numayr.

750. *Dūn al-amwāl*; possibly we should translate *amwāl* as "property," but the meaning proposed would place 'Aqrabā' in a logical defensive situation—far enough out to defend the cultivated land (*rīf*), but still firmly within the territory controlled by the Banū Ḥanīfah and/or its pastoral allies.

751. Cf. Ibn al-Athīr, *Kāmil*, II, 362–63; p. 131, below; Nuwayrī, 91.

752. Reading *ghayr khatībāt* with Cairo, Ibn al-Athīr, *Kāmil*, Wellhausen, *Skizzen*, VI, 149, and *Emendanda*; possibly "without being honored" or "not esteemed" (*ghayr ḥaẓiyyāt*), as in text, Nuwayrī, 91, and Ibn Ḥubaysh, 45 bottom.

753. Cf. p. 105, above and p. 121, below; Ibn Ḥubaysh, 39 top, 40 bottom.

754. A Persian slave from Istakhr, he was one of the favored companions; he was later freed, then adopted, by Abū Ḥudhayfah. One of the most knowledgeable reciters of Qur'ān. Cf. Ibn al-Athīr, *Usd*, II, 245–47.

755. The *Muhājirūn* ask Sālim if he thinks he is able to defend their battle standard effectively, or whether he fears he may be incapable of doing it well enough, in which case it is a matter of concern to all of them.

the Qur'ān I would be, then!" The standard of the Anṣār was with Thābit b. Qays b. Shammās,[756] and the nomads (*al-ʿarab*) were [organized] according to their standards, and Mujjāʿah was prisoner with Umm Tamīm in her tent. The Muslims were dealt a setback, and people[757] from Banū Ḥanīfah entered upon Umm Tamīm and wanted to kill her, but Mujjāʿah stopped them, saying, "I am her protector; what an excellent, noble-born woman she is!" So he kept them from her. The Muslims returned, wheeling around against them so that Banū Ḥanīfah was put to flight. At this al-Muḥakkam b. al-Ṭufayl said,[758] "Oh Banū Ḥanīfah, enter the walled garden; meanwhile I will defend your backs." So he fought behind them for an hour; then God killed him (ʿAbd al-Raḥmān b. Abī Bakr[759] killed him). The unbelievers entered the garden; Waḥshī killed Musaylimah just as a man of the Anṣār was striking him, so he shared with him in it.

According to Ibn Ḥumayd—Salamah—Muḥammad b. Isḥāq: a similar account to this account of Sayf, except that he said:[760] When it became morning Khālid called for Mujjāʿah and those who had been taken with him, and said: "Oh Banū Ḥanīfah, what do you have to say?" They replied, "We say, 'A prophet from us and a prophet from you.' So[761] he put them to the sword, until when there remained of them [only] a man called Sāriyah b. ʿĀmir[762] and Mujjāʿah b. Murārah, Sāriyah said to (Khālid), "Oh man, if you wish good or evil in this town
[1941] tomorrow,[763] then spare this man," meaning Mujjāʿah. So Khālid ordered that he be bound in irons; then he sent him to

756. Cf. Balansī, 76.

757. Cf. p. 118, below, and parallels noted there; also Ibn Ḥubaysh, 42, and Ibn al-Athīr, *Kāmil*, II, 363, which have the story as here.

758. Cf. Balansī, 94; Ibn Ḥubaysh, 45 bottom, 47 top.

759. Son of the first caliph.

760. Cf. Ibn Ḥubaysh, 35 middle; Caetani, 642.

761. Cf. Balansī, 72.

762. Ibn Ḥubaysh: Sāriyah b. Maslamah b. ʿĀmir; Caskel, I, Table 156, II, 511: Sāriyah b. ʿAmr of Yarbūʿ clan of Ḥanīfah. According to Caskel, Sāriyah b. Maslamah was not son of ʿĀmir/ʿAmr, but of ʿUbayd b. Thaʿlabah b. Yarbuʿ . . . Ḥanīfah.

763. Ibn Ḥubaysh, 35: "if you wish good or evil with the people of al-Yamāmah."

his wife, Umm Tamīm, and said, "Look after him well." Then he proceeded until he encamped at al-Yamāmah upon a dune overlooking al-Yamāmah, and established his army in it. The people of al-Yamāmah came out with Musaylimah; he had sent ahead with his vanguard al-Raḥḥāl b. ʿUnfuwah b. Nahshal (According to al-Ṭabarī, Ibn Ḥumayd [spells the name] thus, with "ḥ," [not al-Rajjāl as other authorities have it]).[764] Al-Raḥḥāl was a man of Banū Ḥanīfah who had embraced Islām and recited the *Sūrah* of The Cow.[765] Then when he came to al-Yamāmah, he testified to Musaylimah that the Apostle of God had made him a partner in authority, so he was more significant in [sowing] discord[766] among the people of al-Yamāmah than was Musaylimah [himself]. The Muslims were asking about al-Raḥḥāl, fearing that he would dull their cause with the people of al-Yamāmah through his Islām. Then he met them with the first of the army squadrons. Khālid b. al-Walīd, while he was sitting upon his seat in the company of the notables of the people, the people being at their battle stations, had said while he looked at the flashing swords among Banū Ḥanīfah, "Oh company of Muslims, rejoice, for God has protected you from the cause of your enemy. The force has withdrawn, if God wills." At this al-Mujjāʿah looked while he was behind him bound in irons, and then said, "No, by God, but it is the Indian swords; they feared that they would shatter, so they exposed them to the sun so that they would be flexible for them";[767] and it was as he said. Then when they met the Muslims, the first who met them was al-Raḥḥāl b. ʿUnfuwah, whereupon God killed him.

According to Ibn Ḥumayd—Salamah—Muḥammad b. Isḥāq—a chief of Banū Ḥanīfah—Abū Hurayrah: The Apostle of God said one day while Abū Hurayrah and Raḥḥāl b. ʿUnfuwah [1942]

764. On the name cf. p. 107, above.

765. The second, and longest, of the chapters or *sūrah*s of the Qurʾān; presumably this means that he could recite it from memory.

766. *Fitnah*.

767. Cf. Balansī, 77, Diyārbakrī, II, 211 bottom: "so that they [we] could meet them." Ibn Ḥubaysh, 39: "to warm up their blades" (*li-taskhuna mutūna-hum*), for the morning was cold. Cf. Ibn Ḥubaysh, 47 bottom; Balādhurī, *Futūḥ*, 88.

were in a group meeting with him, "Oh company, the molar tooth of one of you in hellfire on the Day of Judgment will be larger than Uḥud."[768] Abū Hurayrah said, "The group passed away and only Raḥḥāl b. ʿUnfuwah and I survived, whereupon I remained frightened because of this until I heard of the rebellion of Raḥḥāl, at which I felt secure and knew that what the Apostle of God had said was true." Then the people met [in battle],[769] and no war of the Arabs had ever met them like [this] war;[770] so the people fought intensely until the Muslims were put to flight and Banū Ḥanīfah reached Mujjāʿah and Khālid, so that Khālid left his tent. The people[771] entered the tent in which Mujjāʿah was with Umm Tamīm, and a man attacked her with a sword; whereupon Mujjāʿah said, "Stop! I am her protector, and what an excellent, noble-born woman she is! Attack the men!" So they reduced the tent to tatters with swords. Then the Muslims called to one another; such that Thābit b. Qays said, "How bad is that to which you have made yourselves accustomed,[772] oh company of Muslims! Oh God, I have nothing to do with what these ones worship,"[773] (meaning the people of al-Yamāmah), "and I have nothing to do with what these ones do" (meaning the Muslims). Then he waded into battle with his sword until he was killed. Zayd b. al-Khaṭṭāb, when the people became removed from their saddles, said, "There is no retreating after al-Raḥḥāl." Then he fought until he was killed. Then al-Barāʾ b. Mālik,[774] brother of Anas

768. Cf. p. 114, above.

769. Cf. Ibn al-Athīr, *Kāmil*, II, 363; Diyārbakrī, II, 212.

770. I.e., they had never seen the Arabs (i.e., nomads) fighting this intensely before.

771. Cf. Balansī, 78, 79; Ibn Ḥubaysh, 39–40, Nuwayrī, 91–92.

772. Ibn al-Athīr, *Kāmil*, II, 363: *biʾsa mā ʿawwadtum anfusa-kum*; Diyārbakrī, II, 212, Balansī, 79: *biʾsa mā ʿawwadtum anfusa-kum al-farār*; Ibn Ḥubaysh, 45 bottom: *biʾsa mā ʿawwadtum al-aʿrāb*, said by ʿIyād b. Bishr; Nuwayrī, 92, has *biʾsa mā daʿawtum anfusakum ilayhi*, which means "how bad is that to which you have summoned yourselves."

773. Ibn al-Athīr, *Kāmil*, II, 363: "I have nothing to do with what these ones do."

774. Cf. Diyārbakrī, II, 215–16; Ibn al-Athīr, *Kāmil*, II, 364; Balansī, 90–91; Nuwayrī, 92–93.

b. Mālik,[775] stood up; now whenever he faced battle, he used to be overcome by tremors so that men [had to] sit upon him; then he would shake violently beneath them until he urinated in his trousers. When he urinated he would be aroused as a lion is aroused. Now when he saw what the people had done, he was overcome in this manner so that the men sat upon him; then, after he had urinated, he sprang up saying, "Where [are they], oh company of Muslims? I am Barā' b. Mālik, come on with me!" A group of the rear guard of the army returned and fought the enemy until God killed them and they reached Muḥakkam al-Yamāmah, who was Muḥakkam b. al-Ṭufayl. When the fighting reached him, (Muḥakkam) said,[776] "Oh company of Banū Ḥanīfah, now the noble-born women will be carried off unwillingly behind [the riders as captives], and will be taken as wives without being requested in marriage.[777] So display whatever nobility you have." Then he fought intensely; 'Abd al-Raḥmān b. Abī Bakr al-Ṣiddīq shot him with an arrow, hitting him in his throat and killing him. [1943]

Then[778] the Muslims advanced until they made them take refuge in the walled garden, the "garden of death," in which was the enemy of God, Musaylimah the liar. So al-Barā' said, "Oh company of Muslims, throw me onto them in the garden," but the people told Barā' that they would not do so. Whereupon he said, "By God, you surely shall cast me upon them in it!" So he was hoisted up until, when he overlooked the garden from the wall, he leapt down, fighting them from the gate of the garden in order to open it for the Muslims. The Muslims entered upon them in [the garden] and they fought until God killed Musaylimah the enemy of God. Waḥshī,[779] *mawlā* of Jubayr b.

---

775. Ibn al-Athīr, *Kāmil*, has "Asad b. Mālik." Anas b. Mālik, an Anṣārī and early companion of the Prophet, was considered an important source of prophetic traditions: cf. Ibn al-Athīr, *Usd*, I, 127–29; *EI*², s.v. "Anas b. Mālik," (A. J. Wensinck and J. Robson).

776. Cf. Diyārbakrī, II, 216; Balansī, 93–94.

777. Cf. p. 115, above.

778. Cf. Ibn al-Athīr, *Kāmil*, II, 364; Ibn Ḥubaysh, 46 top, 47; cf. references at p. 125, below.

779. Cf. Diyārbakrī, II, 216; Balansī, 95.

Muṭʿim,[780] and a man of the Anṣār were partners in killing him, both of them striking him; as for Waḥshī, he thrust his javelin against him, whereas the Anṣārī struck him with his sword. Waḥshī used to say, "Your Lord knows which of us killed him."

According to Ibn Ḥumayd—Salamah—Muḥammad b. Isḥāq—
[1944] ʿAbdallāh b. al-Faḍl b. al-ʿAbbās b. Rabīʿah—Sulaymān b. Yasār —ʿAbdallāh b. ʿUmar:[781] I heard a man crying out that day, saying, "The black slave killed him."

According to al-Sarī—Shuʿayb—Sayf—Ṭalḥah—ʿUbayd b. ʿUmayr: Al-Rajjāl was opposite Zayd b. al-Khaṭṭāb, so when their two battle lines drew near, Zayd said, "Oh Rajjāl, God! God! For by God, you have abandoned the faith. Truly what I summon you to is nobler for you and greater for your present life." But he refused; so the two drew [their swords]. Then al-Rajjāl and the zealous supporters of Musaylimah's cause among the Banū Ḥanīfah were killed; but [the enemy] encouraged one another and each group attacked [those] in its vicinity, so that the Muslims retreated as far as their camp. Then they fell upon them, cutting the tent ropes, slashing them, and busying themselves with the army. They struggled with Mujjāʿah, intending [to seize] Umm Tamīm, but he protected her, saying, "How excellent is the mistress of the tent!"

Zayd and Khālid and Abū Ḥudhayfah urged each other on and the people backed them up with words.[782] Now it was a day of south wind with lots of dust, so Zayd said, "No, by God, I will not speak today, until either we defeat them or I meet God so that I may tell him of my devotion.[783] Grit your teeth, oh

780. Wahshī b. Ḥarb, an Abyssinian slave, was one of Mecca's blacks; he was famed for having killed the Prophet's uncle Ḥamzah at the battle of Uhud. Cf. Ibn al-Athīr, *Usd*, V, 83–84. Jubayr b. Mutʿim, of the clan of Nawfal of Quraysh, was a diplomat famed for his forbearance and firm, calm manner (*hilm*); he embraced Islam relatively late, at the conquest of Mecca or just before. Cf. Ibn al-Athīr, *Usd*, I, 271–72.

781. Cf. Ibn al-Athīr, *Kāmil*, II, 364–65; Diyārbakrī, II, 216; Nuwayrī, 95.

782. Lit., "the people spoke," which is hardly clear. Wellhausen, *Skizzen*, VI, 149 considered "the people spoke" to be a "fairly unnecessary preparation" for Zayd's statement, "I will not speak today."

783. Lit., "tell Him of my evidence (*ḥujjatī*)," i.e., make evident my devotion to Him through my martyrdom.

people, and strike your enemy and proceed straight ahead." So they did that, driving them back to their ranks until they made retreat farther than they had advanced from their army [in the first place].[784] Zayd was killed. Thābit spoke, saying, "Oh company of the Muslims, you are the party of God, and they are the parties of Satan; glory is to God and to His Apostle and to His parties. Advise me as I advise you." Then he began striking [1945]
among them [with the whip] so that he drove them on. Abū Ḥudhayfah said, "Oh people of the Qur'ān, ornament the Qur'ān with [your] deeds." Then he drove them on until he penetrated them. [Then] he was struck down. Khālid b. al-Walīd attacked, saying to his bodyguards, "Let no one approach me from behind," until [when] he was opposite Musaylimah, he sought his opportunity and lay in wait for Musaylimah.

According to al-Sarī—Shuʿayb—Sayf—Mubashshir b. al-Fuḍayl—Sālim b. ʿAbdallāh: When Sālim was given the battle standard on that day, he said, "How acquainted I am with the reason why you gave it to me! You said a bearer of the Qur'ān,[785] and [that] he should stand fast just as the bearer of it before him stood fast, unto death." They replied, "Yes." Then they said, "Look how you should [do it]." At this he said, "What a bad bearer of the Qur'ān I would be if I did not stand fast!" The standard bearer before him had been ʿAbdallāh b. Ḥafṣ b. Ghānim.[786]

According to ʿAbdallāh b. Saʿīd b. Thābit and Ibn Isḥāq: When Mujjāʿah said to the Banū Ḥanīfah, "Attack the men,"[787] and after a group of the Muslims had incited one another to fight, (Banū Ḥanīfah) affected a show of generosity and all the Muslims did likewise. Some of the companions of the the Apostle of God made addresses. Zayd b. al-Khaṭṭāb said, "By God, I shall not speak until I am victorious or until I am killed.

784. The Arabic phrase is awkward, but I believe it means this. Cf. Ibn al-Athīr, *Kāmil*, II, 363, ll. 15–16.

785. I.e., one who had memorized and could recite all or a large part of the holy text.

786. Cf. pp. 105 and 115–16, above, and Balansī, 79. According to Balansī the standard bearer had been Zayd b. al-Khaṭṭāb.

787. See the earlier account in which this episode occurs, pp. 117–18, above.

Do as I do!" Then he attacked, and his companions attacked [also]. Thābit b. Qays said, "How bad is that to which you have accustomed yourselves, oh company of Muslims! Now get away from me,[788] so that I can show you [how to] fight!" Zayd b. al-Khaṭṭāb was killed.

According to al-Sarī—Shuʿayb—Sayf—Mubashshir—Sālim:[789]
[1946] When ʿAbdallāh b. ʿUmar returned [to ʿUmar], ʿUmar said, "Why weren't you killed before Zayd?[790] Zayd has died and you are still alive." Whereupon he replied, "I coveted that that should come to pass, but my soul drew back, whereas God honored him with martyrdom."

According to Sahl, [ʿUmar] said: "What brought you [back] even though Zayd was killed? Why didn't you hide your face from me?" [ʿAbdallāh b. ʿUmar] said, "He asked God for martyrdom, and it was given to him. I strove that it should be sent to me, but I was not granted it."

According to al-Sarī—Shuʿayb—Sayf—Ṭalḥah b. al-ʾAʿlam—ʿUbayd b. ʿUmayr:[791] The *Muhājirūn* and the *Anṣār* accused the people of the desert of cowardice, and the people of the desert accused them of cowardice, saying to one another, "Organize yourselves separately[792] so that we may shun those who flee on the day [of battle], and may know on the day [of battle] from where we are approached [by the enemy]."[793] So they did that. The settled people said to the people of the desert, "We know more about fighting settled people than you do." Whereupon the people of the desert replied, "Settled people do not excel at fighting, and do not know what war is; so you will see, when you organize us separately, from where weakness comes." So they organized separately. No day [of battle] more intense or

788. *Hākadhā ʿannī.*

789. Cf. Ibn al-Athīr, *Kāmil,* II, 365–66.

790. Zayd was ʿUmar's brother; ʿAbdallāh, ʿUmar's son.

791. Cf. Ibn al-Athīr, *Kāmil,* II, 363–64.

792. Here and in the following passages, *imtāza,* lit., "distinguish, discriminate." The subsequent passages make it clear that the idea was to place members of particular groups together, so that the relative performance of each group in battle would be more readily apparent.

793. I.e., so that we may know who has failed to hold the enemy confronting him.

greater in casualties was ever seen than that day. It was not known which of the two groups inflicted heavier casualties [on the enemy], but the wounded were more numerous among the *Muhājirūn* and the *Anṣār*[794] than they were among the people of the desert, and those who survived were always in distress.[795] ʿAbd al-Raḥmān b. Abū Bakr[796] shot al-Muḥakkam with an arrow, killing him while he was delivering a speech; whereupon he cut his throat. Zayd b. al-Khaṭṭāb killed al-Rajjāl b. ʿUnfuwah. [1947]

According to al-Sarī—Shuʿayb—Sayf—al-Ḍaḥḥāk b. Yarbūʿ—his father—a man of Banū Suḥaym[797] who witnessed [the battle] with Khālid:[798] The advantage on that day was sometimes against the Muslims and sometimes against the unbelievers. When the fighting became intense, Khālid said, "Oh people, organize separately so that we may know the valor of each clan and know from where we are approached [by the enemy]." So the people of the settlements and of the desert organized themselves separately; the tribes of the desert people and of the settled people organized themselves separately, the descendants of each ancestor standing behind their banner to fight together. On that day the people of the desert said, "Now the killing will grow intense among the weaker flock";[799] then the killing did become intense among the people of the settlements. Musaylimah stood firm, and he was in the eye of the storm;[800] at which Khālid realized that it would not abate except through the death of Musaylimah, as long as the Banū Ḥanīfah took no heed of the death of those who had been killed among them. Thereupon Khālid came out against the enemy until, when he was opposite the [enemy] line, he put out a challenge for single combat and raised his lineage, saying, "I am the son of al-Walīd

794. Ibn al-Athīr, *Kāmil*, II, 364: among the *Muhājirūn*, *Anṣār*, and the villagers.

795. I.e., they were in the most intense fighting.

796. Cf. Ibn al-Athīr, *Kāmil*, II, 365.

797. Probably Suhaym b. Murrah, a branch of Ḥanīfah: Caskel, II, 516.

798. Cf. preceding account and Ibn al-Athīr, *Kāmil*, II, 363–63; Nuwayrī, 92.

799. Reading *ajzaʿ*, "flock," with Wellhausen, *Skizzen*, VI, 149, *Emendanda*, and Cairo, for the text's *ajdhaʿ*.

800. Lit., "their mill turned around him."

the experienced,[801] I am the son of 'Āmir and Zayd," and he shouted their battle slogan of that day. Their slogan that day was "Oh Muḥammad!" So he killed everyone who came out against him in single combat. All the while he was reciting,

I am the son of chiefs, and my sword is the Vehement,
all the greater when rage overcomes you.

Whatever came out in single combat against him he defeated. The Muslims fought intensely and effectively.[802] Then, when Khālid drew near to Musaylimah, he called out [to him]. Now
[1948] the Apostle of God had said, "With Musaylimah is a devil that he does not disobey, and whenever (the devil) comes to him, he foams [at the mouth] such that his cheeks are two gobs of froth; (Musaylimah) never forms the intention of doing any good thing, but (this devil) diverts him from it. So when you should see this opening[803] with him, seize the opportunity!"[804] So when Khālid drew near to (Musaylimah), he was searching for that. He saw [Musaylimah] standing fast with the [battle] swirling around him, and he knew that it would not cease unless (Musaylimah) was killed. So he called to Musaylimah, searching for his opening, upon which (Musaylimah) answered him. Then (Khālid) showed Musaylimah some things he liked, saying, "If we agree to half, then which half would you give us?"[805] Now when he was considering his answer, he had turned his face away in seeking advice, but his devil for bade him to accept; so he turned his face away [another] time because of that.[806] Khālid followed him closely on his mount to overtake him, so that he retreated and [his followers] yielded. Then Khālid incited the army, saying, "Here you are! Don't let them go!" They rode closely after them, and routed them. As Musaylimah stood up after the people had fled from him, some people said,[807] "Where

801. *Al-'awd,* "the aged"; cf. Ibn Manẓūr, III, 321.
802. Lit., "The mill of the Muslims turned, and ground."
803. *'Awrah,* lit., "opening in the defenses of an enemy," or possibly, "shameful thing."
804. Lit., "do not forgive him his error!"
805. A reference to Musaylimah's alleged offer to divide the earth with the Prophet; cf. p. 133, below and p. 93, above.
806. The text of this sentence is awkward.
807. Cf. Diyārbakrī, II, 216; Balansī, 94.

is what you used to promise us?" To which he replied, "Fight for your own reputations!"

Al-Muḥakkam[808] cried, "Oh Banū Ḥanīfah, the garden! the garden!" Now Waḥshī was coming upon Musaylimah while he was foaming [at the mouth], barely able to stand and unthinking from the fit [that had overtaken him], so he bared his lance on him and killed him. The people stormed upon them [in] the "garden of death" from its walls and gates, so that 10,000 fighting men[809] were killed in the battle and the "garden of death."

According to al-Sarī—Shuʿayb—Sayf—Hārūn and Ṭalḥah—ʿAmr b. Shuʿayb and Ibn Isḥāq: After they had organized themselves separately and had stood fast and Banū Ḥanīfah had retreated, the Muslims pursued them, killing them until they got them to the "garden of death." Then they differed [in opinion] regarding the killing of Musaylimah there; some say that he was killed in it, whereupon (the Banū Ḥanīfah) entered it and (the Muslims) locked them in it and surrounded them. Al-Barā' b. Mālik[810] screamed, "Oh company of Muslims, lift me onto the wall so that you may throw me onto them." So [1949] they did that, with the result that, when they placed him on the wall, he was thunderstruck at what he saw, and called out, "Lower me [back] down." Then he said, "Lift me up," so they did that again. Then out of fear he said, "Ugh to this!" and asked to be lifted up again. Whereupon when they placed him upon the wall, he leapt upon them to fight them by the gate, until he had opened it for the Muslims, who were by the gate on the outside. At this (the Muslims) entered [the garden]; then he locked the gate upon them and threw the key over the wall. So they fought more bitterly than has ever been seen. Those of them who were in the garden perished after Musaylimah had been killed. Banū Ḥanīfah had said to him,[811] "Where is what you used to promise us?" To which he had replied, "Fight for your own reputations!"

---

808. Cf. Ibn al-Athīr, *Kāmil*, II, 364; Nuwayrī, 92.

809. That is, on the Muslim side.

810. Cf. p. 119, above; Diyārbakrī, II, 214–15, who attributes this episode to Abū Dajānah; Balansī, 87, another version; Ibn Ḥubaysh, 45, another version; Ibn Ḥubaysh, 46.

811. Cf. p. 125, above.

According to al-Sarī—Shuʿayb—Sayf—Hārūn and Ṭalḥah and Ibn Isḥāq: When someone cried out that the black slave had killed Musaylimah, Khālid went out with Mujjāʿah shackled in irons to show him Musaylimah and the banners of his army. He came across al-Rajjāl and said, "This is al-Rajjāl."

According to Ibn Ḥumayd—Salamah—Ibn Isḥāq:[812] When the Muslims had finished with Musaylimah, Khālid was approached and informed [of this], so he went out, taking Mujjāʿah in irons with him in order to show him Musaylimah. Then he began to show him the slain until he passed Muḥakkam b. al-Ṭufayl—he was a corpulent, comely man—whereupon Khālid said, "This is your companion." He replied, "No, by God, this one is better than he and more noble; this is Muḥakkam al-Yamāmah."

Then[813] Khālid continued showing him the slain until he entered the garden, upon which he rummaged through the bodies for him; then lo, there was a small, yellowish, flat-nosed man, whereupon Mujjāʿah said, "This is your companion, whom you have finished off." So Khālid said to Mujjāʿah, "This is your companion, who did with you what he did." He replied, "[So] it was, oh Khālid; but, by God,[814] only the most expeditious of the people came [against] you; the majority of the
[1950] people are [still] in the fortresses." At this Khālid said, "Woe to you, what are you saying?" He replied, "By God, it is the truth; so come on, let me conclude a treaty with you in exchange for [the safety of] my tribe."

According to al-Sarī—Shu'ayb—Sayf—al-Ḍaḥḥāk—his father: There was a man of the Banū ʿĀmir b. Ḥanīfah, named al-Aghlab b. ʿĀmir b. Ḥanīfah, who had the thickest neck of anyone of his time. When the polytheists had been defeated on that day and the Muslims surrounded them, he pretended he was dead. Then, when the Muslims were inspecting the slain, a man of the *Anṣār* named Abū Baṣīrah and some people

812. Cf. Ibn al-Athīr, *Kāmil*, II, 365; Diyārbakrī, II, 217 bottom; Balansī, 104; Nuwayrī, 93.

813. Cf. Ibn al-Athīr, *Kāmil*, II, 365; Diyārbakrī, II, 218; Ibn Ḥubaysh, 54–55; Balādhurī, *Futūḥ*, 104; Nuwayrī, 93–94.

814. Cf. Ibn al-Athīr, *Kāmil*, II, 365; Ibn Ḥubaysh, 47, 55; Balādhurī, *Futūḥ*, 90; Balansī, 104–5.

along with him came upon [al-Aghlab]. When they saw him lying among the slain, taking him for dead, they said, "Oh Abū Baṣīrah, you are always claiming that your sword is exceedingly sharp; so cut the head off this dead al-Aghlab. If you cut it off, everything we have learned about your sword will be true." So he unsheathed it and then strode toward him. Now they were sure he was dead, but when (Abū Baṣīrah) drew near him, (al-Aghlab) sprang up to run away from him. Abū Baṣīrah followed him and began saying, "I am Abū Baṣīrah al-Anṣārī!"[815] Al-Aghlab began to run quickly and the distance between them only increased; every time Abū Baṣīrah said that, al-Aghlab would say, "What do you think of the running of your brother the unbeliever?" until he escaped.[816]

According to al-Sarī—Shuʿayb—Sayf—Sahl b. Yūsuf—al-Qāsim b. Muḥammad:[817] When Khālid had finished with Musaylimah and the army, ʿAbdallāh b. ʿUmar and ʿAbd al-Raḥmān b. Abī Bakr said to him, "March with us and the army to encamp against the fortresses." But he replied, "Let me [first] deploy the cavalry in order to catch those who were not in the fortresses; then I will see [what] my opinion [is]." Thereupon he deployed the cavalry, so that they rounded up what they found of livestock[818] and women and children, and attached this[819] to the army. He ordered a march to encamp against the [1951]
fortresses, so Mujjāʿah said to him,[820] "By God, only the most expeditious of the people came [against] you, and the fortresses are full of men. So come on, make a truce with my following." So he made a truce with him including everything short of [their] persons. Then he said, "I will go out to them to ask their advice, and we will look into this matter; then I will return to you." So Mujjāʿah entered the fortresses, in which were

---

815. The pre-Islamic Arabs customarily identified themselves to their enemies in the course of battle, often as a form of boasting: "I am so-and-so, take this blow!" (E. Landau-Tasseron, personal communication).

816. Cf. Ibn Durayd, *Al-Ishtiqāq*, 184, for a slightly different version and a *Muhājir* as the hero.

817. Cf. Diyārbakrī, II, 218.

818. *māl*; perhaps, "property."

819. Cf. Manuscript B and Nuwayrī, 94: "attached them."

820. Cf. p. 126, above, and references there.

nothing but women and children and worn-out elders and weak men. So he dressed the women in iron breastplates and ordered them to let down their hair[821] and to make themselves visible from the tops of the fortresses until he should return to them. Then he went back and came to Khālid, saying, "They have refused to permit what I arranged. Some of them had a commanding view of you, in opposing me.[822] They [will] have nothing to do with me." At this, Khālid looked at the peaks of the fortresses, which had become black.[823] Now the war had worn the Muslims down, and the encounter had become drawn out, and they yearned to return in triumph, and did not know what might happen if there were in [the fortresses] men and fighting. There had been killed on that day 360 of the *Muhājirūn* and *Anṣār* of the people of the chief city of Medina.

According to Sahl:[824] Of the *Muhājirūn* not of the people of Medina, and of the children of companions [of the Prophet],[825] 300 of the former and 300 of the latter [were killed, totaling] 600 or more. Thābit b. Qays was killed on that day. A man of the polytheists killed him; his foot was cut off, so his killer threw it
[1952] and killed him.[826] Of Banū Ḥanīfah were killed in the plain at ʿAqrabāʾ 7,000, and 7,000 in the "garden of death," and in pursuit something like that [number]. Ḍirār b. al-Azwar said regarding the battle day of al-Yamāmah:[827]

---

821. Presumably young men (e.g., warriors) wore their hair long and flowing, whereas women and older men had their hair bound up and covered.

822. Mujjāʿah suggests that the people in the fortress could see the strength of Khālid's forces, and implies that they rejected Khālid's offer because they were not intimidated by his forces.

823. I.e., with people.

824. The text of the following paragraph—especially the numbers—is confused. Cf. Ibn al-Athīr, *Kāmil*, II, 365: "360 of *Muhājirūn* and *Ansār* of the people of Medina had been killed, and of the *Muhājirūn* of places other than Medina, [another] 360."

825. *al-tābiʿūn bi-ihsān*, lit., "those who follow in good works," refers to the offspring of the *Muhājirūn*, *Ansār*, and other "companions of the Prophet" (*sahāba*).

826. Cairo and Ibn al-Athīr, *Kāmil*, has "his foot was cut off, so Thābit took it and beat (the attacker) with it until he killed him."

827. Cf. Ibn Ḥubaysh, 65, which has verses 1, 3, 4, and 5, as well as four additional verses.

If the south wind were asked about us, it would tell;
in the evening 'Aqrabā' and Malham[828] flowed.
And it flowed in the side branches of the watercourse, so that its rocks
dribbled in it from the people with blood.
In the evening, the spear is not satisfied with its place,
nor the arrows, except the bone-cleaving Mashrafī[829] sword.
So if you seek unbelievers free of blame,
[oh] south wind, indeed I am a follower of the faith, a Muslim.
I strive[830] [in God's way], because striving (*jihād*) is [itself] booty, and God knows best the man who strives.

According to Ibn Ḥumayd—Salamah—Ibn Isḥāq:[831] Mujjā'ah said what he did to Khālid because he had told him, 'Come on, so that I conclude a treaty with you in exchange for [the safety of] my tribe," [saying this] to a man whom the war had exhausted, and with whom many leaders of the people had been struck down. He had weakened, and yearned for rest and truce. So he said, "Come on, so that I may reconcile you," and then made a truce with (Khālid) on condition [of paying] gold, silver, suits of mail, and half the captives. Then he said, "I shall go to the tribe to present them what I have arranged." So he [1953]
went out to them and said to the women, "Put on the armor and then make yourselves visible from atop the fortresses." So they did that; then he returned to Khālid. Now Khālid thought that what he had seen on the fortresses, wearing armor, were men, so when (Mujjā'ah) got to Khālid he said, "They rejected [the conditions] upon which I made a truce with you. But if you wish, I will arrange something and then entreat the tribe [to accept it]." (Khālid) said, "What is it?" He replied, "That you should take from me one quarter of the captives, and let a

828. A fortified village in a date-palm oasis, ca. 75 km northwest of Ḥajr: Thilo, s.v.; Yāqūt, s.v.; *TAVO* B VII 1. Ibn Ḥubaysh reads "in the evening 'Aqrabā' flowed with blood."

829. So called because they were made in the highlands (*mashārif*) of Syria or Yemen. Cf. Lane, *Arabic-English Lexicon*, IV, 1537 and 1539.

830. Ibn Ḥubaysh: we strive.

831. Cf. Ibn al-Athīr, *Kāmil*, II, 365; Diyārbakrī, II, 218; Nuwayrī, 94.

quarter of them go."[832] Khālid said, "Done," and (Mujjāʿah) said, "Agreed, then." Subsequently, after the two of them were finished, the fortresses were opened and lo! there was no one in them but women and children. Whereupon Khālid said to Mujjāʿah, "Woe to you! You deceived me!" He replied, "[They were] my own kinsmen, I had to do what I did."

According to al-Sarī—Shuʿayb—Sayf—Sahl b. Yūsuf:[833] The second [thing] Mujjāʿah said on that day [was], "If you wish to accept from me half the captives and [all] the gold and silver and suits of mail and the horses, I shall entreat [my tribe to accept], and will draw up a truce between me and you." So Khālid did that, making an agreement with him on condition of [payment of] the gold, silver, suits of mail, and horses, and of half the captives, and of a garden of Khālid's choice in every settlement and of a farm of Khālid's choice; whereupon they concluded the truce mutually on those terms. Then he released him and said, "You[834] have three [days] to choose: by God, if you do not complete and accept I shall attack you; then I shall never accept from you any terms except death." So Mujjāʿah came to them and said, "Accept for now." But[835] Salamah b. 'Umayr al-Ḥanafī replied, "No, by God, we shall not accept. We shall send to
[1954] people of settlements and to slaves [for reinforcement], and we shall fight and not make terms with Khālid. For the fortresses are strong and the food plentiful, and winter has come." So Mujjāʿah said, "You are an unlucky man, and you are kidding yourself; [in fact] I deceived the people[836] so that they would agree with me in the truce. Does there remain among you anyone worth anything or who has any [power of] resistance [left]? I went ahead of you [in making the truce] only [to act] before what Shuraḥbīl b. Musaylimah said should befall you."[837]

So Mujjāʿah went out as the seventh of seven [men] until he came to Khālid and said, after he had affirmed what they had

832. I.e., an additional quarter?

833. Cf. Ibn Ḥubaysh, 47, 55; Nuwayrī, 94–95.

834. The pronoun is plural, indicating that Khālid is addressing these words to Mujjāʿah's tribe, not to Mujjāʿah himself.

835. Cf. Ibn Ḥubaysh, 55–56; Balansī, 107.

836. I.e., the Muslims.

837. Cf. p. 115, above, for Shuraḥbīl's warning.

approved, "Write your document." So he wrote: "This is what Khālid b. al-Walīd made a truce with Mujjā'ah b. Murārah and Salamah b. 'Umayr and So-and-so and So-and-so about: he bound them to [payment of] gold, silver, half the captives, suits of mail, horses, a garden in every village, and a farm on condition that they embrace Islam.[838] Then you will be secure in God's safety; you will have the protection of Khālid b. al-Walīd and the protection of Abū Bakr, successor of the Apostle of God, and the protections of the Muslims in good faith."

According to al-Sarī—Shu'ayb—Sayf—Ṭalḥah—'Ikrimah—Ibn Hurayrah: When Khālid made a truce with Mujjā'ah, he did so on [condition of payment of] gold, silver, coats of mail, and every garden that pleased us in every district, and half of those enslaved;[839] but they rejected that, so Khālid said, "You have three days to decide." Then Salamah b. 'Umayr said, "Oh Banū Ḥanīfah, fight for your reputations and do not make a truce on any terms, for the fortress is strong, the food plentiful, and winter has come." To this Mujjā'ah replied, "Oh Banū Ḥanīfah, obey me and defy Salamah—for he is an unlucky man—before [the fate] of which Shuraḥbīl b. Musaylimah spoke befalls [1955] you, before the women are carried off against their will on the backs of horses and are taken to wife without being demanded in marriage."[840] So they obeyed him and renounced Salamah, and accepted his decision.

Now[841] Abū Bakr had sent Salamah b. Salāmah b. Waqsh[842] with a letter to Khālid, ordering him, if God had given him victory, to execute everyone of Banū Ḥanīfah over who[se face] a razor had passed. So he arrived, but found that [Khālid] had concluded a truce with them. Then Khālid observed [the truce] for them and kept to [the terms] that were in it. Banū Ḥanīfah were made to congregate before Khālid for the oath of allegiance and to renounce what they had formerly done. Khālid[843] was in

838. Or: "on condition that they submit."
839. *al-mamlūkīn*, i.e., the captives of war.
840. Cf. p. 115, and note 752, above.
841. Cf. Ibn al-Athīr, *Kāmil*, II, 365; Ibn Ḥubaysh, 56; Balansī, 108.
842. An early Medinan convert to Islam from the Aws tribe; later appointed governor of al-Yamāmah by 'Umar: Caskel, II, 505; Ibn al-Athīr, *Usd*, II, 336–37.
843. Cf. Balansī, 113–14.

his camp, so when they gathered, Salamah b. ʿUmayr said to Mujjāʿah, "Ask permission for me to have an audience with Khālid, so that I may speak to him about a matter of mine that concerns him and for advice"; but he had resolved to assassinate him. So [Mujjāʿah] spoke to him so that he gave him permission [to enter]; then[844] Salamah b. ʿUmayr approached with the sword hidden in his clothing, intending [to carry out] what he wished. At this, [Khālid] said, "Who is this approaching?" Mujjāʿah replied, "This is the one I spoke to you about, to whom you gave permission [to enter]." Khālid said, "Get him away from me!" So they expelled him from (Khālid's) presence; then they searched him and found the sword on him, whereupon they cursed and vilified him and tied him up. They said, "You wanted to destroy your tribe, by God! You wanted nothing less than that Banū Ḥanīfah be extirpated and [their] children and women be captive, by God! If Khālid had known that you carried weapons, he would have killed you. We are not free from fear that, if he learns of it, he may yet kill the men and take the women captive for what you did, reckoning that it was done in
[1956] consultation with us." So they bound him and put him in the fortress. Banū Ḥanīfah continued to make their renunciation of what they had previously done and to make their conversion to Islam. Salamah promised them that he would do nothing else if they would forgive him, but they refused, for they did not feel safe accepting a promise from him on account of his stupidity. Then one night he escaped and headed for the camp of Khālid; so the guards cried out to him. Banū Ḥanīfah were terrified and pursued him. They caught up with him in one of the gardens, whereupon he attacked them with his sword; so they surrounded him in the rocks. He passed the sword around his own throat, cutting his jugular veins. Then he fell into a well and died.

According to al-Sarī—Shuʿayb—Sayf—al-Ḍaḥḥāk b. Yarbūʿ—his father: Khālid concluded a treaty with all of Banū Ḥanīfah except those who were in al-ʿIrḍ and al-Qurayyah;[845] they were

844. Cf. Ibn Ḥubaysh, 57–58.

845. Al-ʿIrḍ (Wādī Ḥanīfah) was the fertile main valley of the Yamāmah district. Al-Qurayyah was an oasis village ca. 60 km northwest of Ḥajr. Cf. Yāqūt, s.vv; Thilo, s.vv; TAVO B VII 1.

taken captive when the raiding parties were sent out. So he sent to Abū Bakr 500 [persons] of those who had undergone the division [of booty] from al-ʿIrḍ and al-Qurayyah, of the Banū Ḥanīfah or Qays b. Thaʿlabah or Yashkur.[846]

According to Ibn Ḥumayd—Salamah—Muḥammad b. Isḥāq:[847] Then Khālid said to Mujjāʿah, "Give me your daughter in marriage." At this, Mujjāʿah said to him, "Take your time. You are destroying my reputation, and with mine, yours, in [the eyes of] your leader." [But Khālid] said, "Marry [her] to me, man!" so he did. News of that reached Abū Bakr, whereupon he wrote him a bloodcurdling letter:[848] "Upon my life, oh son of Khālid's mother, are you so free as to marry women, while in the court of your house is the blood of 1,200 men of the Muslims that has not yet dried?" When Khālid looked into the letter he began to say, "This is the work of the little left-handed man," meaning ʿUmar b. al-Khaṭṭāb. Now Khālid b. al-Walīd had sent a delegation of Banū Ḥanīfah to Abū Bakr. They came before him, so Abū Bakr said to them, "Woe to you! What made you do [1957]
what you did?"[849] They replied, "Oh successor of the Apostle of God, what you learned about what befell us was a man, upon whom and upon whose tribe God bestowed no blessing." He responded to that, "What was it that attracted you to him?" They said, "He used to say, [850] 'Oh frog, croak, croak, you do not bar the one drinking, nor do you make the water turbid; to us[851] half the earth, and to Quraysh half the earth, but Quraysh is a tribe that commits aggression.'" Abū Bakr said, "May God be exalted and woe to you! This talk comes neither from sacredness nor from piety, so where does it get you?"

When[852] Khālid b. al-Walīd was done with al-Yamāmah, his

---

846. Both Qays and Yashkur were tribes of the Bakr b. Wāʾil group, genealogically related to Ḥanīfah, who lived near al-Yamāmah. Cf. Donner, "Bakr," 17–18.

847. Cf. Diyārbakrī, II, 218 bottom; Ibn Ḥubaysh, 56; Balansī, 109; Nuwayrī, 96.

848. Lit., "a letter dripping blood."

849. Lit., "What is this that made slip from you what slipped?"

850. Cf. p. 109, above.

851. Cf. Balansī, 57, 118.

852. Cf. Nuwayrī, 97.

camp in which he used to meet people was Ubāḍ, one of the watercourses of al-Yamāmah. Then he moved to one of its watercourses called al-Wabar,[853] and it became his camp in it.

The People of al-Baḥrayn, the Apostasy of al-Ḥuṭam, and Those Who Joined with Him in al-Baḥrayn

Abū Ja'far said: Among the things we learned about the people of al-Baḥrayn and the apostasy of those who apostatized among them is the following:

According to 'Ubaydallāh b. Sa'd—his uncle Ya'qūb b. Ibrā-
[1958] hīm—Sayf:[854] Al-'Alā' b. al-Ḥaḍramī went out toward al-Baḥrayn. Part of the story of al-Baḥrayn was that the Prophet and al-Mundhir b. Sāwī fell ill in one and the same month; subsequently al-Mundhir died a little after the Prophet, and the people of al-Baḥrayn apostatized after [his death]. As for 'Abd al-Qays,[855] they returned [to the fold]; but Bakr[856] persisted in their apostasy. The one who persuaded 'Abd al-Qays to turn back was al-Jārūd.[857]

According to 'Ubaydallāh—his uncle—Sayf—Ismā'īl b. Muslim—al-Ḥasan b. Abī al-Ḥasan:[858] Al-Jārūd b. al-Mu'allā came to the Prophet, seeking him out, so he said, "Embrace Islām, oh Jārūd!" But Jārūd answered, "I [already] have a religion."[859] The Prophet replied to him, "Oh Jārūd, your religion is really nothing; it is not a religion." So Jārūd said to him, "And if I were to embrace Islam, then whatever consequence [that might have] in

853. Yāqūt has "Wabarah," a village of al-Yamāmah; Hamdānī, 102, has "Wabrah."

854. Cf. Ibn al-Athīr, *Kāmil*, II, 368; Nuwayrī, 99–100; cf. note 53, above.

855. A major tribe of eastern Arabia, partly settled and partly nomadic, centered in the island Uwal (modern Bahrayn) and Qaṭīf on the coast. See *EI*², s.v. "'Abd al-Ḳays" (S. M. Stern).

856. I.e., the Bakr b. Wā'il tribes; the rebel al-Ḥutam was of a Bakrī tribe, Qays b. Tha'laba (cf. p. 137, below).

857. Bishr "al-Jārūd" b. al-Mu'allā was a Christian of 'Abd al-Qays who came to the Prophet in A H 10 and embraced Islam. His name is given variously. Cf. p. 137, below; Caskel, II, 227, s.v. "Bishr b. 'Amr al-Jārūd"; Ibn al-Athīr, *Usd*, I, 260–61.

858. Cf. Nuwayrī, 99.

859. *Dīn*.

Islam would be your responsibility?"[860] (The Prophet) replied that it was so. So he embraced Islām and remained in Medina until he became learned [in the faith]. Then, when he wanted to leave, he said, "Oh Apostle of God, can we find among one of you camels on which we might reach [our destination]?" He replied, "We have no camels." He said, "Oh Apostle of God, I shall find on the road some of these strays." (Muḥammad) replied, "They are the burning of hellfire; beware of them!"[861]

When[862] (al-Jārūd) came to his people, he invited them to Islām, whereupon they all responded to him. Then it was only a short time before the Prophet died and they apostatized; ʿAbd al-Qays said, "If Muḥammad had been a prophet, he would not have died," and they apostatized. (Al-Jārūd) learned of that, so he sent to them to gather them together; then he stood up to address them, saying, "Oh company of ʿAbd al-Qays! I shall question you about things, so tell me about them if you know about them, and do not respond if you do not know." They [1959]
replied, "Ask about whatever crosses your mind." He said, "Do you know that, in the past, God had prophets?" They said, "Yes." He went on, "[And] do you know it [from what you have learned from others], or have you seen it [with your own eyes]?" They said, "No, rather we know it [from others]." He continued, "Then what became of them?" They replied, "They died." He said, "In truth, Muḥammad has died just as they died, and I bear witness that there is no god but God and that Muḥammad is His Servant and His Apostle." They said, "And we [also] bear witness that there is no god but God and that Muḥammad is His Servant and His Apostle, and that you are our chief and the best of us." So they stood firm in their Islām, and did not extend

---

860. *Famā kāna min tabiʿatin fī al-islām fa-ʿalayka.* Cf. Wellhausen, *Skizzen*, VI, 149.

861. According to Lane, *Arabic-English Lexicon*, II, 551 col. 3, this refers to the tradition stating that "the stray animals of the believer are a cause of the burning of hellfire," i.e., that anyone taking possession of the Muslims' stray beasts is in danger of hellfire. Hence in the preceding sentences, one must assume that the Prophet is stating only that there were no riding camels actually in the town at the moment, the Muslims' extra mounts being allowed to roam freely in the surroundings of Medina.

862. Cf. Ibn al-Athīr, *Kāmil*, II, 368; Balansī, 136–37; Caetani, 584–85.

[their hands in evil to anyone], nor was [an evil hand] extended toward them; they did not get involved between the rest of Rabīʿah,[863] on the one hand, and al-Mundhir[864] and the Muslims, on the other. Al-Mundhir was busy with them [for the rest of] his life; then, after al-Mundhir died, his companions were besieged in two places until al-ʿAlā' saved them.

Abū Jaʿfar said: as for Ibn Isḥāq, he said the following about that, according to Ibn Ḥumayd—Salamah—Ibn Isḥāq: When Khālid b. al-Walīd was finished with al-Yamāmah, Abū Bakr sent al-ʿĀlā' b. al-Ḥaḍramī. Al-ʿĀlā' was the one whom the Apostle of God had sent to al-Mundhir b. Sāwī al-ʿAbdī, with the result that al-Mundhir embraced Islām. So al-ʿĀlā' stayed with them as commander for the Apostle of God. Then al-Mundhir b. Sāwī died in al-Baḥrayn after the death of the Apostle of God. Now ʿAmr b. al-ʿĀṣ was in ʿUmān, the Apostle of God passing away while ʿAmr was there, whereupon ʿAmr approached, passing by al-Mundhir b. Sāwī while he was on the point of death. So (ʿAmr) visited him, so that al-Mundhir said to him, "How much of his property did the
[1960] Apostle of God assign to the dying person[865] of the Muslims at the time of his death?" ʿAmr replied, "He used to stipulate a third." He said, "Then what do you advise me to do with a third of my property?" ʿAmr replied, "If you wish, you may divide it among your close kinsmen, assigning it by way of welfare; or, if you wish, you may grant it as *ṣadaqah*, thereby assigning it as an inviolable grant of alms that will be paid after you to those upon whom you bestowed it." [Al-Mundhir] said, "I would not like to make my property into something restricted, like the *baḥīrah*, the *sā'ibah*, the *waṣīlah*, and the *ḥāmī*;[866] rather, I shall divide it and transmit it to those to whom I bequeath it,

---

863. ʿAbd al-Qays was classified genealogically as part of Rabīʿah b. Nizār.

864. I.e., al-Mundhir b. Sāwī of ʿAbd al-Qays.

865. Lit., "the dead person." The question involves how much of his property the dying person was allowed to distribute to heirs of his choice.

866. Cf. *Qur'ān* 5:103. The words refer to four types of camels which, for various reasons, it had been prohibited during the *jāhiliyyah* to ride, to milk, to eat their flesh, to restrict in grazing, etc. These customs were prohibited by Islām. For the details, see Lane, *Arabic-English Lexicon*, I, 187 (s.v. *baḥīrah*); IV, 1481 (s.v. *sā'ibah*); II, 652 (s.v. *ḥāmī*); and Ibn Manẓūr, II, 729 (s.v. *waṣīlah*).

that they may do with it as they please." So ʿAmr used to marvel because of what he said.

Rabīʿah[867] apostatized in al-Baḥrayn among those Arabs[868] who apostatized, except for al-Jārūd b. ʿAmr b. Ḥanash b. al-Muʿallā, who stood firm in Islām along with those of his tribe who were with him. When he learned of the death of the Apostle of God and of the apostasy of the Arabs, he stood up and said, "I bear witness that there is no god but God; and I bear witness that Muḥammad is His Servant and His Apostle; and I declare those who do not [so] bear witness to be unbelievers." Rabīʿah gathered in al-Baḥrayn and apostatized, saying, "Let us return the kingship[869] to the family of al-Mundhir."[870] So they proclaimed al-Mundhir b. al-Nuʿmān b. al-Mundhir to be king. He[871] used to be called al-Gharūr ("the deceiver"); but when he had come to embrace Islām, and the people had embraced Islām and the sword had subdued them, he used to say, "I was not the deceiver, I was the deceived."

According to ʿUbaydallāh b. Saʿd—his uncle—Sayf—Ismāʿīl b. Muslim—ʿUmayr b. Fulān al-ʿAbdī:[872] After the Prophet died, al-Ḥuṭam b. Ḍubayʿah, a tribesman of Banū Qays b. Thaʿlabah, [1961]
rebelled with those of Bakr b. Wā'il who followed him into apostasy, and with nonapostates who were still unbelievers who gathered ʿround him, until he alighted at al-Qaṭīf[873] and Hajar. He stirred up al-Khaṭṭ[874] and those Zuṭṭ and Sabābijah[875] in it to

---

867. Cf. Ibn Ḥubaysh, 73; Iṣfahānī, XIV, 46; Nuwayrī, 100.

868. Here and below, possibly "nomads."

869. Ibn Ḥubaysh: "the kingship has returned. . . ."

870. Presumably the Lakhmids of al-Ḥīrah, the most prominent of whom, al-Mundhir III (ruled A D 503–554) is referred to here; the last Lakhmid king was al-Nuʿmān b. al-Mundhir (IV), ruled 580–602, whose son is mentioned in the next sentence. Cf. *EI*², s.v. "Lakhmids" (I. Shahid); Wathīmah, 24/66.

871. Cf. p. 146, below, with different opinion on the name; Ibn al-Athīr, *Kāmil*, II, 368; Balādhurī, *Futūḥ*, 84; Balansī, 145–46.

872. Cf. Ibn al-Athīr, *Kāmil*, II, 368–69; Iṣfahānī, XIV, 46; Balādhurī, *Futūḥ*, 83; Nuwayrī, 100–101. Cf. note 53, above.

873. Large oasis on Persian Gulf coast, possibly the ancient Gerrha. Cf. *EI*², s.v. "Al-Ḳaṭīf" (G. Rentz).

874. The east Arabian coastal strip in Baḥrayn and ʿUmān; cf. Yāqūt, s.v.; *EI*², s.v. "Al-Khaṭṭ" (A. Grohmann); Wüstenfeld, 181.

875. Text has "Sayābijah." The Zuṭṭ and Sabābijah were people of Indian origin who had settled around the Persian Gulf littoral (and later in Baṣrah); cf.

rebel, and sent an army to Dārīn.[876] So they rose up on (al-Ḥuṭam's) behalf, in order to put ʿAbd al-Qays between him and them. (ʿAbd al-Qays) was opposed to (these rebels), reinforcing al-Mundhir[877] and the Muslims. And (al-Ḥuṭam) sent to al-Gharūr b. Suwayd,[878] brother of al-Nuʿmān b. al-Mundhir, and dispatched him to Juwāthā,[879] saying, "Stand fast, for if I am victorious I shall make you king in al-Baḥrayn, so that you may be like al-Nuʿmān in al-Ḥīrah." He sent[880] to Juwāthā; then he besieged [the Muslims] and pressed them, so that the siege became intense upon them. Among the besieged Muslims was one of their righteous men, called ʿAbdallāh b. Ḥadhaf, one of the Banū ʿAbū Bakr b.Kilāb.[881] Now he and they were extremely
[1962] hungry, so that they were on the verge of dying. About that ʿAbdallāh b. Ḥadhaf said,[882]

Make a messenger reach Abū Bakr
 and all the young men of Medina.[883]
Do you want to come to the aid of the noble tribe,[884]
 sitting in Juwāthā, besieged?
[It is] as if their blood [is] on every path
 [like] the rays of the sun, bedazzling those who watch.
We relied on the Merciful One;[885] Indeed
 we found that forbearance [is] for those who rely [on Him].[886]

Manẓūr, II, 294 and VII, 308; Balādhūrī, *Futūḥ*, 162 ("Sayābıjah"); Pellat, *Milieu basrien*, 40–41.

876. A small ısland wıth port off the Arabıan coast near al-Qaṭīf. Cf. Thilo, s.v.

877. I.e., al-Mundhir b. Sāwī.

878. Cf. Iṣfahānī, XIV, 46 and 48 on his name.

879. Citadel of ʿAbd al-Qays in al-Khaṭṭ. Cf. Thilo, s.v.; Yāqūt, s.v.; Wüstenfeld, 176, 178, 181.

880. *Baʿatha*; one expects something like *dhahaba*, "he went."

881. A branch of the Kilāb of ʿĀmir b. Ṣaʿṣaʿah; cf. Caskel, I, Table 94 and II, 222.

882. Cf. Ibn Ḥubaysh, 71; Balansī, 139; Isfahanī, XIV, 46–47. Wathīmah, 25/67–68 drops verse 3, and adds after the last verse here: "We said: we were content with God as Lord/and with Islam as a relıgıon we were content."

883. Ibn Ḥubaysh and Balansī: "and all the resıdents of Medina."

884. Balansī: of a small troop.

885. *al-raḥmān*.

886. Ibn Ḥubaysh: "profit [is] for those . . .;" Balansī, Wathīmah, Ibn al-Athīr, II, 369 and Iṣfahānī, XIV, 47: "victory [ıs] for those . . . ."

According to al-Sarī—Shuʿayb—Sayf—al-Ṣaʿb b. ʿAṭiyyah b. Bilāl—Sahm b. Minjāb—Minjāb b. Rāshid:[887] Abū Bakr sent al-ʿĀlāʾ b. al-Ḥaḍramī to be in charge of fighting the apostates in al-Baḥrayn. So when he approached it and was opposite al-Yamāmah, Thumāmah b. Uthāl joined him with the Muslims of Banū Ḥanīfah, from Banū Suḥaym[888] and from the people of the settlements of the rest of Banū Ḥanīfah; he had been waiting in uncertain expectation. (Abū Bakr) had dispatched ʿIkrimah to ʿUmān and then to Mahrah, and he had ordered Shuraḥbīl [1963] to remain where he was until Abū Bakr's order should reach him, then [to go to] Dūmah[889] to raid the apostates of Quḍāʿah with ʿAmr b. al-ʿĀṣ. As for ʿAmr b. al-ʿĀṣ, he was raiding Saʿd and Balī;[890] and he ordered this one to [march against] Kalb, and mixed groups joined to them. Then, when (al-ʿĀlāʾ b. al-Ḥaḍramī) drew near us[891] while we were in the high part of the country, there was no one of al-Ribāb or ʿAmr b. Tamīm who had a horse who did not lead (his horse) beside him, going out to receive (al-ʿAlāʾ). As for Banū Ḥanẓalah, they played for time. Mālik b. Nuwayrah was in al-Buṭāḥ with groups with whom we contended,[892] and Wakīʿ b. Mālik was in al-Qarʿāʾ[893] with groups that contended with ʿAmr.[894] As for Saʿd b. Zayd Manāt,

887. Cf. pp. 76–86, above; Ibn al-Athīr, *Kāmil*, II, 369; Iṣfahānī, XIV, 47; Nuwayrī, 101.

888. Suhaym b. Murrah, a branch of Ḥanīfah, lived in the oases of al-Jaww, Malham, and Qurrān; cf. Caskel, II, 516.

889. Dūmat al-Jandal, a town in northern Najd, modern al-Jawf. Text is awkward; Wellhausen, *Skizzen*, VI, 149, wanted to delete Dūmah; editor, on basis of comparison with Ṭabarī, I, 2083, wanted to retain it.

890. I.e., the tribes of Saʿd Hudhaym b. Zayd and Balī, both of the northern Ḥijāz, or Saʿd Allāh of Balī and the rest of the tribe? Cf. Donner, *Conquests* 102–5.

891. The narrator, Minjāb b. Rāshid, was of Banū Ḍabbah, part of the confederation of al-Ribāb, closely connected with Tamīm; cf. Caskel, I, Table 90 and II, 408.

892. Cf. p. 53, above: Khālid b. al-Walīd is ordered to move against Mālik b. Nuwayrah at Buṭāḥ. The narrator now portrays himself and his group, al-Ribāb, as part of the Muslims.

893. A stop on the Mecca-Kufa road near the fringes of Iraq, in northernmost Arabia; cf. Yāqūt, s.v.

894. The identity of the ʿAmr is unclear. E. Landau-Tasseron (personal communication) suggests that he cannot be ʿAmr b. al-ʿĀṣ, but might be ʿAmr b. al-Ahtam, on whom see note 631, above.

they were two divisions: ʿAwf and the Abnāʾ obeyed al-Zibriqān b. Badr, standing firm in their Islām; they were free of fault and defended it. The Muqāʿis and the Buṭūn [on the other hand] listened but did not comply, except for those with Qays b. ʿĀṣim, for he divided the *ṣadaqah* taxes that had been gathered to him among the Muqāʿis and the Buṭūn when al-Zibriqān marched[895] with the *ṣadaqah* taxes of ʿAwf and the Abnāʾ. ʿAwf and the Abnāʾ were occupied [in fighting] with the Muqāʿis and the Buṭūn, but when Qays b. ʿĀṣim saw how al-Ribāb and ʿAmr [b. Tamīm] had received al-ʿĀlāʾ, he regretted his earlier hasty actions; whereupon he received al-ʿĀlāʾ by making ready what he had divided from the *ṣadaqah* taxes. He shunned the business he had been involved in [before] and drove [the *ṣadaqah* camels] so that they reached him.[896] [Then Qays] went out with (al-ʿĀlāʾ) to fight the people of al-Baḥrayn. He recited poetry
[1964] about that, as did al-Zibriqān about his *ṣadaqah* tax when he sent it to Abū Bakr. Al-Zibriqān said about that:

I paid in full the several camels [due to] the Apostle, when [other] collectors of *ṣadaqah* tax had refused,
and not a camel had been returned [to him] by its trustee.[897]
Together we defended (the tax) from all the people;
the enemy's shooting at [it while it is with] us does not harm it.
So I paid it, in order not to betray my covenant—
lean camels, their backs not [yet] broken in for riding.
By doing so I sought piety and the glory of its reputation,
[against a time] when the boastful [man] of a company vies with my kind.
In truth I am from a clan which, when their efforts[898] are reckoned,
their living and their dead[899] see glory in it.
Neither their young nor their old have been humbled,
they are firmly anchored and their breasts are pure.

---

895. I.e., marched to Abū Bakr.
896. I.e., reached al-ʿAlāʾ.
897. Cf. p. 86, above.
898. *Saʿyu-hum*; Kos has *shaʿbu-hum*, "their people."
899. Lit., "their living and their graves."

I claimed my due from an ungrateful clan;
their barking and mewing did not turn my sword back.
For God, I have entered [the domain] of kings, and many a knight
I speared whenever the cavalry's raiding became intense.

So I broke through their front line[900] with a bloody thrust, [1965]
in such a way that he who wished for life injures it.[901]
Many a spectacle of bravery[902] have I borne witness to, not idle in it; but today its fate is turned away.
I see my fear of the enemies as [a kind of] daring;
we weep[903] whenever the inmost thought of the soul is exposed.

Qays said, upon bringing the *ṣadaqah* tax to al-ʿĀlā':

Send Quraysh a letter from me, you two,
when proofs of the payments have reached them.
Many a time, over the ages, have I brought them to the sides of a well,
driving every covetous man of evil conduct to despair [of seizing] them.
I found[904] that my father and maternal uncle were safe
in a plain in which those whom I fended off did not alight.

So al-ʿAlā' honored him. There[905] went out with al-ʿAlā' as many [men] from ʿAmr and Saʿd and al-Ribāb as [there were regular troops in] his army. He crossed the Dahnā'[906] with us until when we were in the heart of it, with the whistling hills and sighing dunes to the right and left, and God wished to show us his signs. (Al-ʿAlā') dismounted and ordered the people to [1966]

---

900. Lit., "I opened her first one."
901. I.e., the one who flees to save his life damages his reputation by fleeing.
902. Reading *mashhad ṣadq* for the text's *mashhad ṣidq*; cf. Ibn Manẓūr, X, 196, for *ṣadq* as "bravery." Or, perhaps, something like "moment of truth?"
903. Reading with Manuscript C, rather than "he weeps" in the text and Cairo.
904. Reading with Cairo, for the text's "I gave generously to . . . ."
905. Ibn al-Athīr, *Kāmil*, II, 369–70; Isfahānī, XIV, 47; Nuwayrī, 101–3.
906. A long, narrow stretch of sand desert in east-central Arabia, separating al-Yamāmah from Baḥrayn. Cf. *EI*², "al-Dahnā'" (C. D. Matthews).

dismount, whereupon the camels bolted from fright in the depths of the night, so that there remained with us neither camel, nor provisions, nor a water bag, nor a tent, unless he came upon it in the middle of the sands, that [happening] when the army had dismounted but before they had unpacked [the camels]. I have not known a group that was so beset by anxiety as we were, one of us appointing another his executor.[907] The herald of al-ʿAlāʾ cried out, "Assemble!" So we gathered to him; then he said, "What is this that has appeared among you and overcome you?" Whereupon the people answered, "How can we be blamed, [seeing that] even if we reach the morrow, the sun will not have waxed hot before we will have become [the subject of] a story?"[908] But he replied, "Oh people, do not be afraid. Are you not Muslims? Are you not on the path of God? Are you not the helpers of God?[909] They said, "Indeed." He went on, "Then rejoice, for by God, He will not forsake someone in a situation like yours." The herald called for the morning prayer when the dawn arose, some of us doing our ablutions with sand and others still being in a state of ritual purity.[910] After he had performed his prayer, he assumed a kneeling position and the people kneeled; then he exerted himself in praying, and they with him. Whereupon a mirage of the sun [as if reflecting off water] shimmered for them, so he turned to the row [of people] and said, "A scout to see what this is!" So (the scout) did so; subsequently he returned saying, "[It is] a mirage." Whereupon he occupied himself [again] with praying. Then it shimmered for them again, but the same thing happened. Then it shimmered for them a final time, whereupon (the scout) said, "Water!" So he got up, and the people got up, and we walked to it until we encamped at it and drank it and washed. The day was not
[1967] advanced before the camels approached, driven from every

---

907. I.e., in anticipation of death.

908. I.e., before we will have died.

909. *Anṣār Allāh.*

910. Ablutions with sand or dust (*tayammum*) are permitted when there is insufficient water to do normal ablutions by washing. Those who were still in a state of ritual purity at the morning prayer had, by implication, not slept the night before, as sleep causes the believer to enter the state of lesser impurity, necessitating ablutions before prayer.

side; then they kneeled for us, so each man went to his mount and took it. We had not lost [so much as] a thread.[911] We watered them and made them drink the second drinking after the first drinking, and we watered ourselves; then we left.[912] Abū Hurayrah was my companion, so when we had left that place he said to me, "How [well] do you know the location of that water?" So I replied, "I am one of the best of the Arabs as guides to this country." He said, "Be with me so that you may bring me straight upon it." So I came back to it, bringing him to that same place; but lo, there was no pool there, nor any trace of the water. So I said to him, "By God, if I had not seen the water I would have told you that this was the place; I have not seen any drinking water in this place before today." But lo, there was a small water bag, filled up. Whereupon (Abū Hurayrah) said, "Oh Abū Sahm, this is the place, by God; and for this I returned and brought you back. I filled my water bags, then I placed them on the edge[913] saying [to myself], 'If this was some act of [divine] grace and a sign [from God] I shall know, and if it was [merely] rainfall[914] I shall know.' Lo! It is an act of grace!" So he praised God. Then we marched until we came to Hajar.

Al-'Alā'[915] sent to al-Jārūd and to another man to betake themselves to 'Abd al-Qays so that they could attack al-Ḥuṭam from [districts] adjacent to them. (Al-'Alā') went out with those who came with him and those who came to him, until he attacked him from what is adjacent to Hajar. All the polytheists gathered to al-Ḥuṭam except the people of Dārīn, and all the [1968]

---

911. I.e., although the camels were wandering untended all night, nothing was lost from their baggage.

912. Diyārbakrī, II, 221 offers a somewhat different miracle story, involving the sudden appearance of rain clouds.

913. Ibn al-Athīr, *Kāmil*, II, 369, adds "of the pool"; Iṣfahānī, XIV, 47, adds "of the valley."

914. The text reads *ghiyāthan*, "divine aid," but the context of the story clearly requires some test between divine grace and accidental encounter of natural water, the idea being that naturally occurring water would still be there when Abū Hurayrah returned. I suspect that the text originally read *ghaythan*, "rain," and have translated accordingly. Ibn al-Athīr, *Kāmil*, II, 369, has *'aynan*, "a spring," which in unpointed texts would appear identical with *ghaythan*. The whole phrase is missing in Iṣfahānī.

915. Cf. Ibn al-Athīr, *Kāmil*, II, 370; Iṣfahānī, XIV, 47–48; Nuwayrī, 103.

Muslims gathered to al-ʿAlāʾ b. al-Ḥaḍramī. The Muslims and the polytheists dug trenches; they used to fight in turns and return to their trench. They were thus for some months.[916] While[917] the people were [in that state], one night the Muslims heard a tremendous racket in the camp of the polytheists, like the clamoring of a rout or of fighting; so al-ʿAlāʾ said, "Who will bring us news of the enemy?" Whereupon ʿAbdallāh b. Ḥadhaf said, "I will bring you news of the enemy." Now his mother was a woman of ʿIjl; so he went out until, when he drew near their trench, they seized him and said to him, "Who are you?" So he related his genealogy for them, and began calling, "Oh Abjar!" At this, Abjar b. Bujayr[918] came and identified him; then he said, "What is your business?" So [ʿAbdallāh] replied, "May I not perish among the Lahāzim![919] Why should I be killed while there are all around me troops of ʿIjl, Taymallāt, Qays, and ʿAnazah? Is al-Ḥuṭam playing tricks on me, while strangers[920] of the tribes and you are witnesses? Stop it!" He said, "By God, I think you are the worst nephew to your uncles tonight." So he said, "Let me go[921] and give me [something] to eat, for I am dying of hunger." So he brought
[1969] food for him, whereupon he ate. Then he said, "Give me provisions and a riding camel and let me go to my home." He said that to a man overcome by drink, who did so. He mounted him on his camel, and gave him provisions, and let him [go]. ʿAbdallāh b. Ḥadhaf went out until he entered the camp of the Muslims; then he informed them that the enemy was drunk. So the Muslims went out against them so that they rushed upon their camp, putting them to the sword at will. [The enemy] rushed into the trench in flight. [Some] were thrown down,

916. Ibn al-Athīr, *Kāmil*, and Nuwayrī: "a month."

917. Cf. Ibn Ḥubaysh, 71ff.; Balansī, 139–40; Nuwayrī, 103–4.

918. Thus text, but we should probably read Abjar b. Jābir, a Christian chieftain of ʿIjl, as given by Balansī. Cf. Caskel, II, 134; Donner, "Bakr," 31.

919. Lahāzim was an alliance of the Bakrī tribes of ʿIjl, Qays b. Thaʿlabah, and Taymallāt b. Thaʿlabah with the ʿAnazah b. Asad b. Rabīʿah, a non-Bakrī tribe. Cf. Donner, "Bakr," 17 and 32.

920. *Nuzzāʿ*; people living in a tribe under protection who are not of the tribe itself. Cf. Ibn Manẓūr, VIII, 350.

921. *Daʿnī min hādha.*

[others] escaped; [some stood] dumbfounded, [and were] killed or taken prisoner. The Muslims seized what was in the camp, no man escaping except with what was on him. As for Abjar, he fled; whereas al-Ḥuṭam became confused and mixed up, and his courage left him. So[922] he went up to his horse while the Muslims were all around them slaying them, in order to ride it; but when he placed his foot in the stirrup, he was unable to proceed. Then ʿAfīf b. al-Mundhir, one of the Banū ʿAmr b. Tamīm, passed him while al-Ḥuṭam was calling for help, saying, "Isn't there a man of Banū Qays b. Thaʿlabah who will lift me onto my mount?" Then he raised his voice, so that (ʿAfīf) recognized his voice; whereupon he said, "Abū Ḍubayʿah?" (Al-Ḥuṭam) replied, "Yes." He said, "Give me your foot so that I may lift you up." So he gave him his foot so he could lift him, but he struck it from the side (with his sword), severing it from the upper leg, and left him. At this (al-Ḥuṭam) said, "Finish me off!" Whereupon (ʿAfīf) replied, "I do not want you to die until I have made you suffer." Now with ʿAfīf were a number of his father's offspring; they were killed that night. Al-Ḥuṭam began [1970]
to say to every Muslim who passed by him in the night, "Would you like to kill al-Ḥuṭam?", saying that even to those he did not know, until Qays b. ʿĀṣim passed him. So he said that to him, whereupon (Qays) turned to him and killed him. Then, when he saw that his thigh had been severed,[923] he said, "Oh vile one! If I had known what [a wound] he had, I would not have touched him." After the Muslims had secured the trench against the enemy, they went out in search of them, pursuing them. Qays b. ʿĀṣim caught up with Abjar; but Abjar's horse was stronger than the horse of Qays, so when he feared that he might escape him, he speared him in the hamstring, severing the tendon while the sciatic nerve remained unharmed; so that did it.[924] ʿAfīf b. al-Mundhir said,

If the tendon pulses [with the heartbeat] the sciatic nerve does not;
not everyone who falls knows about that.

---

922. Cf. Balansī, 140–41.
923. So text; i.e., that the lower leg had been severed from it.
924. *fa-kānat rāddah.*

Did you not see that we subdued their guards
in the lineage of ʿAmr, and noble al-Ribāb?

ʿAfīf b. al-Mundhir took al-Gharūr b. Suwayd prisoner, so al-Ribāb negotiated with him on his behalf; his father was the nephew of Taym, and they asked him to grant him protection. So he said to al-ʿAlā', "I have taken this one under my protection." (Al-ʿAlā') said, "And who is he?" He replied, "Al-Gharūr." (Al-ʿAlā') said [to al-Gharūr], "You misled these [people]!" (Al-Gharūr) replied,[925] "Oh king, I am not the deceiver (*al-gharūr*), rather the deceived." (Al-ʿAlā') said, "Embrace Islam!" So he embraced Islām and remained in Hajar. Al-Gharūr
[1971] was his proper name; it was not a nickname. ʿAfīf killed al-Mundhir b. Suwayd b. al-Mundhir.

In[926] the morning Al-ʿAlā' divided the spoils. He awarded some of the men of valor garments as booty; among those who were awarded booty were ʿAfīf b. al-Mundhir, Qays b. ʿĀṣim, and Thumāmah b. Uthāl. As for Thumāmah, he was given as booty some garments among which was a robe with ornamental borders of which al-Ḥuṭam had been very proud; he sold the garments.

The majority[927] of those who fled headed for Dārīn, and then rode boats to it; the rest returned to the country of their tribe. So al-ʿAlā' b. al-Ḥaḍramī wrote to those among them of Bakr b. Wā'il who had stood by their Islām, and sent to ʿUtaybah b. al-Nahhās[928] and to ʿAmr b. ʿAbd al-Aswad[929] to stick to what they were doing and to waylay the apostates on every road.[930] He ordered Mismaʿ[931] to surprise them, and sent to Khaṣafah al-Taymī and al-Muthannā b. Ḥārithah al-Shaybānī,[932] so that they took up positions against them on the road. Some

925. Cf. p. 137, above.

926. Cf. Ibn al-Athīr, *Kāmil*, II, 370; Iṣfahānī, XIV, 48.

927. Cf. Ibn al-Athīr, *Kāmil*, II, 371; Iṣfahānī, XIV, 48–49.

928. A Muslim of Banū ʿIjl; cf. Ibn Ḥajar, *Iṣābah*, s.v.

929. Possibly ʿAmr b. al-Aswad b. ʿĀmir (Ibn al-Athīr, *Usd*, IV, 84); he is, however, said to have been one of the martyrs at al-Yamāmah.

930. Or "in every way."

931. Possibly Mismaʿ b. Shaybān of Qays b. Thaʿlabah: cf. Caskel, II, 409.

932. Chieftain of Shaybān and early ally of Muslims in Iraq. Cf. *EI*^{2}, s.v. "Al-Muthannā b. Ḥāritha" (F. M. Donner).

of (the fugitives) repented, so (the Muslims) accepted them and included them [in their forces]. Others refused and were stubborn; they were prevented from returning [to Islam], so they went back where they had come from until they crossed over to Dārīn. Thus God gathered them [all] in it. A man of Banū Ḍubayʿah b. ʿIjl called Wahb said about that, reproaching those of Bakr b. Wā'il who apostatized:

Do you not see that God tests his creatures
so that [some] peoples become wicked even as [another] group becomes pure?
God disgraces peoples afflicted by immorality;
Zayd al-Ḍallāl and Maʿmar fell upon them.[933]

Al-ʿAlā' remained lodged in the camp of the polytheists until the letters came back to him from those of Bakr b. Wā'il to whom he had written, and he had learned from them of [their] support for God's cause and zeal[934] for His religion. So when he had gotten what he desired from them in this regard, he felt sure that nothing untoward would take him from behind on the part of anyone of the people of al-Baḥrayn. He summoned the people to Dārīn; then he gathered them together and addressed them, saying: "God gathered for you in this sea the troops[935] of the devils and those fleeing in fright from the war; He has shown you His signs on land, so that you may consider them on the sea. So arise against your enemy, then cross the sea to them.[936] For in truth, God has gathered them." At this they said, "We shall do it, and by God we shall not feel any fear after [what happened in] the Dahnā' as long as we live." So he set out and they did likewise until, when they reached the seashore, they plunged in, [mounted upon] whinnying stallions, pack camels, bellowing mules, and braying donkeys, the rider and the infantryman [alike]. (Al-ʿAlā') gave a call, and so did they; his call and [1972]

933. According to p. 151, below, Zayd amd Maʿmar were the killers of al-Ḥuṭam; this, of course, contradicts the account in pp. 144–46, in which ʿAfīf b. al-Mundhir and Qays b. ʿĀṣim are responsible for al-Ḥuṭam's death.

934. Literally, "passionate anger" (*ghaḍab*).

935. Or "companies, parties" (*aḥzāb*).

936. Lit., "make the sea broad (or ask it to be broad) to them."

theirs was, "Oh Most Merciful of forgivers! Oh Noble One! Oh Mild-tempered One! Oh Unique One! Oh Everlasting One! Oh Living One! Oh Reviver of the dead! Oh Living One! Oh Eternal One! There is no God but Thee, oh our Lord!"[937] Then they all passed over that gulf, by the will of God, walking as if on soft sand upon which was water that [only] covered the hooves of the camels.[938] In truth, between the coast and Dārīn is a trip of a day and a night for a ship of the sea under some conditions. So they reached it and fought so intensely that they did not leave anyone there to relate [what had happened]. They took as captives the offspring [of the vanquished] and drove off the
[1973] flocks. The booty of the horseman reached 6,000,[939] and that of the foot soldier 2,000. They crossed over to them and marched on that [same] day;[940] then when they were done, they returned as they had come so that they crossed [back]. About that ʿAfīf b. al-Mundhir said:[941]

Did you not see that God subdued His ocean,
and has sent one of the momentous happenings down among the unbelievers?
We called on Him Who divided the seas, so He brought us
something more amazing than the dividing of the first seas.

After al-ʿAlāʾ returned to al-Baḥrayn and Islām became established in it, and Islām and its people grew strong and polytheism and its people were abased, those who had something [evil] in their hearts engaged in evil rumors, so the rumor mongers spread their lies. They said, "That one, Mafrūq,[942] has

937. The epithets given in the call are all among the Qur'ānic "beautiful names" of God.

938. Cf. Balansī, 143; Diyārbakrī, II, 221, gives a different version of this miraculous crossing.

939. Presumably dirhams, a silver coin.

940. Cairo, without explanation of source, has "they passed the night and marched the next day."

941. Cf. Diyārbakrī, II, 221; Iṣfahānī, XIV, 49; Balansī, 143.

942. Al-Nuʿmān "Mafrūq" b. ʿAmr of Banū Abū Rabīʿah of Shaybān of Bakr is said to have died ca. 615 at Yaum al-ʿUẓālah (Yawm Iyād); Cf. Caskel, I, Table 149, and II, 451; Balansī, 141, whose editor confirms it to have been Mafrūq b. ʿAmr al-Shaybānī. E. Landau-Tasseron suggests that either the person referred to here is a descendant of the deceased Mafrūq, or the narrator uses the name of a

gathered his kinsmen of Shayban and Taghlib and al-Namir." But groups of Muslims said to them, "Then the Lahāzim will take care of them for us." Now the Lahāzim at that time had agreed to assist al-ʿAlāʾ, and they obeyed [him]. About that ʿAbdallāh b. Ḥadhaf said:[943]

Do not threaten us with Mafrūq and his family;
if he comes to us, he shall suffer among us the fate[944] of al-Ḥuṭam.
In truth, that clan of Bakr, even if it is numerous,
is [nonetheless] one of the communities entering the fire.
Outside the palm grove are horses, and inside it [1974]
are horses, heavily laden with young men leading camels.

Al-ʿAlāʾ b. al-Ḥaḍramī allowed the people to go home, so the people returned, except those who desired to stay. Then[945] we headed home, and Thumāmah b. Uthāl headed home until, when we were at a spring of the Banū Qays b. Thaʿlabah, they saw Thumāmah with the robe of al-Ḥuṭam on him; they hid a man with him, saying, "Ask him how (his robe) came to be his, and whether he or someone else killed al-Ḥuṭam." So (the man) came to him and asked him about it, whereupon (Thumāmah) replied, "I was awarded it as booty." (The man) said, "Were you the one who killed al-Ḥuṭam?" He replied, "No; but I wish I had killed him." (The man) asked, "Then how is it that this robe is with you?" He replied, "Didn't I just tell you?" At this (the man) returned to them to tell them [what he had said], so they gathered to him; then they went to (Thumāmah) and surrounded him. Whereupon he said, "What do you want?" They said, "You are the killer of al-Ḥuṭam." (Thumāmah) replied, "You lie; I am not his killer, but I was given it as booty." They said, "Is anyone but the killer awarded the spoil [of a slain man]?" (Thumāmah)

---

dead tribal hero (personal communication). Cf. Landau-Tasseron, "The Participation of Ṭayyiʾ in the *Ridda*," 63, which describes how a hero of the tribe, Zayd al-Khayl, appears in some accounts about the *ridda*, even though he had died before it began.

943. Cf. Ibn Ḥubaysh, 72; Balansī, 141–42, which reverses order of verses 2 and 3.

944. *Sunnah.*

945. Cf. Ibn al-Athīr, *Kāmil*, II, 370–71; Iṣfahānī, XIV, 49.

replied, "(The robe) was not on him; it was found in his baggage." [But] they said, "You lie!" and struck him down.

With[946] the Muslims in Hajar was a monk; then he embraced Islām on that day, so he was asked, "What induced you to embrace Islām?" He replied, "Three things. I feared that God would transform me into something hideous after it if I did not do it; a flood in the sands and the smoothing of the highest parts of the sea;[947] and a prayer that I heard in their camp on the winds by dawn." They said, "What was it?" He said, "Oh God, You are the Compassionate, the Merciful; there is no God other than You; [You are] the Original, nothing was before You; the Enduring, not forgetful; the Living, Who does not die; Creator of what is seen and what is not seen; and each day, You are
[1975] [employed] in [some] affair; Oh God, You know everything, without learning." Then I knew that a group was not aided by the angels unless they were in God's cause." The companions of the Apostle of God used to listen to that Hajarī thereafter.

Al-ʿAlā' wrote to Abū Bakr, "Now then: God, may He be blessed and exalted, made the Dahnā' flow for us in an inundation the western side of which could not be seen.[948] And He showed us a sign and a wonderful example after [our] anxiety and distress, so that we might praise God and glorify Him. So pray to God and ask His assistance for His armies and those who help His religion." So Abū Bakr praised God and prayed to Him, and said: "The Arabs still say, when speaking of their country, that when Luqmān[949] was asked whether they should dig the Dahnā" [for water] or leave it, he forbade them and said, 'The well rope does not reach it, and one is not refreshed.' In truth the case of this inundation is one of the great signs; we have not heard of it among any nation before. Oh God, appoint among us a successor to Muḥammad!"[950] Then al-ʿAlā' wrote to him

946. Cf. Ibn al-Athīr, *Kāmil*, II, 371; Iṣfahānī, XIV, 49.

947. A reference to the miracles related at pp. 143 and 148, above.

948. Meaning that the pool was so large one could not see across it; the Muslims were, according to the story, coming from the east; cf. p. 143, above.

949. A legendary pre-Islamic hero and sage. Cf. *EI*², s.v. "Luḳmān" (B. Heller—N. A. Stillman).

950. *Ikhlif Muḥammadan fīnā.*

about the defeat of the people of the trench and the killing of al-Ḥuṭam by Zayd and Maʿmar:[951] "Now then: God, may His name be blessed, robbed the enemy of their wits and took away their good fortune[952] by means of a drink that they took by day; then we rushed upon their trench against them, but found them drunk, so we killed them except for those who fled. Al-Ḥuṭam was killed." So Abū Bakr wrote [back] to him, "Now then: If you learn anything further about the Banū Shaybān b. Thaʿlabah like what you have learned [already], and the rumor mongers plunge into it, then send an army to them to crush them, and [1976]
scatter in flight with them whoever is behind them." But they did not gather, nor did those rumors of theirs come to anything.

The Apostasy of the People of ʿUmān and Mahrah and the Yemen

Abū Jaʿfar said:[953] Differences of opinion exist regarding the date of the Muslims' war [with] these [people]. According to Ibn Ḥumayd—Salamah—Ibn Isḥāq: al-Yamāmah and the Yemen and al-Baḥrayn were conquered and the armies sent to Syria in they year 12. According to Abū Zayd—Abū al-Ḥasan al-Madāʾinī—Abū Maʿshar, Yazīd b. ʿIyāḍ b. Juʿdubah, Abū ʿUbaydah b. Muḥammad b. Abī ʿUbaydah, Ghassān b. ʿAbd al-Ḥamīd, Juwayriyyah b. Asmāʾ—their teachers according to their chains of authority, and from others among the scholars of the people of Syria and Iraq: The conquests among all the apostates by Khālid b. al-Walīd and others were in the year 11, except for the affair of Rabīʿah b. Bujayr,[954] which was in the year 13. The story of Rabīʿah b. Bujayr al-Taghlibī is that Khālid b. al-Walīd, according to what was said in this account of his which I mentioned, was in al-Muṣayyakh and al-Ḥaṣīd;[955] then Rabīʿah rose up [in

951. Text has Mismaʿ; but cf. p. 147 and note 933, above. The form Maʿmar must be the correct one because the poem on p. 147 ends in *r*. Cf. Wellhausen, *Skizzen*, VI, 149; *Emendanda*.

952. Or "took away their power" (*adhhaba rīḥahum*).

953. Cf. Ibn al-Athīr, *Kāmil*, II, 372.

954. A chief of Taghlib; cf. Ṭabarī, I, 2072.

955. Two places in southern Iraq conquered by Khālid b. al-Walīd, at which time the uprising of Rabīʿah b. Bujayr occurred. Cf. Ṭabarī I, 2068–2070; Balādhurī, *Futūḥ*, 110–11.

rebellion] with a group of apostates. So [Khālid] fought him,
[1977] plundering and taking captives. He gained [as booty] a daughter of Rabīʿah b. Bujayr, so he took her captive. He sent the captives to Abū Bakr; subsequently Rabīʿah's daughter became the possession of ʿAlī b. Abī Ṭālib.

As for the case of ʿUmān, according to al-Sarī b. Yaḥyā—Shuʿayb—Sayf—Sahl b. Yūsuf—al-Qāsim b. Muḥammad and al-Ghuṣn b. al-Qāsim and Mūsā al-Jalyūsī—Ibn Muḥayrīz:[956] In ʿUmān appeared Laqīṭ b. Mālik al-Azdī,[957] "the one with the crown." During the *jāhiliyyah* he used to be a rival of al-Julandā, and he preached something like what whoever was a prophet preached. He seized ʿUmān as an apostate and forced Jayfar and ʿAbbād[958] to take refuge in the mountains and the sea; so Jayfar sent to Abū Bakr informing him about that and asking him [to send] an army against him. At this, Abū Bakr al-Ṣiddīq sent Ḥudhayfah b. Miḥṣan al-Ghalfānī of Ḥimyar[959] and ʿArfajah al-Bāriqī of the Azd, al-Ḥudhayfah to ʿUmān and ʿArfajah to Mahrah. He ordered the two of them, when they agreed, to combine against those to whom they had been sent, and to begin in ʿUmān, Hudhayfah [having precedence] over ʿArfajah on his front, and ʿArfajah [having precedence] over Ḥudhayfah on his front. So they set out supporting one another. (Abū Bakr) ordered them to march quickly until they should come to ʿUmān. Then, when they were near it, they corresponded with Jayfar and ʿAbbād and acted on their counsel; so they proceeded to what they had been ordered to. Now Abū Bakr had sent ʿIkrimah against Musaylimah in al-Yamāmah; and he sent Shuraḥbīl b. Ḥasanah after him, and named al-Yamāmah to him [as his goal]. He commanded the two of them [to proceed] just as he had commanded
[1978] Ḥudhayfah and ʿArfajah; but ʿIkrimah strove to precede Shuraḥbīl and sought the favor of victory. Then Musaylimah defeated him, so he drew back from Musaylima and wrote to Abū Bakr

956. Cf. Ibn al-Athīr, *Kāmil*, II, 372.

957. Cf. Balādhurī, *Futūḥ*, 76; Balansī, 148.

958. Text and Cairo have ʿAbbād, here and subsequently; Ibn al-Athīr, *Kāmil*, has ʿIyādh. The proper form may be ʿAbd: cf. p. 70 and note 446, above; Balādhurī, *Futūḥ*, 76; Caskel, II, 104; Wilkinson, "The Julanda."

959. Balansī, 147, has Ḥudhayfah b. al-Yamān al-Azdī sent by the Prophet.

with the news. Shuraḥbīl stood firm where the news reached him. Abū Bakr wrote to Shuraḥbīl b. Ḥasanah to remain in the nearest part of al-Yamāmah until his [further] order should come to him, and gave up making him go to the front he had [originally] sent him to. He wrote to 'Ikrimah, censuring him for his excessive haste and saying, "I shall neither see you nor hear you until after [some act of] valor. Go to 'Umān in order to fight the people of 'Umān; assist Ḥudhayfah and 'Arfajah. Each one of you is in charge of his cavalry; Ḥudhayfah is in charge of the army as long as you are in his district.[960] When you have finished, go on to Mahrah; then let your course from it be to the Yemen until you meet up with al-Muhājir b. Abī Umayyah in the Yemen and in Ḥaḍramawt. Crush whoever has apostatized between 'Umān and the Yemen. Let me learn of your valor." So 'Ikrimah proceeded on the heels of 'Arfajah and Ḥudhayfah, leading those who were with him, so that he joined the two of them before they had reached 'Umān. He[961] had made an agreement with them that, after finishing, they would follow the opinion of 'Ikrimah in marching on with him[962] or staying in 'Umān. Then, after they had joined [forces] and were near 'Umān in a place called Rijām,[963] they corresponded with Jayfar and 'Abbād. Laqīṭ learned of the approach of the army, so he gathered his troops and set up camp at Dabā. Jayfar and 'Abbād came out of the places where they had been and set up camp at Ṣuhār.[964] The two of them sent to Ḥudhayfah, 'Arfajah, and 'Ikrimah [inviting them] to come to them; so they came to them both in Ṣuhār. Then they mopped up those who adjoined them until they were satisfied with [the loyalty of] those who were near them. They wrote to chiefs who were with Laqīṭ, [1979]
starting with a chief of Banū Judayd;[965] they exchanged cor-

960. *fī 'amalihi.*

961. Presumably Abū Bakr imposing an agreement on the three commanders, 'Arfajah, Ḥudhayfah, and 'Ikrimah; the pronoun "them" is plural, not dual.

962. I.e., on to Mahrah and the Yemen. The text hereabouts is not always lucid.

963. A long red mountain on the western fringe of 'Umān: cf. Thilo, s.v.

964. A seaport and sometimes capital of 'Umān, where a Sasanian garrison was stationed on the eve of Islam: cf. Yāqūt, s.v.; Wilkinson, "The Julanda," 99.

965. Probably Judayd b. Ḥāḍir, a large subdivision of the 'Umānī tribe of Daws—Azd.

respondence until they became dispersed from him. They fell upon Laqīṭ, meeting [him] at Dabā. Laqīṭ had gathered the families and then put them behind their lines to provoke them to battle and to protect their womenfolk. Now Dabā is the chief town (*miṣr*) and the most important marketplace. So they fought intensely at Dabā. Laqīṭ was prevailing over the army; but while they were in that situation, the Muslims having experienced disorder and the polytheists anticipating victory, there came to the Muslims their great reinforcements from Banū Nājiyah,[966] led by al-Khirrīt b. Rāshid, and from ʿAbd al-Qays, led by Sayḥān b. Ṣūḥān,[967] and scattered individuals of ʿUmān from Banū Nājiyah and ʿAbd al-Qays. Thus[968] God strengthened the people of Islam through them, and weakened through them the polytheists; so the polytheists turned their backs in flight, so that 10,000 of them were killed in the battle. (The Muslims) pursued them so that they made great slaughter among them and took the offspring prisoner and divided the flocks[969] among the Muslims. They sent the fifth [of booty] to Abū Bakr with ʿArfajah. ʿIkrimah and Ḥudhayfah were of the opinion that Ḥudhayfah should remain in ʿUmān so as to facilitate matters and to calm the people down.[970] The fifth [of booty] amounted to 800 heads;[971] and they plundered the marketplace completely. So ʿArfajah marched to Abū Bakr with the fifth of the captives and the plunder, while Ḥudhayfah remained to calm the people down. He invited the tribes around ʿUmān to settle what God had restored as booty to the Muslims and the expatriates[972] of ʿUmān. ʿIkrimah marched on with the people; he started with Mahrah, about which ʿAbbād al-Nājī said:

---

966. A branch of the old Quḍāʿī tribe of Jarm that had, before Islam, taken up independent residence in ʿUmān. Cf. Caskel, II, 442.

967. Cf. Caskel, II, 502.

968. Cf. Nuwayrī, 104–5.

969. Or "property" (*amwāl*).

970. Balansī, 149, says 700 captives, with Hudhayfah conducting them to Medina while ʿIkrimah remained in Dabā.

971. I.e., 800 people captured? Or 800 head of livestock?

972. *Shawādhib* (sing. *shādhib*), "those separated from their homeland."

By my life, Laqīṭ b. Mālik was met by [1980]
an evil that would make foxes shamefaced.
He challenged in battle Abū Bakr and those who praise [God],
whereupon there were thrown down
two strands of his mighty torrent.
The first one did not thwart him, and the enemies were not defeated;
but then his cavalry took away the straying camels.

The Account of Mahrah in the Uplands[973]

After [974] ʿIkrimah and ʿArfajah and Ḥudhayfah had finished with the apostasy of ʿUmān, ʿIkrimah went out with his army toward Mahrah. He asked those around ʿUmān and the people of ʿUmān for assistance, and marched until he reached Mahrah, with men of Nājiyah, al-Azd, ʿAbd al-Qays, Rāsib,[975] and Saʿd of Banū Tamīm[976] whom he had asked to help him, until he fell upon the territories of Mahrah. He met in [that country] two groups[977] of Mahrah. The first of them was in a place of the land of Mahrah called Jayrūt;[978] that region had been filled up as far as Naḍadūn, [Jayrūt and Naḍadūn being] two of the plains of Mahrah. They were led by Shakhrīt,[979] a man of Banū Shakrāt. As for the other [group], they were in the uplands. Now all of Mahrah had obeyed the leader of this group, which was led by al-

---

973. *Al-najd.*

974. Cf. Ibn al-Athīr, *Kāmil*, II, 373–74.

975. A branch of Jarm, which like Nājiya had settled in ʿUmān before Islām. Cf. Caskel, II, 211, 259, s.v. "Ǧarm"; 485.

976. *Saʿd min banī Tamīm.* Wellhausen, *Skizzen*, VI, 149 felt that text should read simply "Saʿd Tamīm," (i.e., referring to Saʿd b. Zaydmanāt b. Tamīm); in the *Emendanda*, De Goeje proposed that the text should read simply "Saʿd" (referring to Saʿd Hudhaym) and that *min banī Tamīm* should be dropped. Ibn al-Athīr, *Kāmil*, II, 373, has, in fact, only "Saʿd," and also omits mention of al-Azd.

977. Here and elsewhere in the paragraph, *jamʿ*, lit., "gathering," refers to a military force, particularly one of bedouins.

978. Neither Jayrūt nor the next toponym, Naḍadūn, are known to Hamdānī; Yāqūt's information about them is derived from this account and so adds nothing.

979. Ibn al-Athīr, *Kāmil*, II, 373: Sikhrīt.

Muṣabbaḥ, one of the Banū Muḥarib,[980] and all the people were
[1981] with him except those who were with Shakhrīt. So the two of them were in disagreement, each one of the two chiefs calling upon the other to [support] him, and each one of the two armies desiring that victory should be to their chief. That was how God helped the Muslims and strengthened them against their enemy, and weakened [the enemy].

Now when ʿIkrimah saw how few were those with Shakhrīt, he invited him to return to Islām. It was at the beginning of the call,[981] so (Shakhrīt) responded to him; in this way God weakened al-Muṣabbaḥ. Then (ʿIkrimah) sent to al-Muṣabbaḥ inviting him to Islām and to return from his unbelief; but he was deceived by how many there were with him, and moved further away because of Shakhrīt's situation.[982] So ʿIkrimah marched against him, and Shakhrīt marched with him; then they and al-Muṣabbaḥ met in the uplands, and fought more intensely than the fighting at Dabā. Then God put the armies of the apostates to flight and killed their leader. The Muslims pursued them, so that they killed of them what they wished and seized [as captives] what they wished. Among what they seized [as captives] were 2,000 noblewomen. Then ʿIkrimah set aside the fifth of the booty and sent the fifth with Shakhrīt to Abū Bakr, and divided the [remaining] four-fifths among the Muslims.[983] ʿIkrimah and his army grew stronger through the camels and goods and weapons [taken as booty]. ʿIkrimah remained so that he could muster them for whatever [purpose] he wished. The people of the Najd congregated—the people of Riyāḍ al-Rawḍah,[984] the people of the seacoast, the people of the

980. Several tribes with this name exist, most notably a branch of ʿAbd al-Qays in al-Baḥrayn; also bearing this name are branches of Quraysh, Qays (both Ḥijāz tribes) and ʿAnazah (of northeastern Arabia).

981. I.e., the beginning of the period when Islām was preached to the tribes of Arabia by the Muslims.

982. That is, since Shakhrīt had joined Islām, his rival al-Muṣabbaḥ distanced himself from it.

983. During the *riddah* and Islamic conquests, the one-fifth share of booty that in pre-Islamic times had been the share of the raid leader was set aside for the caliph to use for the good of the Muslim community.

984. Thus Yāqūt; text has "Riyāḍat al-Rawḍah." Cf. *Emendanda* and pp. 177–79, below.

islands, the people of [the lands of] myrrh and frankincense,[985]
the people of Jayrūt, Ẓuhūr al-Shiḥr, al-Ṣabarāt, Yanʿab, and [1982]
Dhāt al-Khiyam[986]—to take the oath of allegiance to Islām. Then he wrote about that with a herald—he was al-Sā'ib, one of the Banū ʿĀbid of Makhzūm—so he came to Abū Bakr with [news of] the conquest, and Shakhrīt arrived after him with the fifths [of booty]. About that ʿUljūm al-Muḥāribī said:

May God punish Shakhrīt and the splinter groups of Haysham
and Firḍim,[987] since groups from every quarter came to us.
A punishment deserved, [for] he had taken no heed of protection,[988]
and he did not hope for it in the way that relatives do.
Oh ʿIkrimah, but for the gathering of my tribe and their deeds,
indeed the places [where you could go] would have seemed confining to you.
We would have been like someone who lets a palm [of one hand] follow its mate;[989]
the vicissitudes [of fate] would have descended upon us in time.

---

985. Or "the people of al-Murr/al-Marr and Labbān." Text and Yāqūt have "al-Labbān." However, neither Hamdānī nor Yāqūt know of a place called al-Murr/al-Marr, and Yāqūt's entry for "al-Labbān" simply notes that it is in Mahrah and mentioned in the *riddah*, so his information is probably derived from this very account. The Mahrah and Ḥaḍramawt districts were, of course, well known as sources of myrrh (*al-murr*) and frankincense (*al-lubān*).

986. The four preceding toponyms are known to Yāqūt only as "places in the Mahrah mentioned during the *riddah*"; presumably, he got his information on them from this account.

987. Firḍim b. al-ʿUjayl was, according to Ibn al-Kalbī, from Mahrah (Caskel I, Table 328 and II, 247). Wellhausen, *Skizzen*, VI, 149, proposes to read "Qirḍim"; authorities are divided.

988. *Lam yurāqib li-dhimmatin.* Cf. the phrase *lā yarqubu fīhi illan wa-lā dhimmatan*, "he treated him ruthlessly"; Hans Wehr, *A Dictionary of Modern Arabic*, 352. Ibn al-Athīr, *Kāmil*, II, 373, has "took no heed of his religion (*li-dīnihi*)." Presumably the verse refers to Shakhrīt's betrayal of his tribe, Mahrah.

989. I.e., we would have wrung our hands?

Account of the Apostates in the Yemen

Abū Jaʿfar said: according to al-Sarī b. Yaḥyā—Shuʿayb—Sayf—Ṭalḥah—ʿIkrimah and Sahl—al-Qāsim b. Muḥammad:[990] The Apostle of God died while over Mecca and its territory were ʿAttāb b. Asīd[991] and al-Ṭāhir b. Abī Hālah, ʿAttāb over Banū
[1983] Kinānah and al-Ṭāhir over ʿAkk.[992] That was [because] the Prophet had said, "Put the governorship of ʿAkk among the descendants of his ancestor Maʿadd b. ʿAdnān."[993] Over al-Ṭā'if and its territory were ʿUthmān b. Abī al-ʿĀṣ[994] and Mālik b. ʿAwf al-Naṣrī,[995] ʿUthmān over the settled people and Mālik over the nomads, the hinder parts of Hawāzin.[996] Over Najrān and its territory were ʿAmr b. Ḥazm and Abū Sufyān b. Ḥarb,[997] ʿAmr b. Ḥazm over prayer and Abū Sufyān b. Ḥarb over the *sadaqah* taxes. Over [the territory] between Rimaʿ and Zabīd as far as the border of Najrān was Khālid b. Saʿīd b. al-ʿĀṣ. Over all of Hamdān was ʿĀmir b. Shahr, and over Ṣanʿā' was Fayrūz al-Daylamī, supported by Dādhawayh and Qays b. Makshūḥ. Over al-Janad was Yaʿlā b. Umayyah, and over Ma'rib was Abū Mūsā al-Ashʿarī. Over the Ashʿarīs in addition to ʿAkk was al-Ṭāhir b. Abī Hālah. Muʿādh b. Jabal used to instruct the people, making the rounds in the district of every governor.[998]

Then al-Aswad sprang upon them during the life of the Prophet, so the Prophet waged war against him by means of

---

990. Cf. p. 19, above; Ibn al-Athīr, *Kāmil*, II, 374–75; Caetani, 569–70, 581–82.

991. An Umayyad and late convert to Islam who had been appointed governor of Mecca by the Prophet. Cf. *EI*², s.v. "ʿAttāb b. Asīd."

992. Ibn al-Athīr, *Kāmil*: ʿAkk and the Ashʿarīs. Cf. below, in this paragraph.

993. Maʿadd was the supposed ancestor of all North Arabs. Cf. *EI*², s.v. "Maʿadd" (A. Grohmann—G. R. Smith).

994. A member of the tribe of Thaqīf of al-Ṭā'if, he converted late, just before the Prophet's conquest of his city; he was earnest in teaching the Qur'ān. Cf. Caskel, II, 579; Ibn al-Athīr, *Usd*, III, 272–74.

995. A chief of the Naṣr b. Muʿāwiyah clan of Hawāzin. Cf. Caskel, II, 387.

996. *Aʿjāz Hawāzin.*

997. Abū Sufyān, father of the Umayyad caliph Muʿawiyah, was head of the Umayyah clan of Quraysh at the time of the Prophet; he opposed the Prophet until his conversion to Islam just before the conquest of Mecca. Cf. *EI*², s.v. "Abū Sufyān b. Ḥarb" (W. M. Watt).

998. *Fī ʿamali kulli ʿāmilin.*

envoys and letters until God killed him and the cause of the Prophet returned to what it had been one night before the Prophet's death. However, the arrival [of the Prophet's commanders in Yemen][999] did not stir up the people since the people were prepared for it. Then, when [news of] the death of the Prophet reached them, the Yemen and the countries[1000] rebelled. The horsemen of al-ʿAnsī had been in a commotion in [the country] between Najrān and Ṣanʿāʾ on the side of that sea, not taking refuge with anyone nor anyone taking refuge with them. So ʿAmr b. Maʿdīkarib [was] opposite Farwah b. Musayk,[1001] and Muʿāwiyah b. Anas[1002] [was] leading the fugitive soldiers of al-ʿAnsī, wavering. None of the governors of the Prophet returned [to Medina][1003] after the death of the Prophet, except ʿAmr b. [1984]
Ḥazm and Khālid b. Saʿīd. The rest of the governors took refuge among the Muslims. ʿAmr b. Maʿdīkarib confronted Khālid b. Saʿīd, so he seized as booty from him [ʿAmr's sword] "The Persistent." The messengers returned bearing the news, and Jarīr b. ʿAbdallāh[1004] and al-ʾAqraʿ b. ʿAbdallāh[1005] and Wabr b. Yuḥannis came back. So until such time as Usāmah b. Zayd returned from Syria—that was estimated at three months—Abū Bakr waged war against all the apostates [only] by means of envoys and letters, just as the Apostle of God had done, except for the affairs of the people of Dhū Ḥusā and Dhū al-Qaṣṣah.[1006] Then the first clash upon the return of Usāmah was this.[1007] So

---

999. Cf. pp. 33 and 38, above. The text is problematic; Wellhausen, (*Skizzen*, VI, 149–50) and De Goeje (*Emendanda*) disagree on rendering and reading. I have followed De Goeje.

1000. I.e., the surrounding districts? (*al-buldān*).

1001. Of the Murād group of the tribe of Madhḥij, he came to the Prophet at the end of the latter's life and was sent by him over Madhḥij; cf. Caskel, II, 245; Ibn al-Athīr, *Usd*, IV, 180–81.

1002. Of the tribe of Sulaym; cf. Ibn Ḥajar, *Iṣābah* s.v.

1003. Cf. p. 22, above.

1004. Chief of Bajīlah who came to the Prophet in his last year and was put at head of his tribe by him. Cf. Caskel, II, 218; Ibn al-Athīr, *Usd*, I, 279–80.

1005. Of Ḥimyar; sent by the Prophet to Dhū Murrān. Cf. Ibn Ḥajar, *Iṣābah*, s.v.

1006. In these two instances, Abū Bakr resorted to military confrontation; cf. pp. 40ff., above.

1007. I.e., Dhū al-Qaṣṣah. Cairo, following Kosegarten, reads "the first people to clash . . . were they."

he went out to al-Abraq. He did not face a tribe directly to defeat them; rather, he incited those among them who had not apostatized against the others. So, with a group of the *Muhājirūn* and the *Anṣār* and those who had been aroused among the non-apostates, (Abū Bakr) vanquished those [rebels] who were close to them, until he took care of the last of the business of the army[1008] without asking the [former] apostates for help [against the remaining rebels]. The first who wrote to him was ʿAttāb b. Asīd; he wrote to him about the pursuit of those who had stood firm in Islām by those in his governorship who had apostatized, while ʿUthmān b. Abī al-ʿĀṣ [wrote] of the pursuit of those who had stood firm in Islām by those who had apostatized among the people in his governorship. As for ʿAttāb, he sent Khālid b. Asīd[1009] against the people of the Tihāmah, for there had gathered in it groups from Mudlij; and there congregated to them scattered persons from Khuzāʿah[1010] and splinter groups from Kinānah, commanded by Jundab b. Sulmā,[1011] one of the Banū Shannūq of Banū Mudlij.[1012] In the governorship (*ʿamal*) of ʿAttāb there was no gathering besides this, so they met at al-
[1985] Abāriq, whereupon [Khālid b. Asīd] dispersed them and killed them. The slaughter was great among the Banū Shannūq, so that they remained weak and few in number [after that]. The governorship[1013] of ʿAttāb became free [of rebels], and Jundab escaped. Then Jundab said about that:

1008. *Ākhiri ʾumūr al-nās*, i.e., the last rebels opposing the Muslims. The sentence is difficult; cf. Wellhausen, *Skizzen*, VI, 150; *Emendanda*.

1009. ʿAttāb's brother; he embraced Islam at the time of the conquest of Mecca and was one of those Meccans given special favors by the Prophet in order to win them over; they were called those "whose hearts were reconciled." Cf. Caskel, II, 341; Ibn al-Athīr, *Usd*, II, 76.

1010. An old tribe living between Mecca and Medina, formerly dominant in Mecca before being displaced by Quraysh. Cf. EI^2, s.v. "Khuzāʿa" (M. J. Kister); Caskel, II, 350.

1011. Ibn al-Athīr, *Kāmil*, II, 374, has Salmā.

1012. Shannūq b. Murrah, a section of Kinānah, was, according to Ibn al-Kalbī, not part of Mudlij b. Murrah, but rather a lateral affiliate. Cf. Caskel, I, Table 44, and II, 416 and 526. The conflation may have been introduced to explain the verses below.

1013. *ʿUmālah*.

I repented and knew with certainty in the morning that I
had come to something the disgrace of which remains on a man.
I bear witness that there is nothing beside God.
Banū Mudlij, God is my Lord and my Protector.[1014]

ʿUthmān b. Abī al-ʿĀṣ sent a force against Shanūʾah.[1015] There had gathered in it groups of Azd and Bajīlah and Khathʿam,[1016] led by Ḥumayḍah b. al-Nuʿmān.[1017] In charge of the people of al-Ṭāʾif was ʿUthmān b. Rabīʿah.[1018] So they met in Shanūʾah; then they routed those groups and they dispersed from Ḥumayḍah. Ḥumayḍah fled into the countryside, whereupon ʿUthmān b. Rabīʿah said about that:

We broke up their groups while the pool filled with dust,
and the niggardly clouds may promise relief deceitfully.
A lightning-cloud[1019] flashed when we met,
then those flashings returned as rainless clouds.

The Wicked People of ʿAkk

Abū Jaʿfar said:[1020] The first rebellion in the Tihāmah after the [death of the] Prophet was [that of] ʿAkk and the Ashʿarīs. [1986]
[The story of] that was that, when the death of the Prophet reached them, scattered remnants of them gathered; then scattered remnants and large groupings[1021] from the Ashʿarīs

---

1014. Reading *jāriyā* with Wellhausen, *Skizzen*, VI, 150 and *Emendanda*, against *jāru-hā*, "its Protector" in the text and Cairo.

1015. A district in Yemen. Cf. Yāqūt, s.v.

1016. All three were tribes of the Sarāt region (modern ʿAsīr) of southwest Arabia; Khathʿam was closely associated with Bajīlah. Cf. *EI*², s.v. "Azd" (G. Strenziok), "Badjīla" (W. M. Watt), and "Khathʿam" (G. Levi della Vida).

1017. Cf. Ṭabarī, I, 2218: a Bāriqī (of Azd).

1018. According to Ibn al-Athīr, *Usd*, III, 371, he was from Quraysh and among the emigrants to Abyssinia; according to Caskel, I, Table 115 and II, 579, he was of Hawāzin.

1019. *Bāriq*; perhaps "sword." In either case, evidently a pun on the name of Ḥumayḍah's clan, Bāriq.

1020. Cf. Ibn al-Athīr, *Kāmil*, II, 375.

1021. Reading *khiḍamm* with *Emendanda*, against *khaḍḍama* in text and Cairo; cf. Ibn Manẓūr, XII, 83. Wellhausen, *Skizzen*, VI, 150 proposed *ḥakam*. Cf. also Caetani, 582.

came to them, so they joined with them. Then they remained on al-Aʿlāb,[1022] the coastal road. Parties of men under no leader congregated to them. So al-Ṭāhir b. Abī Hālah wrote about this to Abū Bakr, and marched against them, writing also about his marching against them—with him was Masrūq al-ʿAkkī[1023]—until he came to those parties of men on al-Aʿlāb; then they met and fought, whereupon God routed them. They slaughtered them by every means; the roads stank because of their slaughter. Their killing was a great conquest.

Abū Bakr responded to al-Ṭāhir before [al-Ṭāhir's] letter about the conquest could come to him: "Your letter has reached me, in which you inform me that you have marched against the wicked people in al-Aʿlāb and that you have asked Masrūq and his tribe for assistance. You are right, so hurry [to deliver] this blow; do not deal gently with them. Occupy al-Aʿlāb until the road of the wicked people should become secure and [until] my order should reach you." So those groups of ʿAkk and those who congregated to them have been called to this day "the wicked people," and that road has been called "the road of the wicked people." Al-Ṭāhir b. Abī Hālah said about that:

By God, if not for God, other than Whom there is no thing,
the ʿAthāʿith[1024] would not have been dispersed in the rugged hills.
My eye had never seen a day like the one I saw
beside the sweat of horses among the groupings of the wicked people.
[1987] We slew them from the hilltop of Khāmir[1025]
as far as the red sodden plains strewn with mud dredged from wells.[1026]

1022. Yāqūt knows this as a toponym, but evidently gets his information solely from this account. Cf. Ibn Manẓūr, I, 627, which defines *ʿilb* as "barren place."

1023. Cf. Wathīmah, 31/74, which has "Masrūq b. Dhī al-Ḥarb al-Hamdānī al-Arḥabī."

1024. Possibly a nickname applied to the Shahrān, an important lineage of the tribe of Khathʿam, because several of their chiefs bore the name ʿAthʿath. Cf. Caskel, II, 205; Ibn Manẓūr, II, 168 left.

1025. A mountain in the ʿAkk country, according to Yāqūt, s.v.

1026. Yāqūt, s.v. "Khāmir," reads "having ʿAthāʿith."

We seized as booty the flocks of the wicked ones by force,
fighting openly; we took no heed of the din of battle.

Ṭāhir encamped on the "road of the wicked ones," along with Masrūq leading ʿAkk, awaiting Abū Bakr's order.

Abū Jaʿfar said:[1027] When the [news of the] death of the Apostle of God reached the people of Najrān—they were at that time 40,000 fighting men of Banū al-Afʿā,[1028] the community who were in (Najrān) before Banū al-Ḥārith[1029]—they sent a delegation [to Abū Bakr] to renew the pact. So they came to him, whereupon he wrote for them:

> In the name of God, the Merciful, the Compassionate: this is a document from the servant of God, Abū Bakr, successor of the Apostle of God, to the people of Najrān. He affords them protection from his army and himself, and decrees for them the protection[1030] of Muḥammad, except that which Muḥammad the Apostle of God had revoked on God's command regarding their lands and the lands of the Arabs, that two religions should not dwell in them. Thereafter he gave them protection for their persons, their communities, the rest of their properties,[1031] their dependents, their horses,[1032] those absent of them and those present, their bishop and their monks and their churches wherever they might be; and for what their hands possess whether little or much. They owe what is incumbent upon them; if they pay it, they will not be compelled to emigrate, nor tithed, [1988]
> nor shall a bishop be changed from his bishopric or a monk from his monastic life. He shall fulfil for them everything that the Apostle of God granted them in

1027. Cf. Ibn al-Athīr, *Kāmil*, II, 375; Caetani, 582–83.

1028. Presumably descendants of al-Afʿā ("Viper") b.al-Ḥusayn, a legendary judge in Najrān; cf. Caskel, II, 142.

1029. Banū al-Ḥārith b. Kaʿb (Bal-Ḥārith) was a tribe of the Najrān area allied to Madhḥij; they had negotiated with the Prophet, but later backed al-Aswad. Cf. *EI*², s.v. "al-Ḥārith b. Kaʿb" (J. Schleifer); Caskel, II, 308.

1030. *Dhimmah*.

1031. Possibly "flocks": *amwāl*.

1032. Possibly simply "troops": *ʿādiyah*.

writing, and everything that is in this document by way of the protection of Muḥammad, the Apostle of God, and the covenant of the Muslims. They owe [the Muslims] advice and righteousness in those just duties that are incumbent upon them. Al-Miswar b. ʿAmr and ʿAmr, the client of Abū Bakr, were witnesses [to this agreement].

Abū Bakr sent Jarīr b. ʿAbdallāh back and ordered him to summon those from his tribe[1033] who had remained firm in the cause of God, and then to ask those who could reinforce them for help, so as to fight with them those who had turned away from the cause of God. He ordered him to come to Khathʿam so that he could fight those who rebelled out of zealous attachment[1034] to Dhū al-Khalaṣah[1035] and those who wished to restore it [as their deity], until God should kill them and those who participated with them in that. Then he was to direct himself toward Najrān, to remain in it until (Abū Bakr's) orders should reach him. So Jarīr went out, carrying out that which Abū Bakr had commanded him to do. No one opposed him[1036] except some men leading a small number [of followers]; so he killed them and pursued them. Then he directed himself to Najrān, and resided in it awaiting the order of Abū Bakr.

(Abū Bakr) wrote to ʿUthmān b. Abī al-ʿĀṣ to impose on the people of al-Ṭā'if [the raising of] an army, each district [contributing] according to its ability, and to put in command over them a man in whom he had confidence and whose intentions[1037] he trusted. So he imposed twenty men [as a contribution] on each district, and put his brother in command of them. (Abū Bakr) wrote to ʿAttāb b. Asīd to impose on the

1033. I.e., from Bajīlah.

1034. Lit., "out of anger" (*ghaḍaban*).

1035. A pagan shrine of Bajīlah, Khathʿam, Daws, Azd, and other tribes of al-Sarāt, located near Tabālah, 300 km southeast of Mecca. Cf. *EI*², s.v. "Dhū al-Khalaṣa" (T. Fahd).

1036. Or "detained him?" Text and Cairo read *lam y-q-rr lahu*; Ibn al-Athīr, *Kāmil*, II, 375, has *lam y-q-m*; the editor notes that Ibn Khaldūn has *lam y-m-r bihi*.

1037. *Nāhiyah*.

people of Mecca and its district 500 reinforcements, and to send over them a man in whom he had confidence. So he named [1989] those whom he would send and put Khālid b. Asīd in command of them. He appointed the commander of each tribe, and they stood at the ready for Abū Bakr's order to reach them and for al-Muhājir to come to them.

Apostasy of the People of the Yemen a Second Time

Abū Ja'far said: Among those of them who apostatized a second time was Qays b. 'Abd Yaghūth b. Makshūḥ.[1038]

According to al-Sarī—Shu'ayb—Sayf:[1039] The story of Qays in his second apostasy was that when the news of the Apostle of God's death came to them, [the pact] was violated and he worked for the killing of Fayrūz and Dādhawayh and Jushaysh. Abū Bakr wrote to 'Umayr Dhū Murrān and to Sa'īd Dhū Zūd and to Samayfa' Dhū al-Kalā' and to Ḥawshab Dhū Ẓulaym and to Shahr Dhū Yanāf,[1040] ordering them to stick to their position[1041] and to undertake the cause of God and of the people, and promising them soldiers: "From Abū Bakr, successor of the Apostle of God, to 'Umayr b. Aflaḥ Dhū Murrān, Sa'īd b. al-'Āqib Dhū Zūd, Samayfa' b. Nākūr Dhū al-Kalā', Ḥawshab Dhū Ẓulaym, and Shahr Dhū Yanāf. Now then: assist the Abnā' against whosoever opposes them, defend them, and obey Fayrūz and apply your utmost effort with him, for I have appointed him [governor]."

According to al-Sarī—Shu'ayb—Sayf—al-Mustanīr b. Yazīd—'Urwah b. Ghaziyyah al-Dathīnī:[1042] After Abū Bakr was appointed, he put Fayrūz in command. Before that, they had relied [1990] upon one another—(Fayrūz) and Dādhawayh and Jushaysh and Qays.[1043] He wrote to some of the chiefs of the people of the

---

1038. On his name, see note 145, above.
1039. Cf. Ibn al-Athīr, *Kāmil*, II, 375–76.
1040. Ibn al-Athīr, *Kāmil*, II, 376 has "Dhū Niyāf." On these "Dhūs" see p. 27 and note 168, above.
1041. Lit., "to stick to that in which they were," i.e., to stand fast in Islām.
1042. Ibn al-Athīr, *Kāmil*, II, 376–77 (parallels Ṭabarī through p. 169).
1043. I.e., no one had been in overall command, each leader being equal and supporting the others as need required.

Yemen. When Qays heard about that, he wrote to Dhū al-Kalāʿ and his companions, "The Abnā' are interlopers in your country and foreigners among you. Even if you leave them, they will not cease to be against you. I have come to hold the opinion that I should murder their chiefs and expel them from our country." But they declared themselves clear [of the matter], such that they did not conspire with him nor assist the Abnā', but kept aloof, saying, "We have nothing to do with this. You are their responsibility and they are your responsibility."[1044] So Qays lay in wait for them and prepared to kill their chiefs and to expel their common [followers]. Then Qays corresponded with those defeated Laḥjī troops who were roaming about, while they were going up and down through the country, waging war against all who opposed them. Qays corresponded with them in secret and ordered them to hurry to him, [proposing] that his cause and their cause should be one and that they should unite in exiling the Abnā' from the lands of the Yemen. So they wrote [back] to him responding [favorably] to him, and informed him that they were hastening to him. The people of Ṣanʿā' were taken by surprise, [learning of it] only with the news of their drawing near it.[1045] Then Qays came to Fayrūz about that, as though he were terrified of this news, and came to Dādhawayh and consulted the two of them in order to confuse them so that they would not suspect him; so they took that into consideration and had confidence in him. Then[1046] Qays invited them to a meal the next day, starting with Dādhawayh, and [asking] Fayrūz next and
[1991] Jushaysh [after him]. So Dādhawayh went out to call on (Qays); but when he did so, (Qays) fell upon him quickly and killed him. Fayrūz went out to go [to Qays also] until, when he was drawing near, he overheard two women talking between the rooftops. One of them said, "This one will be killed just as Dādhawayh was killed." So he met the two of them; then he turned aside until he could see the people, high up, gathered together. [When]

1044. Lit., "You are their companion . . ." etc. The idea is that Qays and the Abnā' must settle their relationship themselves.

1045. Lit., "Nothing took the people of Ṣanʿā' by surprise except the news of their drawing near it."

1046. Cf. Ibn Ḥubaysh, 77; he says Fayrūz escaped to Abū Bakr.

they were told of Fayrūz's turning back, they went out running [in pursuit]. Fayrūz ran to meet Jushaysh, whereupon he went out with him heading toward the mountain of Khawlān,[1047] for they were the maternal relatives of Fayrūz. The two of them preceded the horsemen to the mountain. Then the two of them climbed down and up the mountain, wearing only plain boots, so that their feet were cut before they arrived. They reached Khawlān, and Fayrūz entrenched himself among his maternal relatives and swore not to wear plain boots. The horsemen returned to Qays. Then he rose in rebellion in Ṣanʿāʾ and occupied it, and collected what was around it, playing for time.[1048] The horsemen of al-Aswad came to him. Now after Fayrūz had taken refuge with his maternal kinsmen of Khawlān, so that they guarded him and the people flocked to him, he wrote to Abū Bakr with the news. Then Qays said, "What is Khawlān, and what is Fayrūz, and in what abode have they taken refuge?" The common people of the tribes to whose leaders Abū Bakr had written sided with Qays, whereas the leaders remained withdrawn.[1049] Qays sought out the Abnāʾ, dividing them into three subdivisions. Those who remained he safeguarded, and their families he safeguarded.[1050] The families of those who had fled to Fayrūz he divided into two groups; one of them he sent to Aden so that they could be carried [away] by sea, and the other was carried away by land. To all of them he said, "Go to your country!" With them he sent someone to make them go. The family of al-Daylamī was among those who were made to go away by land; the family of Dādhawayh were among those who were made to go away by sea. So when Fayrūz saw that the [1992] majority of the people of the Yemen had gathered to Qays, and that the families had been marched [into exile], and [that] he had exposed them to plunder, and [that] he had not found any way to separate himself from his camp in order to save them, and when (Fayrūz) learned what Qays had said out of contempt for him

1047. A tribe and mountain district southeast of Ṣanʿāʾ in Yemen; cf. Caskel, II, 345; Wilson, 158; Yāqūt, s.v.

1048. Lit., "advancing a foot and withdrawing a foot."

1049. I.e., neutral?

1050. Or "those who remained he settled (*aqarra*)" etc.

[and for his] maternal relatives and the Abnā', he said, by way of tracing his lineage and boasting, and mentioning the departure on a desert voyage:[1051]

Call, you two, for the departure of a woman to the palm-filled sands,
and speak to her, so that there would be no blame on me.
What the enemies say did not harm them, even if they said much;
he came to his tribe with neither excess nor stinginess.
So desist from a woman on the road that is stretched out
toward the object of her desire, as the sands seek the sands.
Even if, indeed, our residence was in Ṣanʿā',
ours are the offspring of a tribe from whose noble chiefs my offspring are.
In truth, strong and stubborn Daylam, after hardship,
refused the life of ease and chose the heat over shade.
Most of the lush places of Iraq belonged
to my close kin, when the cooking pots of Kisrā were boiling.[1052]
My lineage [I trace to] a brave one; no matter how much I have grown, my station [in life]
is just like the end of every stick, at the root.
[1993] (My ancestors) left my way level, and they fortified
my mountain roads with good sayings and abundant noble deeds.
Our glory is not from the ignorance[1053] of those of enmity;
God insisted on being glorious despite ignorance.
(The enemy) did not divert us in times of peace from the family of Aḥmad,[1054]
nor did they detract from Islām since they embraced Islām before me.
And if a bucketful of [the deeds of] my tribe had sprinkled me,
I would want my bucketful to drown them.

1051. The departure on a desert voyage (*ẓuʿn*) is a common part of the classical *qaṣīda* or ode.
1052. I.e., in the heyday of Kisrā.
1053. Or "barbarity, coarseness": *jahl*.
1054. I.e., from Islām; Aḥmad = Muḥammad.

Fayrūz continued in his war and devoted himself to it. He sent a messenger to the Banū 'Uqayl b. [Ka'b b.] Rabī'ah b. 'Āmir b. Ṣa'ṣa'ah[1055] [informing them] that he was taking refuge with them and asking them for reinforcements and assistance in bearing down on those who were disturbing the households of the Abnā'. And he sent a messenger to 'Akk, asking them for reinforcements and assistance against those who were disturbing the households of the Abnā'. So 'Uqayl mounted—they were led by a man of the allies called Mu'āwiyah—so that they confronted the cavalry of Qays and then rescued those families. They killed those who were making them march into exile and barred them from the villages until Fayrūz returned to Ṣan'ā'. 'Akk, led by Masrūq, sprang up to march until they rescued the families of the Abnā', and barred them[1056] from the villages until Fayrūz returned to Ṣan'ā'. 'Uqayl and 'Akk reinforced Fayrūz with men. After their reinforcements reached him among those who had gathered to him, he went out at the head of those who had congregated to him and those who had reinforced him [1994] from 'Akk and 'Uqayl; then he clashed with Qays, so that they met before Ṣan'ā'. Then they fought, whereupon God routed Qays at the head of his tribe and those who had risen up. So he departed in flight with his army until he returned with them; they returned to the place in which they had hurried when they fled after the murder of al-'Ansī. Qays was in command of them. The faction of al-'Ansī, and Qays with them, were in a commotion between Ṣan'ā' and Najrān. 'Amr b. Ma'dīkarib was facing Farwah b. Musayk in obedience to al-'Ansī.

According to al-Sarī—Shu'ayb—Sayf—'Aṭiyyah—'Amr b. Salamah:[1057] Part of the affair of Farwah b. Musayk was that he had come to the Apostle of God as a Muslim. About that he said:

1055. A powerful and wide-ranging tribe of the 'Āmir group, centered around Jabal Ṭuwayq in central Arabia. Cf. Caskel, II, 365, s.v. "Ka'b b. Rabī'a b. 'Āmir."

1056. Presumably referring to those who had been marching the Abnā' families into exile, but who are not mentioned in this sentence as they are in the preceding one. It seems probable that this repeat of the earlier phrase constitutes a dittography, rather than part of Ṭabarī's original text.

1057. Cf. Ibn al-Athīr, *Kāmil*, II, 377.

When I saw the kings of Ḥimyar, they shied away
like the leg whose sciatic nerve betrayed it.[1058]
I steered my she-camel before Muḥammad;
I desire benefits and good praise for her.

Among the things the Apostle of God said to him was, "Did what befell your tribe on the day of al-Razm displease you, oh Farwah, or please you?" He replied, "Anyone whose tribe was afflicted as much as my tribe was afflicted on the day of al-Razm would dislike that." (Now the day of al-Razm was [a battle] between (Murād) and the Hamdān over Yaghūth, an idol that was sometimes with the former and sometimes with the latter. Then Murād desired to take sole control of it from (Hamdān) during their time; but Hamdān slaughtered them and their chief, al-Ajdaʿ, the father of Masrūq.) So the Apostle of God said, "Indeed, that only increased their good standing in Islām." Whereupon (Farwah) replied, "It would please me if that were [so]." So the Apostle of God appointed him over the *ṣadaqah* taxes of Murād and whoever resided with them or dwelt in their
[1995] territory.[1059] ʿAmr b. Maʿdīkarib had abandoned his tribe, Saʿd al-ʿAshīrah, leading Banū Zubayd[1060] and its allies, and he joined (Murād) and embraced Islam with them; he was in charge of them.[1061] Then, when al-ʿAnsī apostatized and most people of Madhḥij followed him, Farwah withdrew, leading those who stood fast in Islām with him, whereas ʿAmr was one of those who apostatized. So al-ʿAnsī appointed him deputy and put him opposite Farwah so that he was facing him. Each one of them stayed put because of his counterpart's being in plain view, so the two of them exchanged poetry. ʿAmr said, mentioning the command of Farwah and denouncing it:

We have found the kingship of Farwah to be the worst of kingships;
[he is] an ass whose nostrils sniff some filth.

1058. I.e., made it unable to walk because of pain.
1059. *Dār*.
1060. Saʿd al-ʿAshīrah was a confederation within Madhḥij, and Zubayd a section within Madhḥij living a sedentary life in the Wādī Tathlīth. Cf. Caskel, II, 493 and 608.
1061. *wa kāna fī-him.*

Whenever you saw Abū ʿUmayr,
you were looking upon the amniotic bag of foulness and afterbirth.[1062]

So Farwah responded to him:

Some talk has reached me from Abū Thawr;
Of old he used to run among the mules.
God used to hate him before
for what there was of foulness and afterbirth.

While the two of them were doing that, ʿIkrimah came to Abyan.[1063]

According to al-Sarī—Shuʿayb—Sayf—Sahl—al-Qāsim and Mūsā b. al-Ghuṣn—Ibn Muḥayrīz:[1064] Then ʿIkrimah went out from Mahrah, marching towards the Yemen, until he came to Abyan. With him were many people from Mahrah, Saʿd b. Zayd,[1065] al-Azd, Nājiyah, ʿAbd al-Qays, and Ḥudbān of Banū Mālik b. Kinānah[1066] and ʿAmr b. Jundab from al-ʿAnbar.[1067] [1996]
Then he gathered al-Nakhaʿ after he struck those of them who had retreated, and said to them, "What was your position[1068] in this matter?" At this they told him, "During the *jāhiliyyah* we were the people of a religion,[1069] not dealing [with people] the way some of the Arabs used to deal with others. All the more so since we have come to a religion whose merit we recognize and which we have come to love."[1070] Whereupon he asked about them, [and found that] the situation was as they said. Their

1062. Or "treachery" (*al-ghadr*); also in poem immediately following.
1063. A place in the mountains near Aden; also a place on the coast near Aden and a district near ʿAden; cf. *EI*², s.v. "Abyan" (O. Löfgren); Yāqūt, s.v.
1064. Cf. Ibn al-Athīr, *Kāmil*, II, 377 bottom.
1065. Either the tribe of Saʿd b. Zaydmanāt of Tamīm, or Saʿd Hudhaym b. Zayd.
1066. Ḥudbān b. Jadhīmah was part of Mālik b. Kinānah; cf. Caskel, I, Table 47, II, 327.
1067. ʿAmr b. Jundab was a branch of Banū ʿAnbar of ʿAmr b. Tamīm; cf. Caskel I, Table 81, II, 173.
1068. Lit., "how were you . . . ?"
1069. *dīn*; presumably meaning here a revealed religion such as Christianity, not pre-Islamic Arabian polytheism.
1070. *Fa-kayfa binā idhā ṣirnā ilā dīnin ʿarafnā faḍlahu.*

common people stood fast [in the faith], and those of their notables who had withdrawn fled. ('Ikrimah) purged[1071] al-Nakha' and Ḥimyar and remained so they could gather 'round him. When 'Ikrimah descended upon the Yemen, Qays b. 'Abd Yaghūth fled to 'Amr b. Ma'dīkarib; but after he had joined him, a dispute broke out between them and they found fault with one another. Then 'Amr b. Ma'dīkarib said, reproaching Qays for his treachery toward the Abnā' and his killing of Dādhawayh, and mentioning his flight from Fayrūz:

You acted treacherously and did not do well in faithfulness; no one can
endure [such] deeds except the one who is accustomed.
How could Qays exalt himself
if he were to compete with a [truly] noble leader?

And Qays said:

I was faithful to my tribe and, preparing for action, I gathered [to meet] a company
that struck 'Amr and Marthad despite the tribes.
When I met the Abnā', I was to them
like a lion who aspires to lionhood through might.

And 'Amr B. Ma'dīkarib said:

Dādhaway[h] is not [a source of] glory for you;
rather, Dādhaway[h] disgraced what must be protected.
And Fayrūz by morning spread affliction among you
and remained in your groups and sought refuge.

[1997] *The Story of Ṭāhir When He Marched to Reinforce Fayrūz*

Abū Ja'far al-Ṭabarī said: Abū Bakr had written to Ṭāhir b. Abī Hālah and to Masrūq to go down to Ṣan'ā' and to assist the Abnā'; so the two of them went out until they came to Ṣan'ā'. and he wrote [also] to 'Abdallāh b. Thawr b. Aṣghar[1072] to gather

1071. *Istabra'a.*
1072. Cf. Ṭabarī, I, 2136: of Ghawth (Ṭayyi').

to himself the Arabs and those people of the Tihāmah who responded to him, and then to remain in his place until his command should reach him. Now[1073] [the story of] the first apostasy of ʿAmr b. Maʿdīkarib was that he had been with Khālid b. Saʿīd, but he clashed with him and responded [favorably] to al-Aswad. So Khālid b. Saʿīd marched against him until he encountered him; then they exchanged two blows. Khālid struck (ʿAmr) on his shoulder, severing the harness for his sword, which fell, and the blow reached his shoulder. ʿAmr struck (Khālid), but did not produce any effect. Then when Khālid wished to [strike him] a second time, (Amr) dismounted and climbed up into the mountains [in flight]. (Khālid) plundered him of his horse and his sword, "The Persistent"; ʿAmr took refuge among those to whom he fled.

Now the estate of the family of Saʿīd b. al-ʿĀṣ the Elder became the property of Saʿīd b. al-ʿĀṣ the Younger;[1074] then, after (Saʿīd the Younger) was appointed [to govern] al-Kūfah, ʿAmr [b. Maʿdīkarib] offered him his daughter [in marriage], but he did not accept her. (Saʿīd) came to (ʿAmr) in his house, bringing a number of swords that Khālid had taken in the Yemen. Whereupon (Saʿīd) said, "Which of them is 'The Persistent'?" (ʿAmr) said, "This one." [So] he said [to ʿAmr], "Take it, it is yours." So he took it. Then he saddled a mule of his and struck the pad [with the sword], severing it and the saddle, and making the mule hurry. Then he returned it to Saʿīd, saying, "If you had visited me in my house and it was mine, I would have given it to you. But I cannot accept it since it fell."

According to al-Sarī—Shuʿayb—Sayf—al-Mustanīr b. Yazīd— [1998]
ʿUrwah b. Ghaziyyah and Mūsā—Abū Zurʿah al-Shaybānī:[1075] When al-Muhājir b. Abī Umayyah left Abū Bakr—he was among the last who left—he took the Mecca road. So he passed by it, whereupon Khālid b. Asīd followed him; and he passed by al-

---

1073. Cf. Ibn al-Athīr, *Kāmil*, II, 377.

1074. Saʿīd b. al-ʿĀṣ the Younger, of the Umayyah clan of Quraysh, was grandson of Saʿīd the Elder; Cf. Caskel, II, 500.

1075. Cf. Ibn al-Athīr, II, 377–78. Text, following Mss, has "al-Saybānī," but cf. p. 34.

Ṭā'if, upon which ʿAbd al-Raḥmān b. Abī al-ʿĀṣ followed him. Then he continued on until, when he was opposite Jarīr b. ʿAbdallāh, he joined him to him[self]; and ʿAbdallāh b. Thawr joined him when he was opposite him. Then he came to the people of Najrān, upon which Farwah b. Musayk joined him. ʿAmr b. Maʿdīkarib abandoned Qays [b. ʿAbd Yaghūth] and approached in response until he entered upon al-Muhājir without any [pledge of] protection. So al-Muhājir tied him up, and he tied up Qays, and wrote of their situation to Abū Bakr and sent the two of them to him. Then, when al-Muhājir marched from Najrān to the Lahjites[1076] and the cavalry gathered against those fugitive soldiers, they demanded protection. But he refused to give them security, whereupon they separated into two groups. So al-Muhājir encountered one of [the two groups] at ʿAjīb,[1077] destroying them. His cavalry found the other on the "road of the wicked ones," destroying them and the cavalry of ʿAbdallāh. He killed the scattered remnants on every byway.

Then Qays and ʿAmr were brought before Abū Bakr; so he said, "Oh Qays, did you wage aggression against the servants of God, killing them and adopting as followers the apostates and polytheists, to the exclusion of the believers?" Now he intended
[1999] to kill him if he found a clear case. Qays denied that he was in any way involved in the affair of Dādhawayh, for that deed had been done in secret, of which there was no evidence. So (Abū Bakr) shrank from [taking] his blood. To ʿAmr b. Maʿdīkarib (Abū Bakr) said, "Aren't you ashamed that you are every day defeated or captive? If you had aided this religion, God would have exalted you." Then he released him, and returned the two of them to their tribes. ʿAmr said, "There is no avoiding it; verily I shall consent [to embrace Islam], and not recant."

According to al-Sarī—Shuʿayb—Sayf—al-Mustanīr and Mūsā: Al-Muhājir marched from ʿAjīb until he descended upon Ṣanʿāʾ. He commanded that the scattered [men] of the tribes who had

1076. *Al-Laḥjiyyah*. Wellhausen, *Skizzen*, VI, 150, wished to read this as "al-Rāfiḍah." Laḥj is a town in southwestern Arabia, ca. 25 km northwest of Aden, and surrounding district. Cf. *EI²*, s.v. "Laḥdj" (G. R. Smith).

1077. Yāqūt, doubtless basing his remark on this account, describes it only as "a place in Yemen."

fled should be pursued, so they killed those of them they could by every means. He did not pardon [any] rebel; [but] he accepted the penance of those who repented without rebellion. They did that to the extent that they saw [justification in] the actions [of the repenting people], and [to the extent that] they held some hope [of finding] them. He wrote to Abū Bakr about his entry into Ṣanʿāʾ and about the consequences of that.

The Account of Ḥaḍramawt during Their Apostasy

According to Abū Jaʿfar—al-Sarī—Shuʿayb—Sayf—Sahl b. Yūsuf—al-Ṣalt—Kathīr b. al-Ṣalt:[1078] [When] the Apostle of God died, his governors over the country of Ḥaḍramawt [were] Ziyād b. Labīd al-Bayāḍī over Ḥaḍramawt, ʿUkkāshah b. Thawr[1079] over the Sakāsik and Sakūn, and al-Muhājir over Kindah. (Al-Muhājir) was [still] in Medina; he did not go out until [after] the Apostle of God died; so Abū Bakr sent him afterward to fight those in the Yemen, and to continue on afterward to his governorship (*ʿamal*). [2000]

According to al-Sarī—Shuʿayb—Sayf—Abū al-Sāʾib ʿAṭāʾ b. Fulān al-Makhzūmī—his father—Umm Salamah and al-Muhājir b. Abī Umayyah:[1080] (Al-Muhājir) had held back from [the raid on] Tabūk, so the Apostle of God returned angry with him. While Umm Salamah[1081] was washing the head of the Apostle of God, she said, "How can I enjoy anything[1082] while you are angry with my brother?" Then she noticed some pity on his part, so she nodded to her manservant; then she left him, and he remained with the Apostle of God seeking[1083] (al-Muhājir's) forgiveness until he forgave him and became pleased with him and appointed

1078. Cf. Ibn al-Athīr, *Kāmil*, II, 378.

1079. Text has ʿUkkāshah b. Miḥṣan, but this seems an error; cf. Wellhausen, *Skizzen*, VI, 150 and pp. 19–20, above. Ibn al-Athīr, *Kāmil*, II, 378, has ʿUkkāshah b. Abī Umayyah, presumably a conflation with the name of al-Muhājir [b. Abī Umayyah] on the next line.

1080. Cf. Ibn al-Athīr, *Kāmil*, II, 378.

1081. One of the Prophet's wives, sister of al-Muhājir. Cf. Ibn al-Athīr, *Usd*, V, 588.

1082. Lit., "How can anything profit me?" Ibn al-Athīr, *Kāmil*: "How can life profit me?"

1083. Ibn al-Athīr, *Kāmil*: mentioning.

him over Kindah. Subsequently (al-Muhājir) fell ill and was unable to go out [to his governorship], so (the Apostle) wrote to Ziyād to occupy his governorship for him. (Al-Muhājir) became well afterward; then Abū Bakr confirmed his command and ordered him to fight whoever was between Najrān and the farthest [corner] of the Yemen. For that reason, Ziyād and ʿUkkāshah were slow to fight the Kindah, as they were waiting for him.

According to al-Sarī—Shuʿayb—Sayf—Sahl b. Yūsuf—al-Qāsim b. Muḥammad:[1084] The cause of the apostasy of Kindah and[1085] their responding [favorably] to al-Aswad al-ʿAnsī, so that the Apostle of God cursed the four kings,[1086] was [as follows]: When they had embraced Islām before their apostasy and all the people of the Ḥaḍramawt country had embraced Islām, the Apostle of God, among what was being imposed by way of *ṣadaqah* taxes, had ordered that the *ṣadaqah* tax of part of Ḥaḍramawt be assigned among the Kindah, and he assigned the *ṣadaqah* tax of the Kindah among part of the Ḥaḍramawt; [likewise he assigned] part of the [tax of] Ḥaḍramawt among the Sakūn, and [the tax of] the Sakūn among part of the Ḥaḍramawt. Then some people of Banū Walīʿah[1087] said, "Oh Apostle of God, we are not possessors of camels; do you think (Ḥaḍramawt) would send (the tax) to us on pack camels?" So he asked [Ḥaḍramawt] what they thought was proper.[1088] They said, "We
[2001] shall look [into it], and if they really have no camels we shall do it." Now after the Apostle of God had died and that time came,[1089] Ziyād summoned the people to [fulfill] that. So they gathered to him, whereupon Banū Walīʿah said [to Ḥaḍramawt], "Pay us [the camels] as you promised the Apostle of God!" But they (Ḥaḍramawt) said, "You have pack camels, so go on!"[1090]

1084. Cf. Ibn al-Athīr, *Kāmil*, II, 378–79.

1085. Reading with Ibn al-Athīr, *Kāmil*, and Wellhausen, *Skizzen*, VI, 150.

1086. On the "four kings" of Kindah, cf. p. 180, below.

1087. A clan of Kindah, according to Ibn Manẓūr, VIII, 411 and Ibn al-Athīr, *Kāmil*.

1088. The text is awkward. Lit., "So he said, 'If you think proper.'"

1089. Presumably the time when the payment of tax was due. *Wa jāʾa dhālika al-ibbān*.

1090. I.e., "so go get it yourselves."

At this (Banū Walīʿah) became angry and quarreled with them, to the point that they quarreled with Ziyād [also], saying to him, "You are [siding] with them, against us." Subsequently the Ḥaḍramīs refused [to send any *ṣadaqah*] while the Kindīs insisted, so they returned to their homes and bided their time. Ziyād kept aloof from (the Ḥaḍramīs), waiting for al-Muhājir. When al-Muhājir reached Ṣanʿāʾ and wrote to Abū Bakr about everything that he had done, he remained [there] until the reply to his letter came from Abū Bakr. Abū Bakr wrote to him and to ʿIkrima that they should march until they reached Ḥaḍramawt, and confirm Ziyād over his governorship, and permit those who were with them from [the country] between Mecca and the Yemen to return home, unless a group preferred *jihād*, [in which case] he would reinforce him with ʿUbaydah b. Saʿd. So he did [that]. Then al-Muhājir marched from Ṣanʿāʾ heading for Ḥaḍramawt, and ʿIkrimah marched from Abyan heading for Ḥaḍramawt; so the two of them met at Ma'rib. Then they entered the desert from Ṣayhad[1091] until they fell upon Ḥaḍramawt, one of them staying with al-Ashʿath[1092] and the other with Wāʾil.[1093]

According to al-Sarī—Shuʿayb—Sayf—Sahl b. Yūsuf—his father—Kathīr b. al-Ṣalt:[1094] When the Kindīs returned [to their homes] and became obstinate and the Ḥaḍramīs became obstinate, Ziyād b. Labīd administered the *ṣadaqah* taxes of Banū ʿAmr b. Muʿāwiyah himself, approaching them while they were in al-Riyāḍ[1095] and collecting the *ṣadaqah* tax from the first of them whom he reached, a youth called Shayṭān b. Ḥujr. He admired one of the young she-camels of the *ṣadaqah* tax and called for fire and put the branding iron to her. Now the she- [2002]
camel belonged to the brother of al-Shayṭān, al-ʿAddāʾ b. Ḥujr,

1091. Text has Ṣahīd, manuscripts have other variants. Cf. note 143, above.

1092. Text has "al-Aswad"; cf. *Emendanda*.

1093. Perhaps Wāʾil b. Ḥujr al-Ḥaḍramī, said by Ibn al-Athīr to have been appointed by the Prophet over the chiefs (*aqyāl*) of Ḥaḍramawt; cf. Ibn al-Athīr, *Usd*, V, 81–82.

1094. Cf. Ibn al-Athīr, *Kāmil*, II, 379–81 (through, p. 185, below); Balādhurī, *Futūḥ*, 100; Balansī, 161–62.

1095. Or "the meadows." Cf. p. 156, above, on Riyāḍ al-Rawḍah.

who owed no *ṣadaqah* tax; but his brother had made a mistake when he gave her out [in payment], thinking that she was another [camel]. So al-ʿAddāʾ said, "This is Nugget," [calling the camel] by her name. At this al-Shayṭān said, "My brother is right; I only gave her to you because I thought she was another. So release Nugget and take another, for she is not one to be relinquished." But Ziyād thought that that was [merely] a pretext of his, and accused him of unbelief and of being estranged from Islām and of intending evil; so he grew hot [with anger], and the two men did also. So Ziyād said, "No, she will not be given up. She is not yours; the branding-iron of the *ṣadaqah* has fallen upon her and she has become God's property.[1096] There is no way to return her, so may Nugget not weigh upon you like al-Basūs."[1097] At this al-ʿAddāʾ called out, "Oh family of ʿAmr in al-Riyāḍ! I am being wronged and oppressed! Contemptible is whoever is destroyed in his own abode!" He called out, "Oh Abū al-Sumayṭ!" So Abū al-Sumayṭ Ḥārithah b. Surāqah b. Maʿdīkarib[1098] approached and headed for Ziyād b. Labīd while he was standing [there], and said to him, "Let this youth have his she-camel, and take a [different] camel in her place, for it is only a camel instead of [another] camel." But (Ziyād) said, "There is no way to [do] that." At this (Abū al-Sumayṭ) replied, "That [would be so only] if you were a Jew"; and he turned to her and released her tether. Then he struck her on the side, sending her off.[1099] He stood up near her while saying:

She is protected by an old man with white hair on his cheeks,
mottled as the robe is mottled.

So Ziyād ordered some youths of Ḥaḍramawt and al-Sakūn on
[2003] him; they roughed him up and trampled him and handcuffed him and his companions and took them hostage, and they seized

---

1096. *ḥaqq Allāh.*

1097. *Fa-lā takūnanna Shadharatun ʿalaykum ka-l-basūs.* Probably a reference to the she-camel of al-Basūs bt. Munqidh, the killing (or wounding) of which precipated a bitter feud between the tribes of Bakr and Taghlib, according to legend. This she-camel became proverbial for something unlucky (*ashʾamu min nāqat al-Basūs*). Cf. *EI*², s.v. "Al-Basūs" (J. W. Fück); Ibn Manẓūr, VI, 28.

1098. Cf. Balansī, 161–62.

1099. Or perhaps, "making her get up" (*fa-baʿatha-hā*).

the she-camel and fettered her as she had been. About that Ziyād b. Labīd said:

A whole company of riders could not protect Nugget [from being taken],
but the old man may turn it back. . . .[1100]

The people of al-Riyāḍ cried out to one another and called each other. Banū Muʿāwiyah [b. Kindah] became angry on behalf of Ḥārithah and openly showed their attitude. The Sakūn became angry on behalf of Ziyād, as did the Ḥaḍramawt, and they stood together to defend him. There gathered two great armies [drawn] from the former and the latter. Banū Muʿāwiyah did not initiate anything because of the existence of their captives, and [so] the companions of Ziyād did not find any pretext for taking on the Banū Muʿāwiyah. Then Ziyād sent to them: "Either put down [your] weapons or give notice of war." So to this they replied, "We shall never put down [our] weapons, until you have sent our [captive] companions." To this Ziyād said, "They shall never be sent until you disperse in abasement and shame. Oh most wicked of people, are you not inhabitants of Ḥaḍramawt, and protected neighbors[1101] of al-Sakūn? Then what can you be and do in the abode of Ḥaḍramawt and at the side of your masters, [except follow them]?" The Sakūn said to (Ziyād), "Rush the group, for only that will disengage them." So he rushed upon them by night, killing some of them, and they fled in groups, going in every direction. Ziyād quoted, when morning found him in their camp:

I was not a man to start war unjustly,
but, when they refused, I was obliging in the War of Ḥāṭib.[1102]

After the group had fled, he let the three people go; and Ziyād returned to his residence in victory. After the captives returned [2004]

1100. The second hemistich reads: *wa al-shaykhu qad yathnī-hi urjūb*. The final word is unknown; cf. manuscript C, which has *arḥūb* or *urḥūb*.

1101. *jīrān*.

1102. The War of Ḥāṭib was a major clash among the Arab clans of Medina on the eve of Islam, which ended indecisively in the bloody battle of Buʿāth. Cf. Watt, *Muḥammad at Medina*, 156–58.

to their companions, they chided them so that they incited one another to fight, saying, "This country is not fit for us or for them until it becomes free for one of the two groups." So they gathered and formed an army together, and called for withholding the *ṣadaqah* tax. But Ziyād left them [alone], and did not go out against them; so that they left off marching against him. He sent al-Ḥuṣayn b. Numayr[1103] to them, and he kept seeking reconciliation of what divided them from Ziyād, Ḥaḍramawt, and al-Sakūn, until they calmed one another down. This was the second secession; about that al-Sakūnī said:

By my life—and my life is not something taken lightly!—
Banū ʿAmr could draw bitter things from it.
You lied; by the house of God, you do not hold it back from
Ziyād after we had come to Ziyād as equals.

They remained a little while after that; then Banū ʿAmr b. Muʿāwiyah especially went out to the reserved places of pasture[1104]—to pastures that they had restricted [from public use]. So Jamad encamped in a reserved pasture, Mikhwaṣ in a reserved pasture, Mishraḥ and Abḍaʿah[1105] in others, and their sister al-ʿAmarradah in a reserved pasture. The Banū ʿAmr b. Muʿāwiyah were under these leaders,[1106] and Banū al-Ḥārith b. Muʿāwiyah encamped in their reserved pastures, such that al-Ashʿath b. Qays encamped in a reserved pasture, and al-Simṭ b. al-Aswad[1107] in a pasture. All of [Banū] Muʿāwiyah agreed to withhold the *ṣadaqah* tax and resolved unanimously to apos-

1103. Two individuals bear this name: one, an Anṣārī, participated in the conquest of Tabūk and may have been ʿUmar's governor of al-Urdunn; the other, of Sakūn, was commander of the army sent against Mecca by the Umayyad caliph Yazīd I in the early AD 680s. Cf. Ibn Ḥajar, *Iṣābah*, s.vv.

1104. *Maḥājir* (sing. *maḥjar*). The following three words, *ilā ʿaḥmāʾ ḥamawhā*, appear to be a gloss clarifying the meaning of *maḥjar* in terms of the more familiar word *ḥimā*, which has the same meaning.

1105. The four kings of Banū Walīʿah/Banū Muʿāwiyah b. Kinda, who embraced Islam and then apostatized. Cf. Caskel, II, 409 (s.v. "Mišraḥ b. Maʿdikarib"); p. 176, above; Balādhurī, *Futūḥ*, 101.

1106. Ibn al-Athīr, *Kāmil*, II, 380: "They were the four kings, the chiefs of ʿAmr whom the Apostle of God had cursed."

1107. Chief of Kindah; his deeds are confused with those of his son Shuraḥbīl b. al-Simṭ. Cf. Caskel, II, 523; Ibn Ḥajar, *Iṣābah*, s.v.v.

tatize, except for Shuraḥbīl b. al-Simṭ and his son; the two of them stood up among the Banū Muʿāwiyah and said, "By God, this is disgraceful for tribes of free men. [For] noble men, even when [committed] to a doubtful [cause], consider themselves more noble than to change from it to a better one, out of fear of the disgrace [of changing sides]. How, then, [can you countenance] turning back from what is proper and true to [2005] what is false and shameful? Oh God, we do not help our tribe with this! We regret their joining together to this day"—meaning the day of the she-camel and the day of the secession.

Shuraḥbīl b. al-Simṭ and his son, al-Simṭ, went out until they came to Ziyād b. Labīd and joined him. Ibn Ṣāliḥ and Imruʾ al-Qays b. ʿĀbis[1108] [also] went out until they came to Ziyād and said to him, "Attack the enemy by night, for groups of al-Sakāsik have joined them, and a group of al-Sakūn and isolated individuals from Ḥaḍramawt have hurried to them. Perhaps we may deliver to them a blow that will bequeath enmity between us and draw a distinction between us. If you refuse, we fear that the people will drift from us to them, while the enemy are raiding the place of those who have come to you, hoping [to conquer] those who remained [behind]." At this, he said, "Carry out your plan." So[1109] they gathered their troop and came on (the Banū ʿAmr b. Muʿāwiyah) by night in their reserved pastures, finding them sitting around their fires. They knew whom they wanted, so they fell upon the Banū ʿAmr b. Muʿāwiyah from five directions in five groups, for they were the majority of the enemy and the strongest[1110] of them. Thus they struck down Mishraḥ, Mikhwaṣ, Jamad,[1111] Abḍaʿah, and their sister al-ʿAmarradah. The curse [of the Prophet] reached them. They killed many, and those who could do so fled. Banū ʿAmr b. Muʿāwiyah were so weakened that they [never] recovered after it.

1108. Poet of Kindah, said to have come to the Prophet in a delegation of his tribe and to have remained loyal to Medina during the *riddah*.

1109. Cf. Balansī, 163.

1110. Or, perhaps, "bravest" or "best armed": *shawkatu-hum*, lit., "their thorn."

1111. Balansī: Jamd.

Ziyād took away the captives and the flocks,[1112] and took a road that brought them to the army of al-Ash'ath and the Banū al-Ḥārith b. Mu'āwiyah. So when they passed by them in it, the womenfolk of Banū 'Amr b. Mu'āwiyah asked Banū al-Ḥārith for help, and called to him: "Oh Ash'ath! Oh Ash'ath! Your maternal aunts! Your maternal aunts!" At this, Banū al-Ḥārith became stirred up to rescue them. This [was] the third [secession]. Al-Ash'ath said:

I defended Banū 'Amr after their troop had come
with more goats and more prisoners than the day of al-Buḍayḍ.[1113]

[2006] Now al-Ash'ath knew that Ziyād and his army, if they learned of that, would not desist from [attacking] him nor from Banū al-Ḥārith b. Mu'āwiyah and Banū 'Amr b. Mu'āwiyah; so he gathered to him[self] Banū al-Ḥārith b. Mu'āwiyah and Banū 'Amr b. Mu'āwiyah and those who obeyed them of al-Sakāsik and small groups[1114] of whatever tribes were around them. Those tribes who were in Ḥaḍramawt became estranged from one another because of this battle. Ziyād's companions stood firm in obedience to Ziyād, and Kindah was unyielding; so after the tribes had become estranged from one another, Ziyād wrote to al-Muhājir and the people[1115] corresponded with him, meeting him with the letter after he had crossed Ṣayhad,[1116] a desert between Ma'rib and Ḥaḍramawt. He left 'Ikrimah in charge of the army and hurried ahead with the fastest troops. Then he marched until he came upon Ziyād, whereupon he rushed upon Kindah, who were led by al-Ash'ath, so that they met in the reserved pasture (*maḥjar*) of al-Zurqān[1117] and fought in it.

1112. Or "property" (*amwāl*).

1113. Possibly a watering place in Ṭayyi' country in north central Arabia; cf. Yāqūt, s.v.

1114. *Khaṣā'iṣ*. This rendering seems more natural to me than that proposed by De Goeje, "[people of] huts"; cf. *Glossary*, s.v. "Khaṣā'iṣ."

1115. Or "the army": *al-nās*.

1116. Mss. B and C have Ṣahbadh and Ṣahyad, respectively, but cf. note 143, above.

1117. Yāqūt's information on al-Zurqān is derived from this account.

Consequently Kindah were defeated and killed. They went out in flight and took refuge in al-Nujayr,[1118] having repaired and fortified it [beforehand]. Al-Muhājir said regarding the day of the reserved pasture of al-Zurqān:

We were at Zurqān when you were dispersed by
    a sea that drives firewood in its waves.
We slew you in your reserved pasture
    until you rode off out of fear of us,
To a fortress the easiest [part] of whose [conquest] is
    capturing the offspring and driving them off at a brisk pace.

Al-Muhājir marched with the people from the reserved pasture of al-Zurqān until he descended upon al-Nujayr, the Kindah [2007] having gathered there and fortified themselves in it. With them were those whom they had asked for help from al-Sakāsik and isolated individuals from al-Sakūn and Ḥaḍramawt. Now al-Nujayr is at [the intersection of] three roads; so Ziyād descended upon one of them, and al-Muhājir upon another, and the third was [free] for them to come and go until ʿIkrimah should arrive with the army. Then he settled (ʿIkrimah) upon that [third] road, so that he cut off (Kindah's) supplies and repulsed them. He divided the cavalry among Kindah and ordered them to crush them. Among those whom he sent was Yazīd b. Qanān of Banū Mālik b. Saʿd;[1119] so he killed those who were in the settlements of Banū Hind[1120] as far as Barahūt.[1121] Among those whom he dispatched to the coast were Khālid b. Fulān al-Makhzūmī and Rabīʿah al-Ḥaḍramī; they killed the people of Maḥā and other clans. Kindah learned what had befallen the rest of their people while they were in their fortress, so they said, "Death is better than the situation you find yourselves in [now]; shear your forelocks, so that you are like a people who have given your souls to God—so may He be gracious to you, and

1118. A famous old fort in Yemen; cf. Hamdānī, 87, 203. Yāqūt, s.v. gives, in a long entry, a summary of the events of this chapter of the *riddah*, but little additional information on al-Nujayr.

1119. A branch of Zaydmanāt of Tamīm; cf. Caskel, I, Table 75 and II, 394.

1120. A branch of Kindah; cf. Caskel, I, Table 234 and II, 283.

1121. An old well in lower Ḥaḍramawt; cf. Hamdānī, 128, 201.

may you return [from God] with His blessings! Perhaps He will assist you against these tyrants." So they sheared their forelocks and made a pact, agreeing that no one of them would flee leaving another behind. Their poet began to recite *rajaz*[1122] in the middle of the night from the top of their fortress:

A morning of evil for Banū Qatīrah[1123]
and for the commander from Banū al-Mughīrah.[1124]

The Muslims' poet, Ziyād b. Dīnār, took to replying to them:

Do not threaten us and endure the confinement.
We are the cavalry of the child of al-Mughīrah.
In the morning the tribe shall be victorious.

[2008] When it was morning, they went out against the people, killing in the courtyards of al-Nujayr until there were many slain opposite each one of the three roads. On that day, ʿIkrimah began to recite *rajaz*, saying:

I pierce them while I am in haste,
A piercing that I will repeat[1125] [when] on the way back.

He also said:

My word was spent; indeed it has effect,
And everyone who seeks my protection is protected.

So Kindah was vanquished, they having killed many of them.

According to Hishām b. Muḥammad:[1126] After al-Muhājir had finished with the enemy, ʿIkrimah b. Abī Jahl came as a reinforcement for him. So Ziyād and al-Muhājir said to those who were with them, "Your brethren have arrived as reinforcement for you [only] after you had [completed] the conquest; but let them share in the booty [anyway]." So they did that and allowed

1122. A common form of verse in iambic meter.

1123. Qatīrah b. Ḥarithah was a branch of Sakūn/Kindah; cf. Caskel, II, 468. Balansī, 164ff., vocalizes the name "Quṭayrah." However, the rhyme makes it obvious that Qaṭīrah is the correct form.

1124. The clan of Makhzūm (of Quraysh) to which ʿIkrimah b. Abī Jahl belonged; cf. Caskel, I, Tables 22 and 23; EI^2, s.v. "Makhzūm" (M. Hinds).

1125. Reading with Cairo, instead of "that I confess" in the text.

1126. Cf. Ibn al-Athīr, *Kāmil*, II, 382.

those who joined them to share [the booty], recommending that to each other. They sent the fifths [of booty] and the captives [to Medina]; the heralds marched so that they got there before them. (The heralds) were spreading the news among the tribes and reading to them [news of][1127] the conquest.

According to al-Sarī: Abū Bakr wrote to al-Muhājir with al-Mughīrah b. Shuʿbah:[1128] "If this letter of mine reaches you before you have achieved victory, then—if you conquer the enemy—kill the fighting men and take the offspring captive if you took them by force, or let them fall under my verdict.[1129] If [on the other hand] you have [already] concluded a treaty with them before (my letter reaches you), then [let it be] on condition that you expel them from their abodes; for I am averse to leaving intact in their homes enemies who have done what they did. Let them know that they had done evil, and let them taste the offensiveness of some of what they did."

According to Abū Jaʿfar:[1130] When the people of al-Nujayr saw that the Muslims' supplies were not cut off and they ascertained that (the Muslims) would not turn back from them, their souls were filled with fear. They feared being killed, and the leaders feared for themselves. If they held out until al-Mughīrah should arrive, they would have been saved because they had [concluded] a treaty for the third time on condition of being expelled. Al-Ashʿath hurried to go out to ʿIkrimah with an assurance of protection. (Al-Ashʿath) did not trust anyone else. That was because (ʿIkrimah) was married to Asmāʾ bt. al-Nuʿmān b. Abī al-Jawn;[1131] he had become engaged to her while he was in al- [2009]

1127. Ms. B adds *kitāb*, "the letter" or "the book" (about the conquest). Cf. Wellhausen, *Skizzen*, VI, 150 on *bashīr* as "heralds."

1128. A felon from al-Ṭāʾif who fled to Medina and attached himself to the Prophet's entourage as bodyguard and military commander; later employed as emissary and governor by the caliphs. Cf. Caskel, II, 419–20.

1129. *Ḥukm*. I.e., let them surrender unconditionally, so that they fall under my verdict.

1130. Cf. Ibn al-Athīr, *Kāmil*, II, 381.

1131. *Emendanda* proposes "... al-Nuʿmān b. al-Jawn," but sources vary on the name; Cf. Caskel, II, 451 ("al-Nuʿmān b. ʿAmr b. Muʿāwiya"); cf. Ibn al-Athīr, *Usd*, V, 396–98; Ibn Saʿd, VIII, 102–5; and p. 190, below. Asmāʾ was a noble Kindite woman whose marriage to the Prophet was never consummated. Subsequently she married both al-Muhājir b. Abī Umayyah and ʿIkrimah b. Abī Jahl.

Janad[1132] awaiting al-Muhājir, so her father presented her to him before they set out. So ʿIkrimah conveyed (al-Ashʿath) to al-Muhājir and asked him to grant him protection for his life and nine people with him, on condition that he should stand as surety for them and their families if they would open the gate for them. So he complied with his [request] in this, and said, "Go away so as to save yourself; then bring me your letter so I may seal it."

According to al-Sarī—Shuʿayb—Sayf—Abū Isḥāq al-Shaybānī—Saʿīd b. Abī Burdah—ʿĀmir:[1133] (Al-Ashʿath) came to him and requested protection for his family, his property, and nine of those whom he wished, on condition that he would open the gate for them so that they could enter in upon his tribe. Whereupon al-Muhājir said to him, "Write down what you want, and be quick about it"; so he wrote his pledge of security and one for them. Among them were his brother and his paternal cousins and their families; but, in [his] haste and perplexity, he forget [to include] himself. Then he brought the letter, whereupon (al-Muhājir) sealed it and went back, letting those [mentioned] in the letter go their way.

According to Al-Ajlaḥ and al-Mujālid: When the only thing remaining was for (al-Ashʿath) to write himself [into the pledge of security], [someone named] Jaḥdam pounced upon him with a blade and said, "Your life unless you write me [into it!]" So he wrote him [into it] and left himself out.

According to Abū Isḥāq:[1134] After (al-Ashʿath) opened the
[2010] gate, the Muslims rushed upon [al-Nujayr], not letting any combatant go, but rather killing them by cutting off their heads while in captivity. One thousand of the women of al-Nujayr and al-Khandaq were counted up, and guards were placed among the captives and booty. Kathīr[1135] agreed with them [in their recounting of events].

According to Kathīr b. al-Ṣalt:[1136] After the gate had been

1132. Or: "with the army." Cf. p. 190, below.
1133. Cf. Ibn al-Athīr, *Kāmil*, II, 381.
1134. Cf. Ibn al-Athīr, *Kāmil*, II, 381.
1135. See following *sanad*.
1136. Cf. Ibn al-Athīr, *Kāmil*, II, 381–82.

opened and whoever was in al-Nujayr had been finished off and after what God had bestowed on (the Muslims) as booty had been calculated, (al-Muhājir) summoned al-Ash'ath with those persons [he had mentioned], and called for his document. Then he reviewed them and pardoned those who were [mentioned] in the document;[1137] but lo, al-Ash'ath was not [named] in it. At this al-Muhājir said, "Praise be to God, who made your star to miss,[1138] oh Ash'ath, oh enemy of God! I had been wishing that God would abase you." Then he bound him in ropes and intended to kill him. But 'Ikrimah said to him, "Grant him a postponement and send him to Abū Bakr, for he is more knowledgeable about judging [cases such as] this. If a man forgot to write his [own] name but was promised good treatment by word of mouth,[1139] does (the oversight) nullify (the promise)?" To this al-Muhājir replied, "His case is perfectly clear, but I will follow [your] advice and show it preference."[1140] He granted him a postponement and sent him to Abū Bakr along with the captives. So he was with them, the Muslims and the captives from his tribe [alike] cursing him. A woman of his tribe called him "favor of fire,"[1141] a Yemenite phrase by which they call a traitor. Now al-Mughīrah was perplexed one night because that was God's will. So he came with the enemy [still stained] with blood and the captives, on camels. The captives and prisoners marched and the group reached Abū Bakr with [news of] the conquest and with the captives and prisoners. Then (Abū Bakr) called for al-Ash'ath, whereupon he said,[1142] "Banū Walī'ah led you astray; you would not lead them astray, [for] they do not think enough of you [to do] that. [So] they were destroyed and destroyed you. Aren't you afraid [to rebel, seeing] that something of the [2011]
message of the Apostle of God had reached you? What do you

1137. Lit., "he declared them legal" (*ajāza*).
1138. I.e., who brought you bad luck.
1139. Lit., "he was the friend of conversation."
1140. Reading, with the text, *u'thiru-hā* rather than the *Emendanda*'s *u'thiru-hu*.
1141. *'Urf al-nār*.
1142. The text of Abū Bakr's comment is problematic, and the Cairo and Leiden editions offer slightly different readings, neither of which is entirely lucid.

think I should do with you? He replied, "I have no idea what you are thinking; you know best what you think." (Abū Bakr) said, "I think you should be killed." (Al-Ashʿath) replied, "I am the one who persuaded the adversary[1143] [to spare] ten [people], so that my blood should not be licit." (Abū Bakr) said, "Did they empower you [to do so]?" He replied, "Yes." (Abū Bakr) said, "Then you brought them what had been entrusted to you, whereupon they placed [their] seal upon it?" He replied, "Yes." (Abū Bakr) said, "Peace is required after sealing of a document only for those [named] in the document; before that, you were only a negotiator." Then, when he feared that (Abū Bakr) would fall upon him, (al-Ashʿath) said, "And do you reckon there to be some good in me? Then release me and forgive my misbehavior, accept my Islām and do with me as you have done with others like me, and return my wife to me"—he had been engaged to Umm Farwah bt. Abī Quḥāfah[1144] when he [first] came to the Apostle of God, whereupon (Abū Bakr) had married him [to her], but withheld her [from him] until he should come a second time; then the Apostle of God had died and al-Ashʿath had done what he did, so he feared that she would not be returned to him—"[should you do these things], you will find me the best of the people of my land in the religion of God." So (Abū Bakr) spared him[1145] and accepted [this] from him. He returned his wife to him, and said, "Go, and let me hear [only] good about you," and let the people alone so that they went away. Abū Bakr divided the fifth [of booty] among the people, and the army distributed the four-fifths [among themselves].

Abū Jaʿfar said: According to Ibn Ḥumayd—Salamah—Ibn Isḥāq—ʿAbdallāh b. Abī Bakr: After al-Ashʿath was brought before Abū Bakr, he said, "What do you think I should do to
[2012] you? For you know what you have done." He replied, "You should be gracious to me and release me from the irons and marry your sister to me, for I have come back and embraced Islām." So Abū Bakr said, "Done," and married him to Umm

1143. *Qawm*; here, referring to the Muslims.
1144. Abū Bakr's sister; cf. Ibn al-Athīr, *Usd*, V, 208.
1145. Lit., "relinquished to him [claim to] his blood."

Farwah bt. Abī Quḥāfah. (Al-Ashʿath) was in Medina until the conquest of Iraq.

Continuation of the Report of Sayf

When[1146] ʿUmar acceded [to the caliphate], he said, "It is disgraceful that one of the Arabs should own another, God having enriched [us] and conquered the non-Arabs." He consulted about ransoming the captives of the Arabs from the *jāhiliyyah* and Islam (except for the woman who had borne a child to her master), and made the ransom of each person seven camels and six camels,[1147] except for Ḥanīfah and Kindah, on whom he lightened [the ransom] because of the slaughter of their men, and [except for] those who were not able [to pay] the ransom because of their great number,[1148] and the people of Dabā. So their men searched for their womenfolk in every place.[1149] Then al-Ashʿath found two women among the Banū Nahd[1150] and the Banū Ghuṭayf.[1151] [The story of] that was that he stopped among them, asking after "Raven" and "Eagle," so he was told, "What do you intend with that?" He replied, "At the battle of al-Nujayr, the eagles and ravens and wolves[1152] and dogs snatched away our women." Whereupon Banū Ghuṭayf said, "This is 'Raven.'" He asked, "What is his position among you?" They replied, "Under protection."[1153] He said, "Good, then," and departed. ʿUmar said, "No one shall be master of an Arab,"[1154] because of that which he and the Muslims agreed upon.

1146. Cf. Ibn al-Athīr, *Kāmil,* II, 382.
1147. I.e., six or seven camels per captive. Kos has "six young camels"; lacking in B.
1148. Reading, with *Emendanda, li-fiʾāmihim* for the text's *li-qiyāmihim.*
1149. Although the word *sabāyā* ("captives") can apply to captives of either gender, the passage implies that the majority of captives were women.
1150. Nahd b. Zayd was a Quḍāʿah tribe with branches in Syria and Yemen. Cf. Caskel, II, 443.
1151. Ghuṭayf b. ʿAbdallāh was a prominent clan of Murād. Cf. Caskel, II, 275.
1152. Manuscript C: flies.
1153. *Fī al-ṣiyānah,* lit., "in keeping."
1154. *Lā mulka ʿalā ʿarabiyyin;* here the word *ʿarab* seems to mean not "nomad," but rather something like "speaker of Arabic."

They[1155] said: Al-Muhājir looked into the case of the woman whose father, al-Nuʿmān b. al-Jawn, had offered her to the Apostle of God, whereupon he described her as having never been ill.[1156] But (the Prophet) returned her, saying, "We have no
[2013] need of her," after he had seated her in front of him; he said, "If she had any merit with God, she would have become ill." Then al-Muhājir said to ʿIkrimah, "When did you marry her?" He said, "While I was in Aden; she was given to me in al-Janad,[1157] whereupon I traveled with her to Ma'rib. Then I brought her to the army,[1158] whereupon some of them said, "Leave her! For she is not fit to be desired." Others said, "Don't leave her!" So al-Muhājir wrote to Abū Bakr asking him about that, whereupon Abū Bakr wrote back to him, "Her father, al-Nuʿmān b. al-Jawn, came to the Apostle of God, having beautified her for him, so that (the Apostle) ordered him to bring her to him. After he had brought her to him, he said, 'I give you in addition [the good news] that she has never suffered pain.'" At this (the Apostle) said, "If she had any merit with God, she would have become ill. He disliked her, so you should dislike her [also]." Then he sent her away.

A number [of women] remained among Quraysh [as captives] after ʿUmar ordered the ransoming of the captives. Among them was Bushrā bt. Qays b. Abī al-Kaysam; she was with Saʿd b. Mālik,[1159] to whom she bore [his son] ʿUmar. [Another] was Zurʿah bt. Mishraḥ, with ʿAbdallāh b. al-ʿAbbās,[1160] to whom she bore ʿAlī.

Abū Bakr wrote to al-Muhājir, giving him the choice [of the governorship] of the Yemen or Ḥaḍramawt; whereupon he chose the Yemen. So the Yemen was under two commanders, Fayrūz and al-Muhājir. Ḥaḍramawt was [also] under two commanders, ʿUbaydah b. Saʿd over Kindah and al-Sakāsik, and Ziyād b.

1155. I.e., the narrators of the account.

1156. Lit., "she had never complained" [*innahā lam tashtaki qaṭṭ*]. This is again Asmā' bt. al-Nuʿmān, cf. p. 185, above, and note 1131. Note that al-Muhājir is said to have married her after the Prophet and before ʿIkrimah.

1157. Or "with the army (*al-jund*)." Cf. pp. 185–86, above.

1158. *Al-ʿaskar.*

1159. I.e., Saʿd b. Abī Waqqāṣ.

1160. Cousin of the Prophet, later famed as Qurʾān commentator.

Labīd over Ḥaḍramawt. Abū Bakr wrote to the governors of the apostasy:[1161] "Now then: The dearest to me of those whom you have brought into your cause are those who did not apostatize. So gather together whoever did not apostatize, then garner recruits[1162] from them; but grant leave to whoever [of them] wishes to depart.[1163] Do not ask aid of a [former] apostate in fighting against an enemy." [2014]

Al-Ash'ath b. Mi'nās al-Sakūnī, lamenting the people of al-Nujayr, said:[1164]

By my life—and my life has not been easy to me—
 I was really niggardly concerning the slain.
No wonder, except the day lots were cast among them;
 after them, fate is not secure for me.
Would that the flanks of the people were under their flanks;
 after them, no female walked with an embryo.
I am like the she-camel whose young one has died who, when
 frightened, came up
 to her dummy calf[1165] as she cried out in yearning for her
 young one.

According to al-Sarī—Shu'ayb—Sayf—Mūsā b. 'Uqbah—al-Ḍaḥḥāk b. Khalīfah: There arrived before al-Muhājir two singing women. One of them sang reviling the Apostle of God, so he cut off her hand and pulled her front tooth. Then Abū Bakr wrote to him: "I have learned what you did regarding the woman who sang and piped with abuse of the Apostle of God. If you had not beaten me to (punishing her), I would have ordered you to kill her, for the punishment [for abuse] of prophets is not like [other] punishments. So whoever does [something like] that among those claiming to be Muslims is [actually] an apostate; or among [2015]

1161. That is, to the governors ('*ummāl*) placed over tribes, some of whom had apostasized.

1162. *Ṣanā'i'*, lit., "protegés."

1163. I.e., those who do not wish to join the army should not be required to do so.

1164. Cf. Wathīmah, 29/72, which has the same first half-line but is different thereafter.

1165. *Baww*, the skin of the deceased young stuffed with grass and made available to soothe the mother.

those claiming to be at peace with the Muslims[1166] is [actually] at war [with them] and a traitor." Abū Bakr wrote to him about the woman who had sung satirizing the Muslims, "Now then: I have learned that you cut off the hand of a woman because she sang satirizing the Muslims, and that you pulled her front tooth. If she was among those who claim [to have embraced] Islam, then [it is] good discipline and a reprimand, and not mutilation.[1167] If she was a *dhimmī* woman, by my life that which you forgave [by way] of polytheism is greater [than what she was punished for]. If I had [had a chance to] precede you [to punishment] in [a cause] like this, I would have done something loathsome; so undertake to be gentle and beware of mutilation among the people, for (mutilation) is an offense and generates fear [among the people], unless [made] in chastisement [for a crime]."

In this year[1168]—I mean year 11—Mu'ādh b. Jabal left the Yemen, and Abū Bakr appointed 'Umar b. al-Khaṭṭāb judge. He was in charge of judgeship for the entire time of (Abū Bakr's) caliphate.

In (this year)[1169] Abū Bakr put 'Attāb b. Asīd in charge of the pilgrimage ceremonies, according to those upon whom 'Alī b. Muḥammad based his account, whose names I mentioned beforehand in this book of mine.[1170] [But] according to 'Alī b. Muḥammad: [Another] group said no, 'Abd al-Raḥmān b. 'Awf led the people on pilgrimage in the year 11, upon Abū Bakr's ordering him to do that.

1166. *Mu'āhid*, a non-Muslim who has concluded a pact (*'ahd*) with the Muslims recognizing their superiority and agreeing to pay tribute. The discussion here uses the vocabulary of, and betrays the influence of, second and third century AH classical Islamic jurisprudence.

1167. The terms involved are *adab*, *taqdimah*, and *muthlah*.

1168. Cf. Ibn al-Athīr, *Kāmil*, II, 383; Caetani, 685.

1169. Cf. Ibn al-Athīr, *Kāmil*, II, 383.

1170. Cf. p. 38, above, for full *isnād* of 'Alī b. Muḥammad al-Madā'inī.

Bibliography of Cited Works

The following list includes works cited in the notes. Most references are self-explanatory, citing page or volume/page of the work. Some biographical and geographical dictionaries that have an alphabetical arrangement (Ibn Ḥajar, Yāqūt) are cited sub verbo *referring to the person or place in question, in order to facilitate reference to various editions.*

Abbott, Nabia. Unpublished marginal notes in the Leiden edition of al-Ṭabarī's text held in the Joseph Regenstein Library, The University of Chicago.

Abū Zurʿa al-Dimashqī. *Ta'rīkh*. Edited by Shukrallāh b. Niʿmatullāh al-Qūjānī. Damascus: Majmaʿ al-lughah al-ʿarabiyyah, 1980.

al-ʿAskarī, Murtaḍā. *Khamsūn wa mi'ah ṣaḥābī mukhtalaq*. Baghdad: Kulliyat uṣūl al-dīn, 1969.

The Assyrian Dictionary of the Oriental Institute of the University of Chicago. Chicago: The Oriental Institute, 1955–.

al-Balādhurī, Aḥmad b. Yaḥyā. *Futūḥ al-buldān* [= *Liber expugnationis regionum*]. Edited by M. J. de Goeje. Leiden: E. J. Brill, 1866; reprinted 1968.

al-Balansī, Sulaymān al-Kalāʿī. *Ta'rīkh al-riddah*, gleaned from *al-Iktifā'* by Khurshīd Ahmad Fāriq. New Delhi: Indian Institute of Islamic Studies, 1970.

Becker, C. H. "Ubi sunt, qui ante nos in mundo fuere," in his *Islamstudien*. Heidelberg: Quelle und Meyer, 1924. Vol. 1, 501–19.

Bellamy, James. "Arabic Verses from the First/Second Century. The Inscription of ʿEn ʿAvdat," *Journal of Semitic Studies* 35 (1990), 73–79.

Bibliotheca Geographorum Arabicorum. 8 vols., edited by M. J. De Goeje. Leiden: E. J. Brill, 1870–1894.

Caetani, Leone. *Annali dell' Islam*. 10 volumes; volume 2. Milano: Ulrico Hoepli, 1907.

Caskel, Werner, and G. Strenziok. *Ǧamharat an-Nasab. Das genealogische Werk des Hišām ibn Muḥammad al-Kalbī*. 2 vols. Leiden: E. J. Brill, 1966.

De Goeje, M. J. *Mémoire sur la conquête de la Syrie*, 2nd ed. Leiden: E. J. Brill, 1900.

al-Dhahabī, Muḥammad b. Aḥmad. *al-Mushtabih fī asmā' al-rijāl*. Edited by P. De Jong. Leiden: E. J. Brill, 1881.

al-Diyārbakrī, Ḥusayn b. Muḥammad. *Ta'rīkh al-khamīs fī aḥwāl anfas nafīs*. Cairo: al-Maṭba'ah al-Wahbiyyah, 1283 A.H. Reprinted Beirut: Mu'assasat Sha'bān, n.d. [ca. 1970?].

Donner, Fred M. "The Bakr ibn Wā'il Tribes and Politics in Northeastern Arabia on the Eve of Islam." *Studia Islamica* 51 (1980), 5–38.

———. *The Early Islamic Conquests*. Princeton: Princeton University Press, 1981.

———. "Mecca's Food Supplies and Muḥammad's Boycott." *Journal of the Economic and Social History of the Orient* 20 (1977), 249–66.

———. "The Problem of Early Arabic Historiography in Syria," in Muḥammad 'Adnān al-Bakhīt (ed.). *The History of Bilād al-Shām during the Early Islamic Period up to 40 A.H./640 A.D.* [sic]. Amman: University of Jordan, 1987. Vol. 1, 1–27. [= Fourth International Conference on the History of Bilād al-Shām, Second Symposium, *Proceedings*, vol. 1].

The Encyclopaedia of Islam. New [2nd] edition. Leiden: E. J. Brill, 1960–.

Gil'adi, Avner. "Some Notes on *Taḥnīk* in Medieval Islam." *Journal of Near Eastern Studies* 47 (1988), 175–80.

al-Hamdānī, Abū Muḥammad al-Ḥasan b. Aḥmad b. Ya'qūb. *Ṣifat jazīrat al-'Arab*. Edited by David Heinrich Müller. Leiden: E. J. Brill, 1884–1891. Reprinted 1968 [= Müller, *Al-Hamdânî's Geographie der arabischen Halbinsel*].

Harding, G. Lankester. *An Index and Concordance of Pre-Islamic Arabian Names and Inscriptions*. Toronto: University of Toronto Press, 1971.

Hodgson, Marshall G. S. "Two Pre-Modern Muslim Historians: Pitfalls and Opportunities in Presenting them to Moderns." In *Toward World Community*, edited by John Ulric Nef. The Hague: Carl Junk, 1968, 53–68.

Ibn Abī al-Ḥadīd, ʿAbd al-Ḥamīd b. Hibatallāh. *Sharḥ nahj al-balāghah*. 5 vols., edited by Ḥasan Tamīm. Beirut: Dār maktabat al-Ḥayāh, 1963–1965.

Ibn al-Athīr, ʿIzz al-Dīn ʿAlī. *al-Kāmil fī al-taʾrīkh*. Edited by C. J. Tornberg. Leiden: E. J. Brill, 1868 [= *Chronicon quod perfectissimum inscribitur*]. Reprinted Beirut: Dār Ṣādir and Dār Bayrūt, 1965, with different pagination. Beirut edition is cited here.

———. *al-Lubāb fī tahdhīb al-ansāb*. 3 vols. Beirut: Dār Ṣādir, n.d. [ca. 1965?].

———. *Usd al-ghābah fī maʿrifat al-ṣaḥābah*. 5 vols. Cairo: Maṭbaʿat al-Wahbiyyah, 1280 A.H. Reprinted Beirut: Dār iḥyāʾ al-turāth al-ʿarabī, n.d.

Ibn al-Kalbī, Muḥammad b. Hishām. *Jamharat al-nasab*. (See Caskel and Strenziok.)

Ibn Durayd, Abū Bakr Muḥammad b. al-Ḥasan. *al-Ishtiqāq*. Edited by Ferdinand Wüstenfeld. Göttingen: Dieterischen Buchhandlung, 1854.

Ibn Ḥajar al-ʿAsqalānī, Aḥmad b. ʿAlī. *al-Iṣābah fī tamyīz al-ṣaḥābah*. 4 vols. Cairo: Maṭbaʿat al-saʿādah, 1328 A.H. Reprinted Beirut: Dār Ṣādir, n.d.

Ibn Hishām, ʿAbd al-Malik. *al-Sīrah al-nabawiyyah*. 2 vols., edited by Ferdinand Wüstenfeld. Göttingen: Dieterischen Buchhandlung, 1858–1860 [= Wüstenfeld, *Das Leben Muhammeds*].

Ibn Ḥubaysh, ʿAbd al-Raḥmān b. ʿAbdallāh b. Yūsuf. *Kitāb dhikr al-ghazawāt al-ḍāminah wa al-futūḥ. . . .* Ms. Leiden Or. 343.

Ibn Mājah. *Sunan*. Edited by Muḥammad Fuʾād ʿAbd al-Bāqī. Cairo: Dār iḥyāʾ al-kutub al-ʿarabiyya, 1953.

Ibn Manẓūr, Muḥammad b. Makram. *Lisān al-ʿarab*. 15 vols., n.p., n.d. [ca. 1300 A.H.]. Reprinted Beirut: Dār Ṣādir, n.d.

Ibn Rustah, Abū ʿAlī Aḥmad b. ʿUmar. *Kitāb al-aʿlāq al-nafīsah*. Leiden: E. J. Brill, 1892. Reprinted 1967 [= *Bibliotheca Geographorum Arabicorum* VII].

Ibn Saʿd, Muḥammad. *Kitāb al-ṭabaqāt al-kabīr*. 9 vols., edited by Eduard Sachau et al. Leiden: E. J. Brill, 1917–1940.

al-Iṣfahānī, ʿAlī b. al-Ḥusayn Abū al-Faraj. *Kitāb al-aghānī*. 20 vols. Būlāq, 1284–1285 A.H. Vol. 21 Leiden: E. J. Brill, 1306 A.H.

Justi, Ferdinand. *Iranisches Namenbuch*. Marburg, 1895. Reprinted Hildesheim: Georg Olms, 1963.

Kaḥḥālah, ʿUmar Riḍā. *Muʿjam qabāʾil al-ʿarab*. 3 vols. Beirut: Dār al-ʿilm li al-malāyīn, 1968.

Kister, M. J. "Mecca and Tamīm: Aspects of Their Relations." *Journal of the Economic and Social History of the Orient* 8 (1965), 113–63.

Landau-Tasseron, Ella. "Asad from Jāhiliyya to Islam." *Jerusalem Studies in Arabic and Islam* 6 (1985), 1–28.

———. "The Participation of Ṭayyi' in the *Ridda*." *Jerusalem Studies in Arabic and Islam* 5 (1984), 53–71.

———. "Sayf ibn 'Umar in Medieval and Modern Scholarship." *Der Islam* 67 (1990), 1–26.

Lane, Edward William. *An Arabic-English Lexicon*. 8 vols. London and Edinburgh: Williams and Norgate, 1863–1893. Reprinted Beirut: Librairie du Liban, 1968.

Lecker, Michael. *The Banū Sulaym*. Jerusalem: The Hebrew University, 1989.

al-Mas'ūdī, al-Ḥasan b. 'Alī. *Kitāb al-tanbīh wa al-'ishrāf*. Edited by M. J. De Goeje. Leiden: E. J. Brill, 1984 [= *Bibliotheca Geographorum Arabicorum* VIII].

al-Nuwayrī, Aḥmad b. 'Abd al-Wahhāb. *Niyāhat al-arab fī funūn al-adab*. 26 volumes; volume 19, edited by Muḥammad Abū al-Faḍl Ibrāhīm. Cairo: al-Hay'ah al-Miṣriyyah al-'āmmah li-al-kitāb, 1975.

Pellat, Charles. *Le milieu baṣrien et la formation de Ǧāḥiẓ*. Paris: Adrien-Maisonneuve, 1953.

al-Rāshid, Sa'ad bin 'Abd al-'Azīz [sic]. *Al-Rabadhah. A Portrait of Early Islamic Civilisation in Saudi Arabia*. Riyadh: King Saud University, and Harlow, England: Longman. 1986.

Rosenthal, Franz. *A History of Muslim Historiography*, 2nd ed. Leiden: E. J. Brill, 1968.

al-Ṣan'ānī, 'Abd al-Razzāq. *al-Muṣannaf*. Volume 5, edited by Ḥabīb al-Raḥmān al-A'ẓamī. Transvaal, Karachi, and Gujarat: al-Majlis al-'ilmī, 1972.

Schacht, Joseph. *Introduction to Islamic Law*. Oxford: The Clarendon Press, 1964.

Schick, Robert. *The fate of the Christians of Palestine in the Byzantine-Umayyad transition, 660–750 A.D.* Princeton, N. J.: Darwin Press, forthcoming 1992.

Serjeant, R[obert] B[ertram], and Ronald Lewcock. *Ṣan'ā'. An Arabian Islamic city*. London: World of Islam Festival Trust, 1983.

Shoufani, Elias S. *Al-Riddah and the Muslim Conquest of Arabia*. Toronto: University of Toronto Press, and Beirut: The Arab Institute for Research and Publishing. 1972.

Simonsen, Jørgen Bæk. *Studies in the Genesis and Early Development of the Caliphal Taxation system*. Copenhagen: Akademisk Forlag, 1988.

al-Ṭabarī, Muḥammad b. Jarīr. *Ta'rīkh al-rusul wa al-mulūk*. 15

volumes, edited by M. J. De Goeje et al. Leiden: E. J. Brill, 1879–1901 [= "text"]. Ser. 1, vol. 4 (1890), including the *riddah*, was edited by P. De Jong and E. Prym; the section on the *riddah*, by De Jong.

———. *Ta'rīkh al-rusul wa al-mulūk*. 10 volumes, edited by Muḥammad Abū al-Faḍl Ibrāhīm. Cairo: Dār al-Ma'ārif, 1960–1969 [= "Cairo"]. Vol. 3, including the *riddah*, 1962.

———. *Ta'rīkh al-rusul wa al-mulūk*. Partial edition by Johann Gottfried Ludwig Kosegarten as *Taberistanensis . . . annales regum atque legatorum Dei*. Greifswald: E. Mauritii, 1831–1835 [= "Kos"]. (Not seen; rare partial edition based on Berlin Mss., cited by Leiden and Cairo editions.)

Tübinger Atlas des vorderen Orients. Wiesbaden: Dr. Ludwig Reichert Verlag, 1977–.

al-Wāqidī, Muḥammad b. 'Umar. *Kitāb al-maghāzī*. 3 vols., edited by J. M. B. Jones. London: Oxford University Press, 1966.

Wathīmah b. Mūsā b. al-Furāt. *Kitāb al-riddah*, fragments edited by Wilhelm Hoenerbach as *Waṯīma's Kitāb ar-Ridda aus Ibn Ḥağar's Iṣāba* [= Akademie der Wissenschaft und der Literatur in Mainz. *Abhandlungen der Geistes- und Sozialwissenschaftlichen Klasse*, Jahrgang 1951, nr. 4]. A single number (e.g., "22") refers to Hoenerbach's introduction; a double number with slash (e.g., "7/42") refers to the Arabic text and German translation, in that order.

Watt, William Montgomery. *Muhammad at Mecca*. Oxford: Clarendon Press, 1953.

———. *Muhammad at Medina*. Oxford: Clarendon Press, 1956.

Wehr, Hans. *A Dictionary of Modern Arabic*. Ithaca, N.Y.: Cornell University Press, 1961.

Wellhausen, Julius. *Skizzen und Vorarbeiten*, vol. VI. Berlin: Georg Reimer, 1899 [= *Prolegomena zur ältesten Geschichte des Islams*].

Wensinck, Arent Jan, et al. *Concordance et indices de la tradition musulmane*. 8 vols, Leiden: E. J. Brill, 1936–1988.

Wilkinson, J. C. "The Julanda of Oman." *Journal of Oman Studies* 1 (1975), 97–108.

Wilson, Robert T. O. *Gazetteer of Historical North-West Yemen*. Hildesheim: Georg Olms, 1989.

Wüstenfeld, Ferdinand. "Bahrein und Jemâma. Nach arabischen Geographen beschrieben," *Abhandlungen der königlichen Gesellschaft der Wissenschaften zu Göttingen*, 19 (1874), 173–222.

Yāqūt b. 'Abdullāh al-Ḥamawī al-Rūmī. *Mu'jam al-buldān*. 5 vols. Beirut: Dār Ṣādir and Dār Bayrūt, 1957.

Index

This index includes names of all persons, groups, and places mentioned in the text, as well as most such names mentioned in the footnotes. Entries refer to page numbers only. An asterisk (*) before an entry indicates individuals whose names occur in the isnāds, or chains of transmitters conveying the accounts making up the text. The Arabic definite article al- *and the abbreviations* b. *(ibn, "son of") and* bt. *(bint, "daughter of") have been disregarded in alphabetizing entries.*

B

T

U

V

W

Y

Z